Somatic Experience in Psychoanalysis and Psychotherapy

The body, of both the patient and the analyst, is increasingly a focus of attention in contemporary psychoanalytic theory and practice, especially from a relational perspective. There is a renewed regard for the understanding of embodied experience and sexuality as essential to human vitality. However, most of the existing literature has written by analysts with no formal training in body-centered work. In this book William Cornell draws on his experience as a body-centered psychotherapist to offer an informed blend of the two traditions, to allow psychoanalysts a deep understanding, in psychoanalytic language, of how to work with the body as an ally.

The primary focus of *Somatic Experience in Psychoanalysis and Psychotherapy* situates systematic attention to somatic experience and direct body-level intervention in the practice of psychoanalysis and psychotherapy. It provides a close reading of the work of Wilhelm Reich, repositioning his work within a contemporary psychoanalytic frame and re-presents Winnicott's work with a particular emphasis on the somatic foundations of his theories. William Cornell includes vivid and detailed case vignettes including accounts of his own bodily experience to fully illustrate a range of somatic attention and intervention that include verbal description of sensate experience, exploratory movement, and direct physical contact.

Drawing on relevant theory and significant clinical material, *Somatic Experience in Psychoanalysis and Psychotherapy* will allow psychoanalysts an understanding of how to work with the body in their clinical practice. It will bring a fresh perspective on psychoanalytic thinking to body-centered psychotherapy where somatic experience is seen as an ally to psychic and interpersonal growth. This book will be essential reading for psychoanalysts, psychodynamically oriented psychotherapists, transactional analysts, body-centered psychotherapists, Gestalt therapists, counselors, and students.

William F. Cornell maintains an independent private practice of psychotherapy and consultation in Pittsburgh, PA. He has devoted 40 years to the study and integration of psychoanalysis, neo-Reichian body therapy and transactional analysis. He is a Training and Supervising Transactional Analyst and has established an international reputation for his teaching and consultation.

RELATIONAL PERSPECTIVES BOOK SERIES

LEWIS ARON & ADRIENNE HARRIS
Series Co-Editors

STEVEN KUCHUCK & EYAL ROZMARIN
Associate Editors

The Relational Perspectives Book Series (RPBS) publishes books that grow out of or contribute to the relational tradition in contemporary psychoanalysis. The term *relational psychoanalysis* was first used by Greenberg and Mitchell[1] to bridge the traditions of interpersonal relations, as developed within interpersonal psychoanalysis and object relations, as developed within contemporary British theory. But, under the seminal work of the late Stephen Mitchell, the term *relational psychoanalysis* grew and began to accrue to itself many other influences and developments. Various tributaries—interpersonal psychoanalysis, object relations theory, self psychology, empirical infancy research, and elements of contemporary Freudian and Kleinian thought—flow into this tradition, which understands relational configurations between self and others, both real and fantasied, as the primary subject of psychoanalytic investigation.

We refer to the relational tradition, rather than to a relational school, to highlight that we are identifying a trend, a tendency within contemporary psychoanalysis, not a more formally organized or coherent school or system of beliefs. Our use of the term *relational* signifies a dimension of theory and practice that has become salient across the wide spectrum of contemporary psychoanalysis. Now under the editorial supervision of Lewis Aron and Adrienne Harris with the assistance of Associate Editors Steven Kuchuck and Eyal Rozmarin, the Relational Perspectives Book Series originated in 1990 under the editorial eye of the late Stephen A. Mitchell. Mitchell was the most prolific and influential of the originators of the relational tradition. He was committed to dialogue among psychoanalysts and he abhorred the authoritarianism that dictated adherence to a rigid set of beliefs or technical restrictions. He championed open discussion, comparative and integrative approaches, and he promoted new voices across the generations.

Included in the Relational Perspectives Book Series are authors and works that come from within the relational tradition, extend and develop the tradition, as well as works that critique relational approaches or compare and contrast them with alternative points of view. The series includes our most distinguished senior psychoanalysts, along with younger contributors who bring fresh vision.

[1]Greenberg, J. & Mitchell, S. (1983). *Object relations in psychoanalytic theory.* Cambridge, MA: Harvard University Press.

Somatic Experience in Psychoanalysis and Psychotherapy

In the Expressive Language of the Living

William F. Cornell

Routledge
Taylor & Francis Group

LONDON AND NEW YORK

First published 2015
by Routledge
27 Church Road, Hove, East Sussex, BN3 2FA

And by Routledge
711 Third Avenue, New York, NY 10017

*Routledge is an imprint of the Taylor & Francis Group,
an informa business*

British Library Cataloguing in Publication Data
A catalogue record for this book is available from the British
Library

Library of Congress Cataloging-in-Publication Data
Cornell, William F.
  Somatic experience in psychoanalysis and psychotherapy : in the
expressive language of the living / William F. Cornell.
    pages cm
  1. Psychoanalysis. 2. Psychotherapy. I. Title.
  RC501.2.C67 2015
  616.89'14—dc23
  2014040490

ISBN: 978-1-138-82675-5 (hbk)
ISBN: 978-1-138-82676-2 (pbk)
ISBN: 978-1-315-73899-4 (ebk)

Typeset in Times
by Apex CoVantage, LLC

Printed by Ashford Colour Press Ltd.

In loving and grateful memory of Rose Leopold: For giving me a second chance at life and showing me that a passionate life was possible.

And to Mick Landaiche: For proving Rose so right.

Contents

Acknowledgments

Portions of the following chapters have previously been published and are reproduced here, edited and expanded, with permission from their publishers:

Chapter 1—"My body is unhappy": Somatic foundations of script and script protocol. *Explorations in Transactional Analysis: The Meech Lake Papers*, 159–170, 2008.

Chapter 3—Searching in the "unsaid seen": McLaughlin's unfinished reflections on the place of the body in psychoanalytic discourse. *American Imago*, 515–541, 2010.

Chapter 5—Stranger to desire: Entering the erotic field. *Studies in Gender and Sexuality*, 75–92, 2009.

Chapter 9—The Impassioned Body: Erotic vitality and disturbance. *British Gestalt Journal*, 92–104, 2003.

Chapter 10—Why have sex? A case study in character, perversion, and free choice. *Transactional Analysis Journal*, 136–148, 2009.

With gratitude to the teachers, colleagues, therapists, supervisors, and friends who have informed, shaken, and vitalized my life and work: Mr. Davis, Mr. Utter, Miss Schwartz, Miss Hill, Nicholas Longo, Carol Creedon, Constance Hanf, Virginia Satir, Constance Fischer, Stephanie Neal Cornell, Howard Goodman, Robert Yoder, Lois Johnson, Harry Boyd, Elaine Warburton, Mark Ludwig, Richard Miller, Charelle Samuels, Frances Bonds-White, Stanley Perelman, Mort Johan, Robin Fryer, Mick Landaiche, Robert Marin, Christopher Bollas, James McLaughlin, Sam Gerson, Wilma Bucci, Lew Aron, Muriel Dimen, Ruth Stein, Anne Alvarez, Donnel Stern, Maurice Apprey, Jean-Michel Quinodoz, Danielle Quinodoz, the international Transactional Analysis community, and the Pittsburgh "Keeping Our Work Alive" community. The careful and critical readings of earlier versions of this manuscript by Mick Landaiche, Christopher Bollas, and Lew Aron were vital to my coming to write here in a direct and personal voice.

A special note of gratitude goes to Susan Wickenden, Susannah Frearson, Kate Hawes, Sarah Steele, Laura Emsden, and Abigail Stanley of the Routledge production team whose skills and grace made the final stages of this book a true pleasure.

And to the many clients who over four decades have pushed, shoved, and transgressed the limits of my character, training, and capacity to understand. This book is most of all the story of our work and learning together.

Introduction

The Flesh of Life

What does it mean to live in one's body? How do we bring language that is adequate to the experience of one's body? While there is Freud's oft-quoted phrase that the ego is first and foremost a body ego, the place and meanings of bodily experience in psychoanalysis and psychotherapy have been precarious. Psychoanalytic references to the bodily modes of experience within the therapeutic process often link the body to notions of regression, the primitive, the concrete, the unsymbolized, the unmentalized—states of experience that need to be brought into more mature realms of psychic organization.

This book is based on a different premise: the premise that human beings can bear deep and sustaining meaning through the capacity for deep and sustained bodily experience, that our bodies in their sensate and sexual capacities are powerful resources for psychic growth. Our bodies are not simply prisons full of primitive debris or mechanical neuromuscular machines. Our bodies provide us fundamental means for self-development and contact with others. It is a premise of this book that informed and sustained attention to bodily experience can provide an essential bridge between realms of the unconscious and our conscious capacities for understanding, choice, action, and vitality.

Merleau-Ponty's phenomenology was rooted in the primacy of bodily experience. Toward the end of his life he began to articulate the concept of "flesh" so as to evoke a more alive and living sense of the body as "Flesh of the world—Flesh of the body—Being" (1969, p. 248). He had begun to use this sense of *flesh* to attempt to capture and convey more actively the experience of the body's immersion in the world—both material and human. For Merleau-Ponty:

> That means that my body is made of the same flesh as the world (it is a perceived), and moreover that this flesh of my body is shared by the world, the world *reflects* it, encroaches upon it and it encroaches upon the world (the felt [senti] at the same time the culmination of subjectivity and the culmination of materiality), they are in a relation of transgression or of overlapping. (p. 248)

His sudden death at age 53 in 1961 cut short his development of these ideas, but he left behind a unique philosophy which embedded the structure of human experience in the sensate body. Merleau-Ponty suggests that flesh is like a sensate tissue that extends beyond the physical body, touching and being touched by others, touching and being touched by the material world. It encompasses the spaces between oneself and others, creating a kind of unthought, visceral knowing. *Flesh* conveys the essential physicality of intersubjective experience.

When I discovered this term, *flesh*, I found it deeply evocative of how I understand my work as a body-centered psychotherapist. It evokes both the vitality and the frailty of the body, a sense of the lived and living body (Gilbert & Lennon, 1988). Lucian Freud, in a discussion of his approach to painting, captures this sense of flesh:

> I want paint to work as flesh. [. . .] As far as I'm concerned the paint is the person. I want it to work for me as flesh does. (2010, p. 146)

Flesh is a medium of contact. Flesh is skin with depth, movement, and vitality. Skin and muscle become flesh when intermingled/infused with the flesh of another. There is, too, the aggressive excitation of the flesh: the capacity to excite and disturb, the desire to get to and under another's skin, to get into the other in such a way that one will not be forgotten, to be taken over and filled up by another, to penetrate and be penetrated in our intimate relations.

But flesh also bruises. Flesh decays. Michael Bronski vividly conveys the realities of flesh:

> Flesh is what joins us and what keeps us apart.
> I always thought Hamlet's line was, "Oh, that this too, too solid flesh would melt." But someone just told me it is "sullied," not "solid," and that made sense. Flesh isn't solid; it isn't marble, or noble, or pure, but tender and ready to bruise, and tear, and hurt. Like "truth" and "honesty" and even "love," it can be inexplicably ruptured, ripped, and torn apart. (2002, p. 291)

Flesh is alive. Flesh remembers. Flesh holds desire. And dread.

Since the very beginnings of my work as a psychotherapist, I have been immersed in body-centered modalities. As I began to think of how I might introduce this book, I found myself returning to an earlier description (Cornell, 2008a) of one of my very first therapeutic experiences. I was exploring very early, long-remembered and quite disturbing memories in a workshop with Christopher Whitmont (1972, 1973), a Jungian analyst involved in my early training in transactional analysis.

There were but two memories, both in the upstairs living room of my maternal grandparents' house, from which my mother, father, and I moved before I was four.

The first was a visual image of the brown slats of my wooden playpen. There was no narrative, no sequence of events, only the image of the slats and the sensation of my back pressing against the wood. The other, taking place in the same room, was the music of the refrain of "Hernando's Hideaway," and the sensation of being carried in my mother's arms as she danced.

I presented these memories in a workshop at the very beginning of my training in transactional analysis psychotherapy. Whitmont noted that my memories were held more in physical sensations than in visual images or narrative stories. He explained that in working with early memories or dreams, he attended to the primary mode of experience in the memory/dream: be it somatic sensation, visual imagery, or narrative. He then worked to explore the material, using Jung's concept of active imagination, within the primary mode of experience with which the memory or dream was organized.

He suggested we work with my memories as sensate experiences and see what we might discover. He asked that I sit with my eyes closed, centering my attention on the sensation of the slats against my back, and notice any inclination of my body to move. He encouraged me to inhabit each sensation and movement. The sensations were startlingly vivid and profoundly disturbing. Without actually knowing what my body was doing, I stood, arching backward, pressing into the air with my back, the sensation of the slats sharpening. I wanted to bang my head. I wailed. The only movement available to my body was to press backward and against the no-longer-existing slats. With these sensations came a deep and familiar ache of loneliness. I finally collapsed to the floor in tears, feeling lonely to the core.

Whitmont waited in silent attention for my distress to subside. He then pointed out that I had presented two memories and asked if I would like to move into the other. Again he asked not that I remember and tell the memory, but that I *move into* it, that I let *it move within* me. He asked that I hear the music and feel the sensation of the music in my body. It was immediate. In my mental recall of this experience, I remembered the music sweetly. I had associated it with older childhood memories of dancing the jitterbug with my mother, to an LP that I still have. But the experience in my body as I moved into the music was not so sweet. I felt a deep tenderness toward my mother. I felt the sensation of the dance, held to my mother's body. And I felt the intense, melancholic loneliness of her body. I wept again and felt lonely still. I felt loneliness alone and loneliness with and in my mother. Here was the life of the flesh between my mother and me—forming, informing, drenching my bodily experience of what it meant to bring myself to another.

I had entered psychotherapy training in transactional analysis after a highly intellectual graduate program in phenomenology. I was in a phase of an overworking, overly responsible early adult life, following an adolescence of drug dependency and heroin addiction. In these embodied memories I got my first glimpse of the functions of both my manic and my addictive efforts to ward off the profound loneliness that had permeated my early years.

It was in this singular piece of body-centered psychotherapy that I learned something about myself in relation to my intimate others that I would return to again and again, with deepening layers of meaning, over the course of my subsequent body psychotherapy and later psychoanalyses. The sensations of that bodily exploration of those two memories informed me of something fundamental to my unconscious relational field. I remembered it in my body, explored it through my body, and the experience was an essential one in the shaping of my development as a psychotherapist. I did not yet know any theory or techniques of body psychotherapy, but I knew that the direct engagement of the body would be an essential element in my work as a psychotherapist.

Over dinner, after the workshop, I asked Whitmont how he came to develop his rather unusual approach to working with dreams. He told me that early in his career, he had met both Jung and Reich. He was strongly attracted to Reich's work, its physicality, but he found Reich a rather brutish and unappealing fellow. Jung, in contrast, had a touch of class, and that, Whitmont confessed, appealed to his ego ideal, and so he pursued Jungian rather than Reichian training. Nevertheless, Whitmont found ways to bring an active sense of bodily experience into his work.

My own introduction to Reich's work was completely unexpected. Through a series of fortuitous incidents, while attending Reed College in Portland, Oregon, I had taken a job at a residential treatment program for severely disturbed children and their parents. To work there, I was required to take a week-long training/ treatment workshop with Virginia Satir. I had the very good fortune that this workshop was held at the Esalen Institute. I was all of 18, and this was my first therapeutic experience. It was the late 1960s and Esalen was in its earliest stages of development as the birthplace of the human potential movement. It was at that time a rather casual and free-spirited place, rife with the fevers of discovery and revolution. Satir, then the director of the residential training program at Esalen, took me under her wing. As I had no money, she arranged for me to attend workshops in trade for working on the grounds. I would hitchhike to Big Sur as often as I could and attend whatever was going on. I became a kind of mascot at the Esalen Institute in Big Sur, California.

One weekend, having no idea what I was about to experience, I attended a Bioenergetic workshop led by three men. It was notable for a number of reasons, the first of which was that while the leaders remained clothed, the participants were naked. My skinny, anxious, inept body was thrown into a different universe. I could barely breathe. One of the activities of the workshop consisted of one of the leaders taking a participant through a series of strenuous postures called "stress positions" (Lowen, 1975; Lowen & Lowen, 1977), with the leaders closely observing body patterns and reactions. After a few of these, one of the leaders would narrate, as if by magic, the person's infantile and childhood histories, speculating on the person's character structure and defenses. It was quite a show. The spectacle was both magical and humiliating. I did not dare to put myself forward. The workshop leaders repeatedly mentioned Wilhelm Reich as the creator of this kind of psychotherapy, so I knew that once I returned to Reed, I would be doing some reading.

Upon returning to Reed, while all of Reich's books were in the card catalogue, none was on the shelves. When I inquired, the head librarian told me the story of

Reich's persecution by the U.S. government and the seizure and destruction of all his books. She went into her office and returned with Reich's *The Mass Psychology of Fascism* (1970), handing me the Orgone Institute Press edition: "I couldn't let the bastards take this one." Reich wrote this book on the eve of Hitler's rise to power, a brilliant, provocative book that was shockingly relevant to the revolutionary spirit of the late '60s. I was then lent an Orgone Press edition of Reich's *Cancer Biopathy* (1973). My mother was then dying of cancer. While the book read in part like a delusional science fiction treatise, Reich's vivid descriptions of characterological resignation captured the essence of my mother's being. My mother's profound loneliness and resignation was a part of what I was to later relive in the experience with Christopher Whitmont. I decided that some day I would learn to work in the way that Reich advocated. I gradually assembled a library of Reich's work, but several years were to pass before I could undertake actual training.

Graduate school lay between my undergraduate studies and a return to Reich. The psychology department at Reed was based in Skinnerian behaviorism, rather to my dismay. A philosophical and political debate raged during my undergraduate years, between behaviorism and the humanistic and existential-phenomenological models. I chose the phenomenological psychology program at Duquesne University for my graduate studies. Here I struggled with the dense writings of Merleau-Ponty, Husserl, Heidegger, and others. Merleau-Ponty outlined a model of psychic functioning deeply grounded in sensate, bodily experience, but its translation into clinical application was elusive. I left Duquesne with a profound respect for the powerful effects of the phenomenological inquiry into the subjectivity of another's way of being in the world. My education in phenomenology formed the bedrock of my clinical orientation. But it left me with little sense of what to actually say and do with a client.

Since my teenage years of reading Freud and Jung, I had imagined becoming a psychoanalyst. Still in graduate school I attended various presentations at the Pittsburgh Psychoanalytic Institute. I was dismayed. There was none of the respect that I witnessed at Duquesne for the actual, lived experience of the patient; it was all a matter of defense and psychopathology. The meetings were dominated by men in drab suits, engaged in highly intellectual and nastily competitive, narcissistic debates. I was sure I didn't want to grow up to be like them, so I began to look elsewhere.

I had a second chance encounter with a new way of thinking during my Reed years. The residential treatment center that had sent me to Esalen to work with Virginia Satir held the diagnostic and treatment-planning meetings in a format that I found amazing. Consistent with the milieu treatment model, everyone who had contact with the child being discussed, from psychiatrist to teacher to janitor, was present and involved in the meeting. Moreover, the child being discussed, regardless of his or her age and level of functioning, was also included in these meetings. The child's experience of what was working and what was not, who on the staff was helpful (it might be a janitor or cafeteria worker) and who was not, was actively included in the treatment planning. When I asked the head psychologist where they had come up with this idea, he described the supervision model Eric Berne (1961, 1968) used in psychiatric consultations in which the patient as well as the therapist was in attendance. The therapists discussed their experience of the treatment, with the patients listening; then the patients took the floor, with their therapists listening to *their* experience. It was a remarkable, provocative positioning of therapist and patient. As an undergraduate I then read more of Berne (1963, 1966) and saw him as attempting a kind of melding of psychoanalysis (he was trained as an analyst in the ego psychology model of the '50s) with a phenomenological spirit of investigation. After graduate school I tracked down a trainer in transactional analysis, and in so doing found my professional home. The transactional analysis community was a refreshing contrast to what I had seen in the psychoanalytic institute. While deeply interested in both the inner and interpersonal lives of their clients, TA therapists tended to be much more practical in their approach to psychotherapy.

Leaving graduate school my first job was in an extraordinary community mental health clinic, during the days in which the mental health services were actually delivered in the community—schools, churches, parent groups, a coffee house in the basement for teenagers, support services for the elderly. Our psychiatrist, now semi-retired, had trained with Harry Stack Sullivan (and like Sullivan was a closeted gay man), for whom transactional analysis made immediate sense. Almost the entire staff was trained in TA, and we filled the community with TA courses and groups. It was a perfect time to be a budding young psychotherapist.

It was also during this time that I trained in neo-Reichian body psychotherapy. That proved to be a bit of a challenge in that in TA we were forbidden to ever touch a patient, while in my Reichian training there was never a session in which I did not touch. Years were required to bridge that chasm. And over the years I came to call much of my Reichian training into question. I found rigidity and isolation in the neo-Reichian communities. While I found openness and belonging in the transactional analysis community, a certain kind of questioning was lacking. I returned to an intense reading of psychoanalysis and to psychoanalytic supervision, seeking ways out of my dilemma. Again there were chasms to bridge, but I gradually found how these wildly differing models could both challenge and inform one another. In both contemporary transactional analysis (Morrison & Goodman, 2007) and psychoanalysis (Aron & Anderson, 1998; Orbach, 2006a; Anderson, 2008) there is a growing effort to find ways to work with somatic experience within the psychotherapeutic relationship. This book is a contribution to those efforts. There is a kind of intellectual and professional autobiography underlying this book. It is my hope in the pages ahead to capture aspects of the exploratory edges of current developments in psychoanalysis and psychodynamic psychotherapy as they relate to the growing interest in the body within psychoanalysis and psychotherapy.

The title of this book is taken from Reich's *Character Analysis* (1972, p. 355) and was chosen to express the spirit of this book. It was in this classic volume that

Reich first laid out his radical departure from the psychoanalysis of his day as he sought to grasp and articulate the somatic foundations of human experience and expression:

> ... the beginnings of living functioning lie much *deeper* than and *beyond* language. *Over and above this, the living organism has its own modes of expressing movement which simply cannot be comprehended with words.* (p. 359)

A central project in this book is to present the work of Reich in a renewed, contemporary light. Of the myriad characters with whom Freud surrounded himself, Reich was without a doubt one of the most controversial and most misrepresented. Susan Sontag has observed:

> Certain authors become literary or intellectual classics because they are *not* read, being in some intrinsic way unreadable. Sade, Artaud, and Wilhelm Reich belong in this company: authors who were jailed or locked up in insane asylums because they were screaming, because they were out of control; immodest, obsessed, strident authors who repeat themselves endlessly, who are rewarding to quote and read bits of, but who overpower and exhaust if read in large quantities. (1976, p. lix)

It is my hope that this book, among other things, may stimulate some readers to undertake a closer and better informed reading of Reich's work.

A note on the case material: Each of the extended case examples and those which involve direct quotes have been shared with the client, discussed, and included as part of the ongoing treatment process. Shorter vignettes have fictionalized presentations of client details, but the description of the treatment process is direct from process notes.

Chapter 1

My Body Is Unhappy

From the beginning, working with Pat was an unsettling and challenging experience. Everyone connected to Pat seemed to find the experience of being with Pat rather unpleasant and often shocking. Family and friends over the years had encouraged Pat to enter psychotherapy. It was finally a professional crisis that brought Pat to my office. Working with Pat was like being thrown into an argumentative whirlwind.

Our third session began with Pat, late, rushing into my office, carrying an empty water bottle, pacing rather than sitting, and opening the session with a greeting laced with sarcasm.

PAT: I'm sorry about calling you so much about the appointment. We have so many appointments I can't keep them straight. I hope I didn't bother you. I mean, did I call in time last week when I cancelled? I was pretty sure about this one, but I didn't want to show up and find out I made a mistake. I don't know . . . maybe I've got ADHD, or maybe I'm just OCD. Oh, I didn't have time to get another one (referring to water bottle). Is there a place where I can get some water? I mean, would that be OK? I could just go to the bathroom and use the sink there.

BILL: Or you can use the sink in the kitchen.

PAT: OK, thanks . . . Ugh . . . I know I was supposed to talk about my anger in the marriage. But first something happened at work. A big blow-out. Typical, I guess, but this one really exploded. On one floor at the hospital the nurses never get anything right. I mean, it jeopardizes patient care. I can't stand it. I do things the nurses should be doing. Even filling water bottles. The head nurse just blew up at me, that I'm constantly over-critical. She said everyone hates to work with me, they dread it when I'm on the unit. She said I'm impossible to satisfy, she screamed at me, "Just tell me, does *anybody ever* do *anything* right?!" I yelled right back, "I cannot relieve patients' pain when they're not given breakfast, have no water, aren't turned properly, lie in the same position too long." That was Friday. I haven't heard the fallout from that yet.

BILL: "Over-critical," what do you imagine that means?

PAT: Well, *I* don't know. *She* said it, though *I* hear it all the time. I guess it's the same in the marriage, come to think of it. I'm always accused of being overly critical, seeing everything in black and white. Well, why can't people function like adults? Do their jobs? Anticipate problems and take action. I get really judgmental and impatient. But why not? I don't think what I expect is unreasonable.

BILL: Impatient and judgmental. Are those your words or others'? Is that how "over-critical" feels? What's the push in your impatience?

PAT: I don't know. Nobody ever steps up to the plate. I just want somebody to step up to the plate.

BILL: You talk a lot about the marriage and your work. Do you have relationships that have the capacity for conflict? Where you're not over-critical. Where you can rely on someone stepping up to the plate?

PAT: I already told you that when something goes wrong with a friend, I just cut them off. That's it, no second chances.

I fell silent as Pat went on for another 20 minutes or so, complaining passionately about work and colleagues, an occasional slam at friends thrown in to balance the picture. I may have been silent during those rushing, pressured minutes, but my mind was neither calm nor quiet. It, like Pat, raced, filled with a tumult of reactions and thoughts. On the one hand I heard this whole opening as a statement of the transference expectations that were rapidly unfolding: "*Step up to the plate,* Bill (please). . . . something goes wrong—*no second chances.*" Pat's intensity and aggression simultaneously excited and intimidated me. I wanted my mind to calm my body. I wanted to do something to calm Pat's body. If I confronted the anger and agitation, would Pat burst into tears, collapse into depression? Various, often contradictory, theories raced through my mind, trying to make sense of this shocking barrage. I watched Pat pacing, filling all the space in the room. I couldn't find a space in which to speak. I felt the impact of the utter physicality of Pat's presence.

Finally, Pat said, "The session's nearly over, and I guess I haven't given you the space to say much of anything, have I? I guess I should. There are a few minutes left. They're yours. Better make it good."

"Uh-oh," I thought to myself, "If it's not good . . . TROUBLE." Rather hesitantly, I ventured, "Space. Funny you should use the word space. That's a word that's been in my mind as I've been watching and listening. It's like you fill the space with movement, activity, voice. It's like you expect the space to be snatched away at any moment. I'm pretty good at taking space, but I haven't been able to find a space here with you today. Pace. Space. The plate. At this point I don't really have any idea what we are going to be doing together or how to do it, but it does seem like it's going to have to have something to do with space. *Your* space, *my* space, eventually maybe *our* space."

I wonder, as I write to unseen readers, how you were affected as you read the transcript. How you pictured Pat? Did you create an image of Pat's face?

The sound of Pat's voice or a sense of Pat's body? Did you "hear" Pat's words as demanding, controlling, cynical, desperate, narcissistic, depressed? Did you imagine Pat as male or female? Why do you suppose you chose one gender over another?

There was an urgency in Pat's decision (*finally*, friends, colleagues, and spouse would probably say) to enter therapy. Pat's way of being filled the room, impacted/shocked me. The impacts and shocks communicated a great deal, evoking levels and layers of unconscious reaction and anticipation. A reflective space was not readily available to either of us.

It was when working with patients like Pat that I found my training in body psychotherapy quite lacking. Yes, I could create a diagnosis of character and proceed accordingly, at least succeeding in calming myself down with this illusory sense of knowing and understanding *something*. Yet I knew with Pat that something intense and complex was going on. Pat was not simply acting out a pattern of characterological defense (though there was certainly that element), but was also desperately trying to demonstrate, communicate something to me and others. This session was like being *induced* into a state of being, something I had to *experience with the patient*, rather than use theory and intellect to create a comfortable distance from Pat's intense and affecting distress.

Pat began the next session with a perfunctory, though unconvincing, apology for her behavior the previous week. I asked her what it was that she thought required an apology. She said it had something to do with her agitation and taking up all the space. She was afraid I was angry with her and like so many others would not want to work with her. She'd be damned before apologizing at work, but she barely knew me and felt she needed to apologize for her agitation and aggressiveness. I told her that my sense was that it was exactly this issue of space that would be our working terrain, that I thought her agitated body was communicating things that her mind did not yet understand. I asked her what it might be like when she became so agitated that she couldn't sit if I also stood and moved around the room. "That plate you referred to last week doesn't seem to stay put for long," I joked, "so I think I'll need to move too if I'm going to step up to it." She agreed.

It was a rare session in which Pat could remain in her chair the full hour. Much more often than not, she would be on her feet pacing the office, complaining about her marriage and situations at work, with me soon to be on my feet staying in her vicinity, chasing after "the plate." I found myself identifying rather strongly with her husband as well as her colleagues, feeling myself constantly on a bewildered, agitated edge as I tried, quite literally, to keep up with her. At the same time, I began to sense her acute vulnerability. I had been considering a number of possible directions for our work, but our actual direction emerged from a fantasy/impulse of Pat's.

After a few sessions like this, Pat said, "I keep having the impulse to bang into you, or maybe it's more that you bang into me, kind of bashing shoulders." "You first," I replied. She didn't, that session. But a couple sessions later, Pat suddenly stopped her pacing, turned and bashed into me with her shoulder. I bashed back.

I was anything but tender. She grinned with delight. "Again!" she proclaimed as she bashed into me. "Finally something solid," she said, almost shouting, and then bursting into tears. "My god, how good that feels, someone who stays put, someone who's not afraid. What a fucking relief." I encouraged her to continue to listen to her body, to hear the story it was trying to tell, what it needed to have understood.

For weeks afterward memories and associations to her siblings, their aggressiveness and competitiveness, the lack of protection from her parents, all began to emerge and connect. As she connected to her sibling histories, she also verbalized fantasies of her body coming up against mine in various ways, sitting shoulder to shoulder as we talked, sitting on the floor back to back pressing against (or was it actually toward?) each other. She felt her pleasure of her body's strength and energy being met and enjoyed. We often ended sessions banging shoulder to shoulder, sometimes playfully, sometimes aggressively. As Pat felt my bodily presence, she began to realize how her constant movement and aggression was to avoid her experience of absence and the life-long pains that evoked in her.

Gradually her agitation lessened, her anger was less automatic, opening the way for increasing awareness (and occasional acknowledgment) of her vulnerabilities and wishes. The presence and competence of those around her began to register in her experience, beginning to inform and soften her constant vigilance for absence and incompetence. She could still rather startlingly fly off the handle at points of frustration, but as she became less wedded to her annoyances, she was more often able to backtrack to identify the trigger (and her vulnerability).

Could Pat and I have addressed her agitation without literally bashing into one another? Most certainly. But there was something in the sheer physicality of her presence in the session that called for the direct engagement with her body. It would, of course, have been possible to work with Pat without any direct, physical contact. But I have chosen this as an opening vignette to underscore a central difference between body-centered psychotherapy and more cognitively or analytically oriented approaches. It is my abiding belief that each modality can be deeply instructive to the other. In recent years, the body as a subject of interest, curiosity, and often dismay has emerged in the psychotherapeutic and psychoanalytic literature. It is my hope that this book will lessen the dismay and heighten the interest in the multitude of meanings and opportunities afforded by attention to somatic experience (of both patient and therapist).

Patients who seek a body-oriented psychotherapist, sometimes consciously, sometimes unconsciously, hope to repair life-long ruptures in relationship to their own bodies. Many patients, I believe, seek out a psychotherapist out of their yearning to overcome splits in relation to their own bodies, to begin to take possession of their own somatic and affective experiences. What sets the body psychotherapies apart from the more traditional cognitive, psychoanalytic, and interpersonal models of therapy is the centrality of theory and techniques that more directly address *the body* itself. Body psychotherapies and somatic methodologies offer a vast repertoire of techniques that can facilitate the regaining of one's somatic awareness and vitality.

There is an essential, compelling experience of the body itself. There is the simultaneous force—wish, desire—for contact with others, which in turn further enhances the vitality, the flesh, of the body in relation to itself. These two forces can often seem antithetical. These two forces, for both bodily efficacy and relational contact, remain in a life-long dialectical tension. I see it as the central and enduring task of psychotherapy and psychoanalysis to bring these two forces together into an increasingly functional unity.

There are significant times in the therapeutic endeavor when upon entering emergent and novel realms of bodily experience, words may fail or simply not be available. At these times, the pressure to verbalize may limit rather than deepen or enlighten a patient's experience. Patients may need, at times like this, for the therapist to enter more directly—if temporarily—into the literal syntax and action of the patient's sense and gesture, not in an unconscious enactment, but in a conscious, intentional provision of a wordless, somatic containing, structuring, or formative function.

To offer another example, I will describe an in-person consultation with a colleague and her patient. This format may seem extreme to some, but has been part of the supervisory traditions in both somatic psychotherapy and transactional analysis (Cornell, Shadbolt, & Norton 2007; Cornell, 2008b). Given the importance of bodily movement and touch in body-centered traditions, supervision is done at times with direct observation of a session so that the supervisor is not dependent on verbal reports but can actually see the interactions and qualities of movement in the work.

It had been a year since I last consulted with Lara and Emily. The previous year Lara had asked that I consult with her regarding her patient, Emily, with whom she'd been working quite productively for three years addressing Emily's eating disorder, body shame, and sexual anxieties. Emily was a successful young attorney, then involved in her first serious relationship. She was "fed up" (so to speak) with her constant preoccupation with her eating and her weight and fearful that her bodily shame and preoccupations would ruin this loving relationship. The therapeutic work to this point had enabled Emily to value herself and be able to stand outside her "issues" enough to pursue this relationship. But as this man became more important to her, her body anxieties came flooding back. Lara, deeply saddened by Emily's struggle, became trapped in a cycle of reassurance, while Emily's sense of self-worth seemed to utterly collapse into series of images of a fat, undesirable body. They were at a point of impasse and decided to seek consultation. Emily felt it important to have the point of view of a male therapist; Lara agreed and was particularly interested in a body-centered perspective.

We agreed upon a rather unusual structure for the consultation: Lara and Emily would discuss their experience of their work together and of the current point of impasse, with me listening; I would then do a therapeutic session with Emily, with Lara watching and probably participating; then the three of us would discuss the work together. Listening to the opening conversation between Lara and Emily, two things were immediately apparent: The first was that there was a deep affection and intimacy between the two; the second was that Emily's experience/accounting of her body was almost exclusively in visual terms, i.e., how she saw herself and imagined others saw her. This visual frame of reference unconsciously directed both Emily's and Lara's attention to the surfaces of her being. Emily's use of a visual frame of reference was so dominant and familiar that it had become "invisible," unnoticeable to Lara and Emily, which I thought was contributing to the impasse in the therapy. Emily experienced herself only as a visual object, constantly subject to scrutiny. This experience was so familiar and compelling that it was re-created within the therapeutic couple, even though the intentions of their lookings were benign. As I have so often experienced myself in seeking consultation at points of impasse, the consultant (or peer group) is an outside force, not so intimately subjected to the states of being and relatedness induced within the therapeutic relationship, thus more able to see, feel, and imagine things anew. What seemed so familiar to Emily and Lara seemed sad and limiting to me. In keeping with our contract for body-centered exploration, I wondered what it would be like for Emily to use her eyes actively, aggressively in response to those around her.

Eyes became the focus of this first consultation. I worked with Emily to use her own eyes, rather than lose herself in the actual or imagined gaze of others. We experimented with her using her eyes to repel unwanted expressions from others, to make demands upon others, and most importantly to hold Lara's eyes with her eyes. These experiments were a relief and source of excitement for Emily. As the body-centered work came to an end, the three of us then spoke of the meaning of these somatic experiments, both in the literal use of her eyes in relation to those around her and as a kind of metaphor for shifting from passive/receptive reactions to emotionally significant people to active/aggressive engagements.

A year later, Emily's relationship was deepening, the work with her eyes continued to foster a sense of independence and mastery, and eating was not at the center of her concerns. But gradually, as her years-long vigilance about food waned, Emily had put on a few pounds. While virtually invisible to anyone else (except—not coincidentally—her mother and her maternal grandfather), Emily's perceptions of herself became graphically distorted and she once again saw herself held and judged disgusting in the eyes of others. She abruptly canceled a beach vacation with her boyfriend. She knew this time that her reactions were entirely irrational, but was unable to contain them. Lara, for her part, was bewildered and feeling ferociously protective in ways she knew might not be productive. They decided on having another in-person consultation.

As we began the new session, Emily told me that in her mind everyone could see the extra weight, that people stared, joked about her behind her back, and found her disgusting. "I know it's not true, but that is how it feels, and it feels entirely real." She was deeply upset with herself for this setback. She felt it started when she went to lunch with her maternal grandfather, and he commented constantly on how *fat* everyone around them was. She was certain (and very likely correct) that he had noticed her weight gain and was indirectly commenting on it. Her mother (now in her 60s and bulimic for at least 40 years) had immediately noticed the weight gain and told Emily that her boyfriend would soon leave her. As I listened,

I wondered (but did not say) if the deepening intimacy with her lover might also have triggered a step back into the safety and familiarity of a script-based focus on weight and undesirability. Her mother was convinced that Emily's father had abandoned them because he found his wife too fat and that her weight was the fatal cause in the ending of every relationship she'd ever had. Emily described the experience of her sense of her body changing and being invaded again by the gazes of others. She felt helpless, unable to hold her gains from her therapy. She became convinced that Lara was just saying nice things to make her feel better.

And then she said to me, "My body is unhappy when it is fat." I responded with, "You mean that you feel happier with your body when it is thinner. You are unhappy with your body when you put on weight, and you imagine everyone else is, too." "No," she insisted, "my *body* is happier when it is thin, not me. My body is unhappy when it weighs too much. My body knows when it puts on weight." My god, I thought to myself, what an extraordinary statement. I suddenly found myself imagining this body of Emily's literally absorbing the anxiety and disgust of her mother's body toward itself and toward Emily's body when one/the other/ or both were "*too fat.*" I imagined her young body literally an unhappy body in the grip of another's/mother's unhappy body in a symbiotic fusion, the sensations merged, the sensation of literally making her mother's body unhappy, the sensations of disgust. Only thinness brought some possibility of relief, acceptance, fleeting happiness. I imagined the literal, unspoken, flesh-to-flesh transactions that must have impinged upon Emily's body from birth. A phrase kept flashing through my mind, "the *weight* of the gaze of others." I felt that weight in my own body, as well as a sadness and fierce protectiveness toward Emily. I could identify with Lara's wish to ward off the mother by offering a different kind of maternal presence, to reassure Emily of her worth and attractiveness, and to protect her from a vicious parental introject.

I asked Emily to close her eyes and bring our conversation into her body. How was she sensing/feeling our discussion in her body? Could she put words to the experience of her body. "I feel heavy . . . heavy like fat and heavy like sad, weighted down," were Emily's first words, continuing, "The eyes of the others are always so heavy." I repeated her words, slightly amplifying their intensity. I suggested she begin to *feel* the eyes of others surrounding her, intruding, judging, shaming, weighing her down. I asked that she feel how it is to be noticed for her exterior, the surface and size of her body. "What is it that people see and know (or think they know) about you when they see your size and surface?" I asked her quietly, several times over. "What is it about you that is not seen?" "What is it that is of no interest to these eyes at the surface?" I did not want Emily to speak in response to my questions, but to be with these questions in her body. I asked Emily to feel the *weight* of these eyes upon her body. As time passed, I asked her to both *describe* and *show* what was happening in her body. "I'm being crushed. It crushes me." "*Show* me the crushing," I urged Emily. Her body began to collapse, I moved behind her, and Lara moved in front to take my place. As her body began to collapse against me, Emily suddenly said, "*I* want to crush *them*!" She opened her eyes, looked at Lara, took Lara's hands, and began to press her back forcefully into my chest. She pushed long and hard until I finally gave way. Then she pulled herself forward into Lara's arms, crying. Gradually, Emily opened her eyes, locking them on Lara's, challenging her mother in a torrent of words, and speaking of Lara's importance to her with the force of both gaze and voice growing.

In time, she shifted her gaze from Lara to include me and began to reflect on the experience of her body. We spoke of the literalness of her body being happy, rather than she herself being happy, of her sense of herself being so concretely tied to her bodily perceptions and sensations. Emily asked how this was possible and what to do about it. I described to her my fantasy that the "happy/unhappy body" was originally that of her mother, not her, but as her mother could literally not tell herself apart from her daughter, it all felt one and the same. How could her body as a baby, a growing girl, be happy when enveloped, nearly possessed, by her mother's profound anxiety and unhappiness with her own body? I wondered aloud about the confusion she may have felt in the midst of these crazy, destructive projections on her mother's part that were also ferociously loving and protective in their intent. Her mother seemed (and seems) to have had no sense of self separate from the external appearance of her own body, so how could she have helped Emily develop that separation? Emily needed to develop a new relationship to her "unhappy" body and to explore the conflict between these two felt, sensate aspects of her self-experience.

Thirty years after Emily's birth, verbally and nonverbally, Emily's mother was still communicating the same, affect-laden messages to her daughter and her daughter's body. As I reviewed my notes in preparation for writing about this consultation, I asked myself what it was about this single consultation that came to mind as I imagined the issues I wished to address in this chapter. Why did this particular session stay in my mind in such a compelling fashion? I realized that there was something very moving and familiar for me in my own body of the fusion and confusion of love, longing, and anxiety between Emily and her mother within the traces of my own early bodily relations with my mother. I felt a deep, somatic countertransferential identification with Emily's vulnerabilities to her mother's anguished body, which quite literally moved me and informed our work.

In the very midst of the consultation I recalled a disturbing passage from Christopher Bollas' book, *Hysteria*:

> As maternal love is the first field of sexual foreplay, the hysterical mother conveys to her infant's body an anguished desire, as her energetic touches bear the trace of disgust and frustration, carrying to the infant's body communication about sexual ambivalence, "rolfed", as it were, into the infant's body knowledge, part of the self's unthought known. (2000, p. 48)

Whose body is Emily actually experiencing within herself? Her own, her mother's, some amalgam of the two? Who is in treatment? Emily, her mother, her maternal grandfather, the dyad of Emily and her mother, perhaps all of them?

My interventions with Emily were fundamentally somatic and experiential, sensing and feeling our conversation and the eyes of others in her body, in a subsymbolic communication. In my mind were notions of hysterical Rolfings, enigmatic signifiers, maternal narcissistic possession, all of which helped open my body to Emily's struggles and to find a way to bring that struggle alive in the room within her body and among the three of us.

The focus in my first consultation with Lara and Emily had also been at a somatic level, working directly with her eyes. The work was quite useful and self-sustaining until strained and ultimately overwhelmed by the deepening erotic intimacy with her boyfriend (my interpretation) and the continuing encounters with her mother and grandfather. Emily could not sustain her ownership of her body. As we all do so often, Lara sought to relieve Emily's suffering. I think we have all experienced the limits of those interventions. When the impasse is rooted in the flesh, patient and therapist must typically enter the suffering, live it together, to experience an understanding in the mode in which the problem is being held and enacted. Emily captured this level of reality when she said, "I know it isn't true, but that is how it feels, and it feels entirely real."

When Emily said, "My body is unhappy," I redefined what she meant by saying "*You* are unhappy with your body." But Emily meant what she said, in the way she said it—this was a description of experience at the level of the subsymbolic. I realized then that a different level of intervention and involvement would be needed. I slowed myself down, shifting my attention into myself, noticing the ideas, fantasies, images, body sensations that came up in me as I stayed with this statement, "My body is unhappy." Bits and pieces of things I've read came to mind, as did a few of my own patients. The phrase "the weight of the gaze" kept floating through my mind. I began to feel a continuity of the previous year's session with what was happening now, i.e., a shift from Emily's experience of her own eyes, to the impact of the eyes of others, real and imagined. As I often do, I was trying to experience in my own body what Emily was describing in hers, and I began to sense a place to start, the sense of being *weighted down*.

We shifted to the subsymbolic (Bucci, 1997a, 1997b, 2008) level of experience as I asked Emily to bring our conversation into her body, to *feel* our conversation in her body. I was, in essence, inviting her to think *with and through* her body, rather than think *about* it. This was a grounding in the subsymbolic, a grounding for an evolving referential process of connecting to other modes of experience. *"Show me the crushing"* is a very different intervention than "tell me about . . .," anchoring the work in her body and body movement. We reached an understanding in her body, through her somatic experience, rather than through her (or my) cognition.

Emily's spontaneous rush of words against her mother and her physical move toward Lara, unleashed by the expression of aggression in her body, began the shift from the sensate/somatic subsymbolic experience to that of the nonverbal symbolic and then to the verbal symbolic (Bucci, 2011). She was then able to spontaneously include me in the dialogue with Lara, and the three of us could begin to reflect on the meaning of what had happened and to look to the future. It is a testimony to the quality of the work and the level of trust between Emily and Lara that we were able to cover so much ground in a single session. It is probably no coincidence that given her absent father, the presence of a third, especially a male, helped to open the physical, sexual space between Emily and Lara for action and exploration.

Emily had had little experience at a body level that others' perceptions were different from her mother's, that others' bodies could receive her body differently from how she was perceived/received through her mother's body. Something new needed to be known at a body level as well as at a cognitive level. Verbal permission, empathy, or attunement may be rendered useless by the depth and pervasiveness of the unconscious underpinnings of the somatic/relational "protocol" (Berne, 1963; Cornell & Landaiche, 2006), the subsymbolic levels of psychical organization set wordlessly within one's primary relationships. Over and over again, in the face of anxiety, shame, and doubt, Emily will need to slowly experience her body evoking responses in the eyes and touch of others different from those that have been forever known through her mother.

I think not only of my experience as a psychotherapist but also of my experience as a father. Each of my sons, whose very distinct personalities (differences that were quite apparent virtually from birth) needed me to be a different kind of father in the service of their becoming different kinds of selves, now very different kinds of young men. Each has quite unconsciously but very persistently forced me to be the particular kind of father, the sort of father they needed to be able to internalize, grow through, push against, and differ from. The father that each of my sons has at various times needed me to be has been rather different from the one I had imagined I would be. Sometimes I have succeeded with each of them; other times I have failed. But always there has been this force of shaping and using each other.

Central in Winnicott's (1971) writings on the mother/infant relationship and its evocation within the therapeutic relationship is the concept of the baby's *use* of the mother during a crucial developmental phase in which the baby relates to the parent less as an "other," but more as an instrumental extension of the self, and so, too, at times between patient and analyst. Of course, as with my sons, we see the importance also of the father and the father's body. Bollas (1989) extends and elaborates Winnicott's observations of object usage to argue that each patient must be free to use and shape the therapist into forms and functions which help the patient to first discover and then give expression and form to an emergent "true self."

Pat needed to quite literally push and shape me as an instrument for her self-experiencing—moving, looking, speaking, often not knowing what we might find but exploring the spaces of the yet-to-be-known. Emily was able to begin challenging and experimenting with the very literal, deeply habituated, experiences of her body in relation to others.

Within the fields of body-centered psychotherapies, there has been a profound change in the understanding of what it means to work at the level of somatic organization, both with our patients *and* within ourselves as practitioners. Working with the body is now understood as the provision of systematic attention not only to patterns of movement and muscular action (or inaction), but also to subtle states of affect, sensation, and fantasy. Psychotherapeutic attention to the body seeks to deepen self-awareness, emotional capacities, and integrate different levels and forms of self-experience. Work with the body may at times involve touch but does not have to. It may involve movement but does not have to. It does require psychotherapists have a genuine comfort with and working knowledge of their own bodily experiences and subjectivity—conscious and unconscious. We do not all need to become fully trained *body* psychotherapists in order to become psychoanalysts, psychotherapists, or counselors who know how to attend to bodily states and communication within more traditional frames of practice.

This is intimate work. This is delicate work. It is work that requires the flexibility and emotional availability of the therapist. It requires the provision of a living space within which there can be the gradual unfolding and formation of meaning and agency within the patient's gestural world. The patient's bodily gesture and activity (both cognitive and somatic) are acknowledged and allowed to exist in their essential physicality, haunted by the ghosts of the historical losses and failures. The gestural field is enlivened in the here and now to be gradually brought into the light of new possibilities, into a grammar of new experiences, through the grammar of movement, into a grammar of relatedness, and into the grammar of language and personal agency.

I am not suggesting that body-centered interventions should supplant cognitive investigation and verbal interpretation. But I am arguing, and hope to illustrate, that more systematic attention to and intervention within patterns of nonverbal, somatic expression can deepen and extend psychoanalytic and cognitively oriented therapies. In the chapters and pages ahead, I shall be discussing and illustrating numerous means of working more systematically and intentionally with patterns of somatic organization through the informed and intentional use of embodied language, sensate experience, movement—with and without direct, physical contact.

Chapter 2

The Radical and Tragic Vision of Wilhelm Reich

The arrangement of Sigmund Freud's consulting room must have evoked an unusual physical intimacy, especially within the times and Victorian culture of *fin-de-siècle* Vienna. Though Freud's chair was positioned at a right angle to the patient, the arm of the chair was directly against the back of the couch, placing Freud's shoulder but inches from the patient's head. The patient would have felt Freud's voice resonating from behind, with a kind of closeness we usually associate with being held. The two would have been near enough for whatever residue of Freud's cigar smoke that permeated his clothing to have drifted to the nostrils of his patient. He could have easily turned slightly, be it in moments of reverie or with conscious intent, to cast his gaze over the patient's body. If Freud turned to look upon his patient, could the patient sense this shift from being heard to being seen? Though Freud's stated preference in psychoanalysis was for mental content, neither Freud nor his patients could ever fully escape the body's presence within the analytic hour. Even as he looked away from his patient, enveloped in his own associative processes, Freud's gaze would have fallen upon hundreds of antique representations of the human body, filling every available surface and cranny (Engelman, 1976). Everywhere in Freud's consulting room were images, artifacts, the presence of the human form.

The body, with the vitality and force of the drives, was central to Freud's thinking, from the very beginnings of his neurological and clinical explorations. Fast (2006) contrasts Freud's historically favored model of primary and secondary processes—which casts the primary process body "developmentally and clinically primitive" (p. 275) which is to be replaced by "body-free, logical-rational secondary processes" (p. 275)—with that of Freud's more radical though undeveloped vision, in which "the mature mind . . . is a body-based organization of increasingly sophisticated and nuanced patterns of experience in which the personal and emotional are of continuing importance" (p. 275).

Attention to the body did not disappear altogether within the early psychoanalytic communities in Austria and Germany. The genesis of psychoanalysis and the early beginnings of bodywork (Brooks, 1974; Weaver, 2004; Heller, 2012) ran in precarious parallels of mutual interest and suspicion. Vienna, Baden-Baden, Budapest, and Berlin were all sites of psychoanalytic excursions into bodywork, which I have delineated in an earlier article (Cornell, 2008a). Groddeck (1977), at his spa and residential clinic, incorporated massage, deep tissue work, sensory awareness, hot baths, special diets, exercise, and his own brand of psychoanalytic inquiry into his therapeutic regimens. He maintained a friendly relationship with Freud, and his work influenced Ferenczi and Reich. Ferenczi, Horney, and Fromm-Reichmann among other analysts were visitors to Groddeck's clinic. Other than in the work and experimentations of Groddeck, Ferenczi, and Reich, the living, breathing, moving body of patient and analyst faded to the fringes of psychoanalytic theories.

Reich, before his Marxist involvements, was a favorite "son" of Freud's, cast by some to be Freud's heir apparent. In Vienna and Berlin at the time of the Weimar Republic was a center of artistic, intellectual, psychoanalytic and somatic experimentation (Danto, 2005); the formative years of psychoanalysis in the first decades of the 20th century were alive with creative fervor. In her translation of a series of letters from Freud to Reich, Elizabeth Danto (2011) characterized their relationship, with Freud as "the benevolent but enigmatic father; Reich the simmering, sensual son" in a "scenario of love and estrangement, suggesting that their fractured relationship" echoes still, in psychoanalysis as in the world (p. 165).

Yet psychoanalytic theory and practice seems to have become so identified with the mind and symbolization, that as a field of practice it has developed a dis-ease with somatic life and sexuality. It has come to the point that André Green (1996), in his Sigmund Freud's Birthday Lecture at the Anna Freud Centre in London, would ask a question now, "Has Sexuality Anything to Do with Psychoanalysis?," that at one time in the history of psychoanalysis would have been absurd. The roots of this gradual disappearance of the body may lie in Freud's abandoning his early experiments with physical contact, hypnosis, cathartic technique, massage, electrotherapy, and possibly genital stimulation (Aron & Starr, 2013), then feeling compelled to develop his talking cure, a method that privileged ears and mind over hands and body as primary therapeutic instruments. The talking cure could well have been a safeguard to ensure the respectability of Freud's emergent science of psychoanalysis. It was Wilhelm Reich, one of Freud's most brilliant and loyal adherents, who continued to embrace Freud's initial interest in and experimentation with soma and sexuality.

World War I had left Freud deeply dispirited. In reaction, Freud determined that his psychoanalytic movement had to have a fundamental social (though not political) responsibility, and at his urging each city with a major psychoanalytic center established a clinic offering free psychoanalysis and education to the poor and working class, first in Berlin in 1920 under Karl Abraham and then in Vienna in 1922. Reich's experience in the Vienna clinic had a profound influence on him. This is how Reich recollected his experience in *The Function of the Orgasm*:

> The psychoanalytic clinic became a fountainhead of insights into the mechanisms of neuroses in impecunious people. . . . The consultation hours were jammed. There were industrial workers, office clerks, students, and farmers

from the country. The influx was so great that we were at a loss to deal with it . . . Work in the clinic soon made the following very clear:

Neurosis is a mass sickness, an infection similar to an epidemic, and not the whim of spoiled women, as was later contended in the fight against psychoanalysis.

Disturbance of the genital sexual function was by far the most frequent reason given for coming to the clinic.

Neither the psychiatrist nor the psychoanalyst thought to inquire into the social living conditions of the patients. It was known, of course, that there was poverty and material distress, but somehow this was not regarded as relevant to treatment. Yet, the patient's material conditions were a constant problem in the clinic. It was often necessary to provide social aid first. All of a sudden there was a tremendous gap between private practice and practice in the clinic. (1961, pp. 74–75)

In this passage we see the themes that came to dominate Reich's work—the influence of people's actual life circumstances on their psychological and emotional wellbeing and the role of sexuality in emotional health. The experiences in the polyclinic radicalized Reich and drew him to Marx and the Communist movement as potential solutions to the mass-social problems he witnessed.

Between 1919 and 1921, Otto Fenichel, an analysand of Paul Federn, was among the young psychoanalysts-in-becoming who were drawn to the left-wing youth movements (Reich, 1983). Fenichel founded a seminar on sexuality, in which Reich became a member (Reich, 1961, pp. 3–19). Fenichel became both mentor and friend to Reich, and both became members of the Psychoanalytic Society of Vienna; both were 23. Reich had a brief analysis with Isodor Sadger and then moved to Fenichel's analyst, Federn (Federn, 1990; Heller, 2012). In 1922 Fenichel moved to Berlin and asked Reich to take over the seminar on sexuality. Karl Abraham had established the first formal psychoanalytic society in Berlin in 1908. After the war, the Berlin society became the most formal and structured psychoanalytic training institute in Europe (Makari, 2009), an analytic center that trained Erich Fromm, Karen Horney, Edith Jacobson, Melanie Klein, Helena Deutsh, Michael Balint, Nic Waal, Ola Raknes, and Trygve Braatoy, among many others. Abraham died in 1925, and by then Fenichel had become established as one of the trainers at the Berlin Institute. In Berlin, Fenichel became acquainted with the body-centered "gymnastics" movement of Elsa Gindler, who was soon to become an influence on Reich and many other analysts. Fenichel began linking the characterological theories of Abraham with muscular patterns (Heller, 2012, pp. 422–428). At the same time, in Vienna, Reich was coming to similar conclusions, first explored in his classic *Character-Analysis* (Reich, 1933). When Reich moved to Berlin in 1930, Fenichel introduced him to Gindler's method.

Reich's decade in Vienna was marked by prolific writing and radical experimentation. The world of psychoanalysis was rather more free-wheeling in the early 1920s than it came to be. As noted by Makari, "Just a year out of medical school, Reich was asked to lecture on clinical method. This was truly a case of the blind leading the blind, for by Reich's own account, he had analyzed four women and slept with two of them" (2009, p. 342). In 1924, now already a training analyst and a favorite "son" of Freud, Reich was asked by Freud to direct the technical seminar of the Vienna Society. Reich insisted that his colleagues present cases of treatment failure, so as to examine the limits of psychoanalytic technique. During this period of time, he began to elaborate his theories of resistance analysis and character analysis (Reich, 1925, 1933, 1949). While psychoanalytic histories expel Reich from sanctioned recognition at various points in his writing and social/political activities, his work during the Vienna period has had lasting recognition (Fenichel, 1945; Braatoy, 1954; Sterba, 1968, 1982; Frank, 1992). Reich's increasing interest in the somatic aspects of character defenses, his publications on sexuality, and his deepening involvement in socialist and Communist activities created anxiety and disapproval from Freud, with his subsequent marginalization within Vienna circles.

By the time Reich moved to Berlin in 1930 and became involved in the free clinic there, he was deeply involved in Marxist politics, to the dismay of many of his psychoanalytic colleagues, including Freud and, especially, Freud's daughter Anna. The German Communist Party set up an organization called the German Association for Proletarian Sexual Politics, under Reich's leadership, and the "Sex-Pol" era of his work was born (Reich, 1972).

Reich believed fervently that the capacity for sexual pleasure within a loving relationship was rendered virtually impossible by authoritarian family, social, and political structures. His passion in this regard is no doubt founded in the tragedy of his adolescence. The young Reich discovered that his beloved tutor was having an affair with his mother, a shocking betrayal that Reich reported to his authoritarian father. His father expelled the tutor from the household and so mercilessly humiliated his wife that she committed suicide by poison. Three years later Reich's haunted, tubercular father, facing financial ruin, stood in a lake, "fishing," in a frigid rain, becoming so ill that he too died. In 1919, then a 22-year-old medical student, Reich (1988) wrote a recollection of his youth and adolescence. Reich described his father's anguish, lurching from plans to shoot the tutor, to kill his wife, to force his wife and tutor to marry, to finally forgive the tutor and turn his blame upon his wife:

> Father unleashed his entire fury on Mother and exonerated [the tutor] of all blame by claiming that any young man would gladly have entered into such a relationship. . . . In senseless attacks of rage which occurred almost daily, he would beat Mother mercilessly. . . .
>
> Thus, the poor woman was driven to death like a hunted animal by her husband and children! None of us saw any way to remedy the situation. We all suffered—and she most of all. I do not hesitate to say that in those months she more than atoned for what she had done. (1988, pp. 33, 36)

By the time of his father's illness, the family had become destitute. Reich begged and borrowed money to send his father to a health spa in the hopes of his recovery. In his diary Reich describes his journey with his father to the spa:

> We spoke very little. I had wrapped him in a plaid blanket; he rested his head on my shoulder, closed his eyes, and appeared to doze. I stole a look at him: once he had been so strong, energetic, full of vigor. But how he looked now! And again I felt those indefinable pangs! What a stranger I remained to him. Had there been no way for us to communicate. . . . I forgot the beatings I had received so often, forgot his furious look, which had frightened me so horribly, forgot his scolding voice. . . . And I cursed the memory of her, for this was her doing! Just as I once blamed Father for Mother's death, I now blamed her. . . .
>
> On my trip home [from the spa], a telegram reached me, informing me of his death. I drove back with both of his brothers and we buried him in Vienna. I have never again seen either my father's or my mother's grave. I was seventeen. (1988, pp. 49, 50)

A year later, Reich (1920/1975) delivered "A case of pubertal breaching of the incest taboo," to the Vienna Seminar Sexology. Allegedly an account of his analysis of a young student from the Technological Institute, it was in fact a disguised self-analysis, with the words attributed to his supposed patient being virtually those from his personal diary (which was not to be published until 30 years after his death). Five years later, now working in Freud's Psychoanalytic Polyclinic, Reich (1925/1974) published "The impulsive character: A psychoanalytic study of ego pathology" in the *International Psychoanalytic Press*. Again this lengthy monograph was a disguised self-analysis. As Freud had anchored his study of dreams in his own self-analysis, so too did Reich (though less honestly) found his theories of character analysis in his efforts to understand his own troubled psyche.

Reich argued passionately that social and political structures had to kill the capacity for healthy sexuality in order to create and sustain the kinds of submissive masochism and hate-filled sadism necessary to maintain authoritarian social structures and economic arrangements. During the Sex-Pol period, he campaigned for the freeing of sexuality from social and governmental restraints, with a program that was decades ahead of its time. Reich demanded the free distribution of contraceptives and public programs for birth control to minimize the need for abortion; elimination of all obstacles to abortion, free abortions in public clinics, and financial and medical safeguards for pregnant and nursing mothers; the guarantee of sexual privacy for adolescents; the abolition of laws against homosexuality; the abolition of legal distinctions between married and unmarried couples; public teaching about venereal disease and maintenance of sexual hygiene clinics; and the training of all health care professionals in matters of sexual hygiene. Three sex education books were published for the public. The first, for mothers, *If Your*

Child Asks You, was written by Annie Reich (Reich's first wife); the second, *The Chalk Triangle*, for children 8 to 12; and *The Sexual Struggle of Youth* written by Reich, which was to be published by the German Communist Party, but it was rejected by the Party, so Reich published it himself.

Within years, Reich (1945) became deeply disenchanted with the gulf between Marxist theory and its practice in the Soviet Union. He was especially dismayed by the Communist turn away from a freer and more informed sexuality, returning to conventional, state-imposed moralities. In speech and writings he began to criticize the Party (1976). In 1933 Reich was expelled from the Communist Party due to his psychoanalytic work. Then in 1934, due to his political writings and activities, he was also expelled from the International Psychoanalytic Association, which—for more than a decade—he had both inspired and always criticized.

Reich became a hero of the student movements in the United States, France, and Germany during the late '60s and early '70s. His work became the hallmark of the movements for sexual freedom and radical, leftist politics. I doubt that most people at that time had ever bothered to read his work in any detail or subtlety. His was not an advocacy for casual or promiscuous sex. While Reich was stridently opposed to the legislation of sexuality, his was a sexuality of passion, tenderness, and mutual responsiveness—freed from the intrusions of Church and state. Reich was keenly aware that intimacy and true political freedom entailed deep interpersonal and social responsibility.

From my first discovery of Reich's work at the Esalen Institute, encountering Reich's writing was a revelation to me and a glorious stimulant for a restless adolescent mind. He was truly radical. He was passionate, a stunning contrast to other psychoanalytic writings I was exploring at the time that seemed to me so often pretentious and distant from lived experience. In stark contrast to other analysts of his time, Reich did not wish to simply understand human misery, he was dedicated to relieving human misery, to eradicating it. And he wrote explicitly about sex. I reveled in his sexual and political writings (1945, 1966, 1970).

After university and graduate school, as a naïve therapist, I aggressively pursued training in neo-Reichian body therapy (Kelley, 2004). My early training was very much in the mode of what Reich came to call "vegetotherapy" (based on the German word for the vegetative or autonomic nervous system), so as to distinguish his somatically based therapy from psychoanalysis. Rather quickly I became dissatisfied with this mode of work, and returned to a more informed reading of Reich's clinical papers. I discovered that the way I had been trained was a significant distortion and simplification of his work.

Crucial to Reich's evolution, and central to the work of body psychotherapists, was what he came to call "the breakthrough into the vegetative realm" (1961, pp. 234 ff.), a realm of psychological and emotional organization operating outside of conscious awareness and reflective cognitions. Reich's "vegetative realm" would now be framed in the language of implicit memory or subsymbolic organization, arenas of contemporary attention within psychoanalytic theory and cognitive research (Bucci, 1997a,1997b; Schore, 2003, 2012), as well as body psychotherapy. Reich first moved from the standard practice centered on dreams and free association to a style that analyzed patterns of resistance. As he began to address resistances more directly, he noticed subtle changes in his patients' breathing, body posture, and movements. He then began to directly address, first verbally and then physically, these unconscious somatic reactions. With this methodological breakthrough, Reich began to create a new psychotherapy, one grounded in precognitive and somatic processes, leaving behind his identification as a psychoanalyst (though never relinquishing his deep admiration for and identification with Freud). He opened a new realm of understanding and technique to the therapeutic process centered in careful attention to shifts in bodily aliveness and movement within the therapeutic hour. Reich was a more active participant in the therapeutic hour than the standard psychoanalyst of his day. He could be direct to the point of sometimes becoming mercilessly confrontive.

What I want to stress here are two aspects of his work, the first being that Reich worked in the here and now, carefully tracking the shifts on the patient's bodily and interpersonal expression that either brought the patient more fully alive in the session or deadened internal and interpersonal contact. He actively called the patient's attention to the interpersonal and somatic/muscular mechanisms, which he called armor, the means by which one deadened and defended one's self. The second is that his work during the character analytic period was, at its heart, profoundly interpersonal. Reich did not simply seek the *discharge* of affect, rather he sought to promote the *expression* of feelings to the therapist. "Show me . . . let me see . . . give me your eyes . . . let me hear it in your voice . . . " The goal for Reich was for his patients to develop the capacity for deep emotional experience and surrender in the presence of another. As much is required of the therapist as of the patient in such an enterprise.

At the heart of Reich's clinical work was his awareness of the body's need and wish for contact and love with another. In his monograph, "Psychic Contact and Vegetative Current," Reich describes the experience of what he called "contactlessness":

> However, we learn much about this phenomenon [of inner emptiness and deadening] if we make the patient relive the transition from the alive to the dead condition as vividly as possible, and if we pay the closest attention to the swings from one condition to the other during treatment. If one does so, one observes very peculiar reactions. One patient, for example, experienced the transition by having to repeat mechanically, "It's no good, it's no good at all," etc. The meaning of this was: "It is no good to try, to make sacrifices, or to try to get love, because I'm not being understood anyhow." Small children have a most tragic experience: Not being able to express their wishes and needs in words, they appeal to the adult in some form for understanding; the adults, as they are, are quite unable to feel what is going on in the child; the child tries and tries to make himself understood, in vain; finally it gives up the struggle for understanding and resigns: "It's no good." The

transition from full living experiencing to inner deadness is usually caused by severe disappointments in love. (1949, pp. 325–326)

"Severe disappointments in love" is an unusually poignant diagnostic statement for Reich. It is rather unusual to hear Reich speaking so directly of love in a clinical discussion, though he often wrote of love between mothers and babies and in the genital embrace. Reich read this paper, one of his most passionate pieces of clinical writing, at the International Psychoanalytic Congress in Lucerne, Switzerland in 1934, the meeting at which he was expelled from the International Psychoanalytic Association. His paper on heartbreak accompanied one of his most heartbreaking professional rejections. Reich's expulsion from the IPA was not only a result of his political views (he had already turned away from Marxist ideology), his clinical work, or his deepening attention to the body. Reich fell victim to both the internal politics of Freud's inner circle, the increasing vulnerability of the Jewish analysts, and the increasingly desperate negotiations of the psychoanalytic institutes with the Nazis (Jacoby, 1983; Cocks, 2001; Lothane, 2001; Reich Rubin, 2003; Makari, 2009; Sletvold, 2011, 2014). The 1920s and early 1930s marked a period of fervent creativity and dissent within the growing community of psychoanalysts. Looking back now, one wonders had it not been for the vicious rise of Nazism and its persecution, slaughter, and dispersal of Jewish citizens throughout Europe (Aron & Starr, 2013; Kuriloff, 2014), would the psychoanalytic community have been able to tolerate, and perhaps even welcome, its more dissident members rather than turn to increasing orthodoxy?

Recognizing that his work had to be rejected by the Marxists in a doctrinaire refusal to acknowledge the existence of the unconscious and sexology, and facing his rejection by his psychoanalytic colleagues, Reich concluded:

> For psychoanalysis, acceptance of my work would have meant the following: unity of social outlook and science; giving up the theory of the biological nature of perversions and of infantile conflicts; acceptance of a plan for an economic order in which the corresponding cultural policies could unfold, i.e., work democracy; giving up the theory of the death instinct and its replacement by my theory of the *social origin of anxiety and suffering*. (1953, p. 235, italics in the original)

Following the Lucerne conference, Reich escaped the growing danger in Germany through Denmark, then to renew life in Norway. The Norwegian psychoanalytic association offered him membership, but he declined. His identification as a psychoanalyst had come to a final end. In later reflection on his expulsion from the International Psychoanalytic Association, Reich wrote:

> I no longer felt bound organizationally, and was forced to loneliness. To be alone is conducive to the ripening of weighty thoughts, which one does not seek, but which force themselves upon one. . . . in 1934 I lost all, literally all friends in the professional circle. (1976, p. 232)

By the time Reich had made his final emigration to the Untied States, he had come to realize that his political involvements had been mistaken. In his 1952 interview with Kurt Eissler for the Sigmund Freud Archives, *Reich Speaks of Freud*, he spoke with frank regret:

> Originally I made one mistake, one great mistake. I set it up as a political movement. Political movements were initiated because of hunger and economic needs. So I created a movement concerned with sexual needs. You see? To begin with, it was wrong to create a movement on political grounds. I know that today, but I didn't know it then. I felt that enthusiasm, that first tremendous response. That kept me going for six years. (1967, p. 80)

This volume also contains the extensive, quite dramatic correspondence that accompanied and surrounded Reich's ultimate expulsion from the IPA.

In the 1934 paper, Reich weaves back and forth between tender and compassionate language on the one hand and his more familiar, distancing language of orgastic anxieties and vegetative currents on the other. One can see in this remarkable passage describing the evolution of his character analytic techniques that Reich's thinking foreshadowed both object relations theory and self psychology, a sense of the relational roots of psychopathology and character formation to which Reich repeatedly alluded but never fully articulated in his work. This passage speaks to the very essence of character analytic technique: not one of attacking armor and eliciting cathartic discharges, but of the delicate and carefully attended experience of shifting *in the present moment* between vitality and deadness, between motility and defense.

Once settled and teaching in Norway, Reich's character analytic techniques were increasingly focused on what he called muscular armoring, the patterns of bodily defense that he saw as the foundation of character. He increasingly *acted upon* his patients' bodies rather than interacting with. It was in this style that he trained many of his most devoted adherents. During his years in Norway, Reich influenced and trained many psychotherapists, and his body-centered style of character analysis lives on until this day (Sletvold, 2011). Sletvold (2014) provides an excellent, detailed accounting of the continuation of the Norwegian character analytic tradition among many creative practitioners. The International Psychoanalytic Association had excluded the Norwegian Psychoanalytic Society from membership throughout and after World War II, largely due to the Norwegian group's affiliation with Reich. I suspect that this exclusion created a certain disidentification with psychoanalysis for many of the Norwegians, creating a freedom of mind from orthodox psychoanalysis such that it was possible to continue thoughtful and systematic explorations of the inclusion of the body within the therapeutic process and relationship.

The IPA was not the only entity to use exclusion as a way of managing difference. Again there was the all-too-often-repeated pattern of Reich's cutting off contact with once-trusted colleagues and friends when they began to differ with him.

After his emigration to the United States and his deepening involvement in his orgone energy theories, his work became increasingly impersonal and mechanistic. His emphasis came to be one of breaking through muscular and energetic defenses through characterological confrontation and physical manipulation of the body. This was the generation of neo-Reichian therapists who subsequently trained me and those of my generation. With his theories of orgone energy, which he conceived of as the fundamental form of life energy, Reich amended his classic work on character analysis to argue:

> What psychoanalytic theory calls the "id" is, in reality, the physical orgone function within the biosystem. In a metaphysical way, the term "id" implies that there is "something" in the biosystem whose functions are determined beyond the individual. *This something called the "id" is a physical reality, i.e., it is cosmic orgone energy.* The living "orgonotic system," the bioapparatus, merely represents a particular embodiment of concentrated orgone energy. (1949, p. 304)

He invented various devices such as the orgone energy accumulator, orgone blankets, and orgone shooters, which he believed could be applied to the body to build up orgone energy to facilitate therapeutic interventions and enhance health (Reich, 1973, 1999). He now conceived of his work as fundamentally energetic and biophysical, the interpersonal dimension of his character analytic work virtually disappearing. Character was an energetic, biophysical system of defenses, acquiescing to socio-familial controls and squashing the life force within the body. The therapist's primary task was to physically and energetically break through the patient's character structure, evoking the discharge of negative emotions, and thereby re-establishing the body's capacity for more open and vital energetic flow and self-regulation.

While many neo-Reichian body therapists in the United States quietly bypassed Reich's orgone theories, they maintained some version of the energetic model and the central focus on breaking through the armor and promoting emotional discharge. Sessions consisted of patients lying on a mattress with little or no clothing, pushed into deep breathing in order to "build a charge," and directed ("mobilized," it was typically called) into vigorous voluntary muscle movement and sound so as to trigger involuntary (autonomic) muscular and emotional discharge. So, typical of the era when I began training, were the cathartic models advocated by Baker, (1967), Liss (1974), Lowen (1975), Pierrakos (1987), and Kelley (2004), here summarized by Liss:

> Emotional discharge is the method. Emotional discharge clears stuck feelings. When feelings "rise and subside," three results emerge:
>
> 1.   Feelings discharge consecutively, one after another.
> 2.   Unpleasant distress transforms into pleasurable warmth.
> 3.   The person's life-energy intensifies.
>
> These dramatic effects are based on direct observation of the emotional discharge process. (p. 38)

In body-centered modalities, especially those with a neo-Reichian bent, there is the risk of the seduction for both therapist and patient by the power and impact of the body and of body-focused interventions. It can be all too easy to position *the* body—treating this body as a kind of disabled "thing," rather than as a living means object of desire: fascinating, erotic, problematic. The therapist and patient work to fix "*it.*" Therapist and patient work on *its* tensions, *its* resistances, *its* armor, *its* collapse, *its* rigidity, or *its* sensorimotor deficits. The body becomes objectified; the work becomes depersonalized. There is an essential task to re-establish the body's relationship to itself, but when the work is a-relational and the body depersonalized, an essential aspect of the body is ignored at the peril of therapist and patient alike.

Reich's absolute confidence in his own thinking, at whatever phase and in whatever style, tended to create loyal, rather mindless acolytes who were not able to critique his ideas or techniques. By the time of his orgone theories, Reich had largely forsaken the subtleties and complexities of transferential dynamics and unconscious functioning; he never developed a theory of countertransference, as he had always conceived of himself as an objective observer and "natural scientist." As I began to question my neo-Reichian training in Radix, and seeing the problems in Reichian certainty of perception and meaning with the resulting objectification of the patient, I found a counterpoint in Winnicott (1971):

> My description here amounts to a plea to every therapist to allow for the patient's capacity to play, that is, to be creative in the analytic work. The patient's creativity can be only too easily stolen by a therapist who knows too much. (p. 57)

There will be much more of Winnicott in subsequent chapters as we explore his theories of play, psychosomatic partnership, and gesture, but for the moment I keep my focus on Reich.

Reich was deeply committed to the alleviation of human suffering. In his quest, Reich flung himself from one solution to another: psychoanalysis, character analysis, Marxism, the Sex-Pol movement, Sex-economic work democracy, vegetotherapy, orgonomy, his laboratory at Orgonon, and ultimately his battle with the emotional plague and cosmic orgone spacemen (Reich, 2012). In each phase of his work, Reich was passionately committed to the improvement of social wellbeing and human life on the planet. Toward the end of his life, Reich devoted himself to research in what he saw as cosmic orgone energy, which he believed could save the Earth from climate change and the pollution of atomic radiation (Reich, 2012).

Peter Reich's heartbreaking memoir (Peter Reich, 1973) of his life with his father captures Reich's final years, as he quotes his father's exhortations to him: "Yes, we are really engaged in a cosmic war. Peeps, you must be very brave and very proud, for we are the first human beings to engage in a battle to the death with spaceships. . . . Here at age eleven you have already disabled a flying saucer using cosmic Orgone Energy. Quite a feat" (p. 27).

Reich was well aware of the rumors and accusations of his being insane, which had followed him since the 1930s, when his former analyst, Paul Federn, argued with Freud that Reich had become schizophrenic. When under persecution by the U.S. government, Reich declared:

> Are men from outer space already living on the planet Earth? On March 10, 1956, at 10 o'clock at night, this almost incredible idea came to me: "Am I really a spaceman? Do I belong to a new race of Earthlings sired by beings from outer space who had intercourse with Earth-women? Are my children the first offspring of an interplanetary race? . . . I claim the privilege of asking these and similar questions without fear of imprisonment by any authority whatsoever. I hate the irrational. However, I believe that even the most flagrant irrationality must contain something of rational truth. (Reich, quoted in Makavejev, 1972, p. 46)

This amazing statement captures both Reich's grandiosity and his life-long sense of being out of place, of having no place. So, perhaps, belonging in outer space may have come to make the best sense to Reich, as a place where he might finally find a home. Only Reich, under indictment by the U.S. federal government, would have entitled his brief to the court "Atoms for Peace vs. Hig (Hoodlums in Government)" (1956).

Reich was a deeply haunted man. He often lived a profound contradiction between his written ideals and his actual life. There was often a naïveté to his thinking and a relentless sense of being driven in his life and work. Reich would become intensely fixated on every new idea he had, always framing them as revolutionary discoveries. His writing was strident and often breathtakingly self-certain. He wrote, for example, in the 1926 preface to the first version of *The Function of the Orgasm*:

> I publish this work fully aware that it deals with very "explosive material" and that I must therefore be prepared for emotionally-based objections . . . there is always danger of distortion or ideological coloring of factual judgment. The question, however, is not the presence or absence of an ideology but rather the type of ideology involved; that is, whether an ethically evaluative attitude toward the problem of sex leads one away from the truth or whether a different moral attitude compels one to pursue it. (1926/1980, p. 5)

Reich was driven by the quest for the "truth" and was willing to suffer repeated ostracism in a relentless quest in which he seemed unable to question himself, his motivations, or the value of his "discoveries."

Reich invited idealization. He longed for it and dreaded it. In *The Murder of Christ*, a deeply personal and anguished diatribe written late in his life, he proclaimed, "Disciples have no hearts. They only want to get inspiration and warmth from the master" (1953, p. 122). The stridency in his writing was, and is, very easily converted into ideology. Few of Reich's friends and colleagues ever challenged him. A.S. Neill, the founder of the radical school Summerhill in England, a former patient, was a life-long friend to Reich, and the protector of Peter during the last months of Reich's fight with the U.S. government. The correspondence between Neill and Reich is a remarkable *Record of a Friendship* (Placzek, 1981). Neill became increasingly dismayed at his friend's intransigence and deepening isolation. In 1956 Neill wrote to Reich:

> I think you have few friends; disciples, yes, enemies, yes, but few who stood outside and were objective. Thus, I was genuinely concerned for Peter and his fears of overhead planes and his grownup-ness which is not real, for he wants to be childish and play a lot all the time. I could speak to you of him where one of your disciples could not. . . . I say you are wrong about Peter. He looks too anxious. I think he is trying to live a part . . . "I am the only one who understands what Daddy is doing." He may understand but his emotions are all mixed up. He isn't Peter Reich; he is Peter Reich plus Wilhelm Reich. (pp. 417–418)

I think Neill was the rare exception from whom Reich would tolerate such a direct challenge. Reich needed more friends like Neill, but that was not the case, which only added to the tragedy of Reich's ultimate fate.

Reich's work changed constantly, but at each stage, those who worked with him far too often idealized him, seemed certain that only they knew the true Reich. Reich's self-proclaimed loyalists and true believers simultaneously enshrined and embalmed his work in idealization and ideology. These were the men (and they were nearly all men) who carried on Reich's work, more as idealizing mimics than curious clinicians.

It was perhaps inevitable—given Reich's personality and his persecution, ultimate imprisonment, and the destruction of his books by the U.S. government (Greenfield, 1974; Sharaf, 1983)—that the neo-Reichian movement went through an intense period of paranoid isolation and self-proclaimed superiority. Reich's model was one of constant conflict between opposing forces, be they intrapsychic conflicts or the conflicts between the individual and society.

Al Alvarez has observed, "Freud may have called his method scientific, but, in practice, he worked more like a novelist than a researcher, creating form and significance out of the chaos of the unconscious" (2005, p. 19). Freud was deeply immersed in the literary culture of his time, and reading him is like witnessing a brilliantly creative spirit constantly calling himself into question. Like Reich, Freud often attempted sweeping efforts to address broad historical and social forces. Reich came to envision himself as a true scientist (Zepf & Zepf, 2010), but unlike Freud did not have the capacity to call his own mind and "discoveries" into question, an attitude fundamental to true scientific research. Perhaps due to the pressures of his own unresolved psychic traumas and repeated expulsions from his professional communities, the brilliant creativity and experimental attitude that fed Reich's early work collapsed. Reich lost track of the profound interiority of the human body. The body became a system of defenses infected with the "emotional plague of mankind" (1948, 1953), to be treated with mechanical interventions and orgone boxes, blankets, and shooters. He surrounded himself with true believers, and to read these first-generation Reichians (Baker, 1967; Raphael, 1970; Konia, 2008) is like visiting a psychic space that is simultaneously a shrine and a crypt.

Contemporary models of body psychotherapy have moved away from this foundation of binary oppositions, to a sense of dialectical tensions between mind and body, symbolic and subsymbolic, cognition and affect, speech and movement. Even more significantly, influenced by mother/infant research, attachment and object relations theories, and relational models of psychotherapy, body-oriented therapists now place much more emphasis on emotional *communication* rather than emotional *expression and discharge*. Reich linked the body to emotional and sexual health. Many body-centered psychotherapists understand the centrality of the somatic experience, movement, and motoric organization in self-agency, coherence, and the development of language and interpersonal skills.

Body psychotherapy today rarely engages in the forceful physical and characterological interventions that have typified bioenergetics, Radix, vegetotherapy, and some periods of Reich's own work, with the therapist as the all-seeing, all-knowing observer. The understanding of the centrality of the body in therapeutic change is now framed in models of the transference and countertransference communications, of implicit memory processes, and of the enduring effects of subsymbolic experience and organization. Body psychotherapists increasingly work with body process and expression as a process of interpersonal communication, often imbued with transferential wishes and distortions, inhibited by shame and anxiety, often delicate and easily disrupted. Somatically based psychotherapists no longer take touch for granted and often work with body process without direct physical contact.

In my own evolution as a somatically based psychotherapist and trainer, there was a period of deep disquiet as I became increasingly aware of the limits of the Reichian model. I considered abandoning body-centered work altogether, as I could not find answers to my questions within the neo-Reichian communities of the 1980s. But I was reluctant to give up on a model that seemed so fundamentally rich and right in spite of its limits. I turned to the contemporary psychoanalytic literature to expand my frame of reference, finding a goldmine of possibilities in the writings of James McLaughlin, Donald Winnicott, and Christopher Bollas.

Chapter 3

To Enter the Gesture as Though a Dream: A Psychoanalyst Encounters the Body

Seeking a bridge between my work as a body-centered psychotherapist and the newer thinking among psychoanalysts, I discovered James McLaughlin's work, reading first his papers in nonverbal communication and infant–mother interaction (McLaughlin, 1989, 1992/2010), which I found rather frustrating and disappointing. What truly captured my attention and imagination were his papers on self-analysis. I was deeply moved by his honesty; only in Harold Searles had I found such personal directness in the writing of a psychoanalyst. As I read McLaughlin, I felt privileged to witness a fine clinical mind at work.

McLaughlin wrote with a frankness that was both revealing and (as I discovered later) rather unsettling to many of the analysts of his generation. His ideas were not always well received. More than once he was told by disapproving colleagues that he should return to personal analysis to resolve his countertransferences rather than broadcasting them in his professional publications. The questions McLaughlin raised through the self-revealing nature of much of his writing—especially those on self-analysis and the meanings of enactment—speak to issues still very much alive in today's analytic communities.

Although I lived in the same city as McLaughlin and had read virtually all of his papers, we never met until brought together by our mutual interest in the place of the body in psychotherapy and psychoanalysis. In 2000 I was invited by the Pittsburgh Psychoanalytic Institute to give a paper, "Entering the gestural field: Bringing somatic and subsymbolic processes into the psychoanalytic frame." Lore Reich Rubin, daughter of Wilhelm and Annie Reich, a psychoanalyst in Pittsburgh, was a discussant. She offered a personal and rather humorous discussion of analytic parameters, arguing on the one hand that touch was outside the analytic frame, while ending her talk with an anecdote from her analysis as an adolescent. A proper Viennese analyst, he remained mostly silent. But he was also a proper Viennese gentleman, so each time she left the session, he rose to help her on with her coat. In so doing, he touched her shoulders: "It was really why I kept coming back. Of course, I never told him, because he would have stopped it immediately and just interpreted it."

McLaughlin, with his well-known interest in nonverbal behavior, had been asked to be my other discussant. After that evening Jim and I agreed that we each had much to learn from the other, and a collegial and creative friendship ensued until Jim's death in 2006.

A year after my presentation to the Pittsburgh Institute, I attended the first conference of the International Association for Relational Psychoanalysis and Psychotherapy in New York. Although McLaughlin's papers were referenced repeatedly, he was not in attendance. Upon my return to Pittsburgh, I told Jim often that his work had been mentioned, and suggested that he put his papers together in a book. My suggestion was met with a resounding, repeated, and heated refusal. Jim was retired and "done" with the analytic community, and feeling more bruised and battered than appreciated in the reception of his work, had no appetite for such an enterprise. Lew Aron, who was enthusiastic about the project for the Relational Perspectives series, informed Jim that his papers were widely read in the independent and relational institutes around the country. Sadly, Jim had not known that. He reluctantly agreed to undertake the book with me as editor, resulting in *The Healer's Bent: Solitude and Dialogue in the Clinical Encounter* (McLaughlin, 2005).

As we combed through talks and manuscripts in preparation for the book, Jim spoke of the psychic cuts and bruises that remained from the disapproval of his challenges to the then theoretical canons of psychoanalysis and ego psychology. Jim came to see the disabling impact of rejection and shame (Thomas, 1997; McLaughlin, 2005, pp. 23–30, 43–44) upon an analyst in his or her professional development, with the consequent foreclosing of the openness and curiosity necessary for true analytic exploration in treatment and in the evolution of theory.

Nowhere in McLaughlin's writings do we see the lingering effects of analytic rigidity and doctrinal thinking more than in his efforts to understand somatic (nonverbal) activity and experience within the analytic process. An interest in the body permeated his work from its beginnings but remained the most unresolved of all his areas of exploration and articulation.

In my paper to the Pittsburgh Institute, I argued that the prefix "pre-"—as in pre-oedipal, pre-genital, pre-object, pre-verbal, and pre-symbolic—was all too common in the psychoanalytic lexicon and introduced a bias that needed to be closely examined. The terms pre-symbolic and pre-verbal, by definition, suggest a developmental pressure and inevitable (desirable) maturation of these realms of experience into the verbal, symbolic realm. In that paper, I drew upon the recent research in the multiple code theory of Wilma Bucci (1997a, 1997b), introducing a rich conceptualization of *subsymbolic* organization, which I saw as an important bridge between my own orientation and more traditional analytic perspectives.

McLaughlin's first efforts to grasp the meanings of the patient's nonverbal activity on the couch began with several years of making—in the margins of his notes of patients' verbal reports—"crude notations about the positions and movements of hands and arms, feet and legs" (2005, p. 142), which were often accompanied by tiny sketches of body positions. He tried to correlate these visual noticings with what he was hearing, but ultimately abandoned his efforts, as he found this dual attention interfering with his capacity to listen in his more familiar analytic mode. He concluded:

> The patterning that can be shaped from my data takes its substance from the concatenation of action, words, and affective music. The totality can be impressive, particularly when repeatedly observed over analytic time, but it remains a web of circumstantial evidence. (2005, p. 143)

Significantly, given his later interest in the meanings of enactments and the mutuality of influence between patient and analyst (McLaughlin, 1987), his early observations included only those of the patients' bodies, not his own. His operating assumptions at the time reflected the traditional view that these bodily signals were signs of primitive, unresolved infantile wounds and longings.

As McLaughlin struggled to give meaning to the unspoken domains of the analytic process, he seemed often in a quandary. At times his language was profoundly distancing, as in "primitive kinaesthetic-proprioceptive-visceral experiences (like the Isakower phenomenon) through postural-gestural kinesics to the quirks of verbalization" (1989, p. 111). Often it seemed that the physicality of his patients on the couch was something to be observed from a careful remove. And, typical of the psychoanalytic bias of the day (Suslick, 1969; Lilleskov, 1977; Anthi, 1983; Kramer and Akhtar, 1992; Shapiro, 1996; Gedo, 1997; Krystal, 1997), he often equated the nonverbal with the pre-verbal and the infantile, a theoretical assumption which he came gradually to call into question but was never able to fully resolve conceptually or translate into effective technique. His ambivalence to his own project is evident:

> I do not wish to suggest that this attention to the nonverbal should, or could, take precedence over the usual analytic devotion to verbal content, nor that the kinetic play provides an alternative royal road to psychic depth. (1989, p. 116)

And yet, later in the same article, he described his persistent efforts to get a patient (Mrs. M.) to attend to her alternately harsh finger picking and soft self-touching, which he ascribes as affording him "a fuller view into her inner experiences of attachment and conflict, particularly in the maternal transference" (p. 118). This patient had for a long while resisted his efforts to call attention to and interpret her nonverbal activities. But "gradually she dealt with the gesture as she had grown accustomed to work on dreams, gingerly, but with some safety in viewing dream and gesture as being a happening slightly removed from her" (p. 120). *Entering her gestures as she might a dream* yielded a rich field of memory, associations, and intense interactions for Mrs. M. with Jim. His case material seemed to directly contradict his cautious, politically correct distancing from the very phenomena he sought to explore and articulate in the paper. Here we glimpse McLaughlin's growing sense that nonverbal behavior might constitute a gestural field rich with unconscious meanings of past and present.

McLaughlin reflected upon the historical biases that have profoundly shaped the dominant psychoanalytic attitude toward bodily expressions on the couch. He noted that from the earliest years of Freud's first explorations in the treatment of hysteria, physicality of expression was equated with hysterical defense and regression to the infantile. Freud valorized words over action. He commented that even as Groddeck and Ferenczi "wrestled with the muscular and gut power of what caught them up, and went off in directions of their own in their struggles to acknowledge the role of the nonverbal aspects of their analytic experience" (1992/2010, pp. 505–506), these pioneers of the body were roundly ostracized from the analytic communities surrounding Freud and relegated to the fringes of psychoanalytic history.

He observed that the century-long consequence "from the beginnings of analysis to this day, was Freud's overriding commitment to the saving power of rationality and to the secondary processes that language provided to ensure the dominance of reason in human endeavors . . . " " . . . out of which rational man, now epitomized by the generic analyst and the well-analyzed patient, was to shape and assert his higher reality view" (1992, p. 152). The fundamental rule was (and is) "*Say* what comes to mind." Action and movement were classically seen as regressive, infantile modes of expressions, actings out, which needed to be tamed and transformed into the verbal domains of rationality. He went on to observe:

> We still accept as valid the proposition that adult thinking is blended from three essential ingredients: a sensori-motor-visceral-affective mix that is the infant's earliest mode of responding; his later, or perhaps simultaneous, imaging in all sensory modes; and gradually, as childhood is traversed, a verbal-lexical capability that achieves relative dominance over human behavior. (1992, p. 152)

Even as McLaughlin struggled to unravel the meanings of what comes through the body, we see the languaged mind cast as the superior, mature mind. The embodied mind remains suspiciously unsavory. In the discussant paper that accompanied the original publication of McLaughlin's paper, Pulver (1992) reinforced Jim's ambivalent conclusions:

> From the standpoint of analyzing, nonverbal behavior functions exactly the same as character traits. First, the patient must become aware of the behavior. . . . Next, the patient must be motivated to understand what the behavior represents. For this to happen, he must become convinced that in fact there is some significance to what he is doing and that it is deleterious to him. . . . My experience agrees with McLaughlin's. It is rarely useful to call a patient's attention directly to any kind of nonverbal behavior, whether subtle or obvious, either by inquiring about it directly . . . or by interpreting it. (p. 175)

McLaughlin's struggles were deeply apparent in his later writings. He would put in quotation marks such evocative phrases as "set into resonance" and "evoked into companionship" (2005, p. 152), hinting at the intersubjective potential and richness of nonverbal communication, yet seeming reluctant to fully step into the experience. He could not quite grasp that, like most everything in our psychic make-ups, while there are often remnants of the infantile past conveyed in our nonverbal, sub-symbolic expressions, there is also a depth of affective experience in the present, as well as unspoken calls to future possibility—"evocations into companionship."

In spite of his interest in nonverbal behavior, McLaughlin was unable to make effective therapeutic work with it, concluding "I have found only limited usefulness in bringing background kinesics to the patient's attention, and not for reasons of resistance" (2005, p. 135). He notes that the limited usefulness of attention in this realm was not the product of the patient's resistance but rather the result of a theoretical field insufficient to facilitate elaboration and understanding. When the analyst is intent on verbalization and cognition as the primary signs and means of health, drawing attention to one's bodily expressions (which are often out of the patient's conscious awareness) can seem bizarre, shaming, or intrusive, as Jim vividly described in the case of Mr. E. (2005, p. 171). If, however, from the beginnings of treatment the understanding is one in which body movement and nonverbal expressions are seen and described to the patient as a form of communication, then the analyst/therapist's attention to the unspoken (in the analyst as well as the patient) can be much more productive. As a body-centered psychotherapist, I learned to tell patients at the beginning our of work together that we communicate not only through the spoken word but also through our bodies, so we will likely have multiple avenues of experience and exploration open to us during our work. Within this frame of reference, bringing attention to one's body (be it that of patient or therapist) does not seem so alien or potentially shocking.

Through my reading of McLaughlin's work and our many discussions on the topic, I saw that he had repeatedly tried to challenge this bias for the supremacy of the verbal order (while fearing the scorn of his analytic colleagues if he went too far out on this treacherous limb of somatic experience), as he argued here:

> It is this perspective that I support and extend: that the nonverbal behaviors of a patient significantly enrich and extend into the experiential dimensions of both what the patient is able to say to the analyst and what the analyst is able to perceive and resonate to as he listens; and that the enrichment is not just a primitive remnant of the infantile past but constitutes an integral and essential component of the full communicative capacities available to both parties in the analytic work. (2005, p. 121)

In his accounting of his "turbulent analysis" with Mrs. T. (1992/2010) McLaughlin described his patient's tendency to suddenly sit up, turning to face him and check out his facial expressions while feeling the floor underneath her feet. He wryly observed:

> I found that my encouraging her to lie down when she could, for the usual good analytic reasons, evoked only dull submission and affectless rumination,

> then mute rage and anxiety that we could not work on. Similarly, when I met her sitting gaze with exploring questions and requests for analytic work, her agitation and motility increased. (1992, p. 147)

He simply had no other available option than to urge the familiar mode of a prone, verbally reflective stillness that provided the reassuring evidence that "analytic work" was at hand.

Mrs. T.'s "motility" threatened McLaughlin and his analytic enterprise, but I would argue that the threat is not in the movement itself but in the lack of understanding of the possible meanings of "motility." In his discussions of movement and play, Winnicott, for example, draws a distinction between *mobility* and *motility*. For Winnicott, mobility had to do with movement from one place to another, the intentionality of getting myself somewhere. Motility, as Winnicott (1950/1992) conceived the term, refers to the literal experience of movement in and of itself, the experience of what he called the "muscle pleasure" of moving. What is central here is not the goal of the action, but the pleasure, the learning in the movement itself. It is a body sense, a body pleasure, a body learning, a body knowing—which can remain quite distinct from a verbalized, cognitive knowing. Verbalization does not necessarily enhance or improve this form of knowing.

Winnicott saw movement (motility) as inherently linked to aggression, not in the sense of the expression of hostility, but as the capacity to explore one's environment (both the impersonal of things and interpersonal of people), as in Joseph Lichtenberg's exploratory/assertive mode (1989) and Jaak Panksepp's seeking/expectancy model (1998, 2009). Like Lichtenberg from an analytic perspective, Panksepp, a researcher in affective neuroscience, does not posit these motivational forces as regressive, infantile, or stage specific but as life long and vitalizing.

Panksepp (2008a, 2008b) differentiates several categories of play, including exploratory/sensorimotor play, rough and tumble play, relational/functional play, constructive play, dramatic/symbolic play, and games-with-rules play. It is perhaps the exploratory/sensorimotor and rough and tumble forms of play that relate most directly to the processes of the activities of the body itself in the psychotherapeutic process. The other forms of play are more socialized and structured from the outside (like much of traditional psychotherapy and psychoanalysis) and are more dependent on instruction and languaged interactions. Panksepp speculates that rough and tumble play does not get the attention—at home, in schools, or in research labs—that other forms of play get, as it is seen by adults as aggressive, boisterous, and potentially dangerous. More organized forms of play, at the surface, may seem more constructive, purposeful, controlled, and thus more socially acceptable. Panksepp suggests that physical play "may be the most underutilized emotional force that could have remarkable benefits in psychotherapy" (2009, p. 21), something demonstrated in my work with Pat as we banged into one another. I will return to a more detailed discussion of the centrality of play from a somatic perspective in subsequent chapters.

Loewald emphasized that "early levels of psychic development are not simply outgrown and left behind" (1980, p. 81), recognizing that in love, sexuality, play, creativity, grief, our passions of all sorts, throughout all phases of life, retain simultaneous realms of the symbolic and subsymbolic. While it is certainly a primary therapeutic task to foster the development of the capacity for symbolic and verbal representation, it is not necessarily true that sensate and unsymbolized experience is in some way regressive or pathological or that it will be improved somehow in achieving the status of symbolic or languaged knowing. Katya Bloom, an analytically trained movement therapist, observes that when "ambivalent feelings are *given form in the present* in movement psychotherapy, they are . . . made more tangible and live than may be possible when using words alone" (2006, p. 182, emphasis added). Bucci argues that:

> . . . Freud was caught in the inconsistencies of the energy theory that he himself formulated, as well as in his implicit valuing of language over nonverbal forms. On the one hand, he characterized the primary process as a systematic mode of thought, organized according to a set of principles that he specified as the laws of the dream work. On the other hand, he also characterized this system as the mode of thought associated with unbound energy, the forces of the Id, chaotic, driven by wish fulfillment and divorced from reality. This inconsistency can be seen throughout psychoanalytic theory. (2010, p. 205)

Bucci's research in subsymbolic processes within the psychoanalytic discourse has led her to a different understanding, and one which I suggest profoundly informs the issues Jim attempted to address in his writings on nonverbal communication. McLaughlin's concerns are articulated anew in Bucci's writing:

> Of greatest interest to psychoanalysis, subsymbolic processing is dominant in emotional information processing and emotional communication—reading facial and bodily expressions of others; experiencing one's own feelings and emotions. . . . We are not accustomed to thinking of processes, including sensory, motoric and visceral processes that cannot be verbalized or symbolized, as systematic and organized thought; the new understanding of subsymbolic processing opens the door to this reformulation. It changes our entire perspective of pathology and treatment when we are able to make this shift.
>   . . . But the specific psychical terrain that we are trying to explore can be mapped only partially onto words; if we try to place the signposts prematurely— apply general mappings that have been used in other terrains—we will find ourselves blocked or lost. (2010, p. 205–206)

Much of what Panksepp and Bucci have discovered and delineated through their research echoes the frames of reference underlying most body-centered psychotherapy and can profoundly inform analytic theory. Panksepp's phrase, "an experience-expectant process," is at the heart of the work in body psychotherapy, this sense of expectation, of the drive, the fundamental need for *experience*, for *experience-based learning* through bodily movement and experimentation. Body-work and body psychotherapy are at their best when they afford a patient the opportunity to *find out* through the letting go of familiar or habitual body patterns into movements, sensations or interactions that are unfamiliar and novel. This is learning through lived experience, which can deeply enhance and enrich the cognitive, spoken functions of therapeutic and analytic processes, for patient and professional alike. Symbolization and cognition may follow, but here it does not lead. Body-centered attention can expand the analytic frame and bring meaningful experience and understanding to the nonverbal domains that McLaughlin so urgently wished to comprehend (Kepner, 1987; Hanna, 1993; Aposhyan, 2004; Ogden, Minton, & Pain, 2006; Fogel, 2009; Heller, 2012).

Over the course of a psychotherapy or psychoanalysis of any depth or intimacy there is a constant to-and-fro between the somatic/subsymbolic realms of organization and the cognitive/symbolic. There is a constant dialectical tension, not only over the course of a psychoanalysis, but also over the course of one's life, between our cognitive symbolic capacities and our sensate, somatic capabilities. Both are the stuff of life. Yet in most traditions of psychoanalysis, verbal interpretation and conceptualization have too often been privileged over somatic and sensate learning. It was this privileging that McLaughlin sought to question and understand in his examinations of nonverbal behavior, but his was a questioning that never came to a full and clear resolution.

There was a remarkable incident with Jim in 2006. He was then fully retired and rather physically frail, but the previous year he had joined, as a participant, a group that Pittsburgh psychotherapists had formed, called "Keeping Our Work Alive." The group sponsored a seminar series with leading writers in relationally based psychoanalysis and body-centered psychotherapy. Though no longer able to practice, Jim refused to stop learning. This particular session, "Enlarging the therapeutic frame (with panache and subtlety)," focused on bringing bodily experience and activity into the therapeutic process, was taught by Angela Klopstech (2000a, 2000b), a Bioenergetic therapist and trainer. As she taught, Angela was on her feet, moving gracefully around the room, interacting with various participants. After some time Jim suddenly burst out, "*I can't stand this any more!!*", which startled the group a bit. Angela inquired, and Jim responded with a verbal outpouring of envy and frustration, literally rocking back and forth in his chair as he spoke. Alternating between an intensely angry voice and a sense of resignation, he spoke at length about his admiration and envy of Angela's freedom of movement as she taught, her obvious skill in both *what* she said and *how* she said it. "I spent fifty years nailed to my seat, like a good little analyst, with my patients glued to the couch. God forbid anyone *moved*! Fifty years. I never got out of my chair in a session, I never moved, but I watch you move all around this room. And I have no question of your competence. I hardly imagine that you are acting out! I am so angry with myself." Angela listened, and she *watched*. "Actually, Jim," she said, "you are in your chair, true, but you are not still. Hardly. You are moving."

Jim did not know what she meant; he was still in his chair. She began to use her own body to replay to him what his body was doing as he spoke: coming forward in the chair, chest out, voice growing deeper and louder when he was angry and expressing his envy—and then collapsing his chest, rolling his shoulders forward, shifting back into the chair, arms collapsing, eyes averted, voice dropping as he spoke of his adapting to the analytic norms of his training. She had him actually repeat his physically shifting back and forth between the two modes of expression, using her own movements to both mirror and lead his, intensifying his affective experience of this conflict between the vitality of his fury and the depressiveness of his compliant adaptation to norms. "Thank you," said Jim, "that was wonderful, competent, and about thirty years too late."

As I listened, worked, and often argued with Jim during the last years of his life, I was repeatedly moved by his relentless willingness to be disturbed in his work self and to learn from his disturbances. This attitude was demonstrated anew in his final two published papers, both of which addressed the issues of movement and physical contact in analytic work: "Touching Limits in the Analytic Dyad" (1995) and "The Problem and Place of Physical Contact in Analytic Work: Some Reflections on Handholding in the Analytic Situation" (2000). In the latter paper, McLaughlin returns to Freud's dictum, "Above all, both parties were to speak, not act," (p. 65), while going on to argue, "I want also to demonstrate that the analyst's resort to preferred theory can be a protective retreat from affective intensities, in self and patient, and thus an impairment to the analyst's capacities to handle ambiguity and uncertainty" (p. 66). In both of these papers McLaughlin describes his struggle with his own affective and bodily urgencies in the face of the touching, and sometimes, bewildering struggles of his patients:

> I have come to see that my hard spots (i.e., allegiances to givens taught me) often provided justification for my blind spots of personal need and bias. . . . At the same time, ethical constraints that warn of the disasters of sexual intimacy and aggressive excess were indeed helpful in those brink moments narrowly averted. (1995, p. 438)

It is, of course, quite possible to attend actively to bodily experience and expression without an inevitable descent into disaster. But his struggles and anxieties were so commonly shared by his analytic colleagues, that he found few resources within the analytic community to help resolve the dilemma. McLaughlin knew well the power of words to touch, to impact the other. He also knew that actions (enactments) were an equally powerful, though an often less conscious form of communication that can affect and infect the other. However, he struggled to actualize the *intentional* use of direct work with the patient's body as a therapeutic intervention.

With his typical humor and self-deprecation he observed, "I do not recall how many volunteered handshakes I flappingly avoided or cut short without even watching for the consequences of my discourtesy" (1995, p. 440). But his patients persisted in various ways to offer or even insist upon a handshake, a hug, a reassuring moment of touch, or direct eye contact up off the couch. McLaughlin gradually relented while then noticing what actually happened (which did not always match the dire consequences so often predicted):

> I live with, and feel I must constrain, and do indeed constrain, the impulse to reach out and touch the hand, the shoulder, the cheek of a patient who is in abject misery. . . . I put these matters vaguely to suggest the powerful ambiguity of such moments when the intentions of the patient and my own press to respond are yet to be named, let alone understood. As experience and age have enhanced my span of ease, I have taken the position that I will make finger or hand contact in match with what is proffered and without requiring that the appeal first be explored and its meaning understood. (1995, p. 441–442)

As he shifted from his "refuge in my presumed detachment," (p. 445) he realized that he and his patients did not collapse into unending boundary violations, though he did notice that his patients were often quite aware of *his* anxiety and discomfort:

> Their actions flushed me out of my illusion of safe distancing and grabbed us too close for (my) comfort. Inside, I had to deal with the fresh surges of these immediacies added to the sexual and aggressive, pleasurable and repulsive, feelings and impulses between us. (1995, p. 445)

I think it no accident that as "experience and age" enhanced his range of emotional and bodily comfort (and discomfort), McLaughlin's interactive and interpretive style shifted from his initial preoccupation with focusing on his patients' psychic realities to one of the acknowledgment of the "dialectics of influence" (2005, p. 185–222) articulated in his later papers. In his final paper discussing Casement's classic 1982 paper addressing the pressures on the analyst by the patient for physical contact, he comes to state plainly, "We are very much at odds, Casement and I, about how we see ourselves in what we did in the critical interactions described" (2000, p. 79). Jim concludes his discussion with an attitude of exploratory openness, arguing that "in these matters I prefer to risk what feels right, to gamble with consequences I do not comprehend to prejudge, and to deal as openly as I can with the consequences of working in a two-part confluence" (2000, p. 80). Still, touch was a "gamble," a step into the unknown. The taboo against touch in the psychoanalytic canon has made informed and intentional interventions with physical contact nearly unimaginable. Jim did not have the opportunity to benefit from the substantial thought and training that goes into physical contact within the body-centered modalities of treatment (Zur, 2007).

Since McLaughlin's last published paper, contemporary analytic theory has increasingly sought to address the place of somatic experience and nonverbal communication within analytic processes and relationships (Aron & Anderson,

1998; Quinodoz, 2003; Bloom, 2006; Fast, 2006; Anderson, 2008; La Barre, 2001, 2005, 2008; Lombardi, 2008; Cornell, 2008a, 2009a, 2009b; Bucci, 1997a, 2001, 2008, 2010; Knoblauch, 2005, 2011; Alvarez, 2010, 2012). There is, of course, an irony—and often a frustration—in the effort to write about the realms of the wordless. How can we as clinicians gradually develop more ease and skill not only in moving from the wordless into the languaged but also from languaged realms into those of nonverbal bodily and gestural experience? How can we as authors and analysts use language and ideas to describe and evoke wordless forms of knowing (Cornell, 2011; Knoblauch, 2011)? A more sensate sensibility is emerging in contemporary analytic literature. Throughout these recent psychoanalytic writings there are important insights into the nature of somatic knowing and organization. The clinical writings of many of the authors referenced in this chapter are like glistening facets of a mosaic that is still forming.

McLaughlin labored within the analytic theories and cultures that formed him and that were slow to be called into question. Now in these more recent analytic explorations we see a shift from the observed/interpreted body to a lived/ phenomenological body. Attention to the immediacy and actuality of sensate experience and bodily activity can now be seen as a means to enhance affective meaning and deepen intersubjective understandings, rather than an unleashing of acting out or unbridled affect. Somatic attentiveness can, quite to the contrary of some of Jim's anxieties, be an effective means of affect regulation. This attentiveness to the subsymbolic may be sufficient in and of itself, or can lay the foundation for further verbal exploration and interpretation. Somatic attentiveness can ground an individual in their here-and-now experience, bringing a certain vitality and immediacy into the work.

There are times in the therapeutic endeavor when words fail, not always out of some defensive reaction, but often in entering emergent realms of experience that are not yet available in words, when the pressure to verbalize may circumscribe rather than elaborate experience. Something new, an emergent possibility, the leading edge of unformulated experience (Stern, 1997) may be evoked within the patient's body (or the analyst's), to be formed and formulated between analyst and patient. This is the territory that Reich proclaimed as "the expressive language of the living" (1972/1949, p. 355). Reich here brought the analytic endeavor into the sensate and nonverbal realms of communication:

> *We work with the language of facial and body expression.* Only when we have *sensed* the patient's facial *expression* are we in a position to comprehend it. . . . The patient's expressive movements involuntarily bring about *an imitation* in our own organism. By imitating these movements, we "sense" and understand the expression in ourselves and, consequently, in the patient. (p. 362)

How do we relate to the actual physicality of body experience within the patient, within the analyst, or between patient and therapist? If we begin to conceptualize somatic experience, at least in part, as a communicative process, the opening of a gestural field, then how do we enter this field? Bucci effectively evokes a sense of the body:

> These sensory experiences occur in consonance with somatic and visceral experience of pleasure and pain, as well as organized motoric actions involving the mouth, hands, and the whole body—kicking, crying, sucking, rooting and shaping one's body to another's. . . . These direct and integrate emotional life long before language is acquired. (1997a, p. 161)

Shaping one's body to another's represents quite a challenge to the classical analytic process. Somatic processes place unique demands upon psychoanalytic theory, the psychoanalyst, and the therapeutic relationship. In these sensorimotoric realms, the therapeutic process becomes a kind of psychosomatic partnership that can often be wordless, entering realms of experience that may not easily come into the comfort and familiarity of language. We experience the successful or unsuccessful shaping of our bodies in all of our vital, intimate relationships of any age and developmental stage. There is a fundamental knowing of self and other which forms first through the experience of one's body with another's. In life, and in psychoanalysis, healthy development involves the integration of motoric and sensate processes within the context of a primary relationship, establishing subsymbolic, somatic schemas of the self in relation to one's own body, to cognitive and symbolic processes, and to the desire for and experience of the other.

Central to psychoanalytic inquiry, to the process of the "talking cure," is the question "What comes to your mind?" and the freedom to speak it. In the exploration of subsymbolic realms, I would suggest that other questions may need to be asked (and *experienced*): "What comes to your body?" "What might you need to *do*?" "How might your body need to *move*?" "Can you describe any sensations in your body as you speak of this?"

In hindsight I can see that it was no accident that Jim and I came to work together so intimately. At the surface, we were an unlikely pair to embark on a project like *The Healer's Bent*. Here was a classically trained psychoanalyst forged in the decades of medical and analytic authority and convention, partnering late in his life with a neo-Reichian, body-centered psychotherapist trained during the '60s and '70s, immersed in anti-authority and relentless dissent.

We were each profoundly shaped by absent fathers and dependent mothers. Jim's physician father died in the 'flu epidemic of 1918 just six weeks after Jim's birth. Jim was raised by his melancholic mother and older sisters, with such results that "When the father dies, the mother is lost, at least for the length and depth of her mourning, and the gap compounded" (2005, p. 25). But he spent summers with a paternal uncle and cousin, who introduced him to the skills and satisfactions of woodshop and garden, which were to become the "transference sanctuaries" (1993, p. 79; Cornell, 2005, p. 6) of his later life. "When I'm in the shop," Jim told me, "it is as though the place says 'You belong here. You are alive,' and I come alive with the smell of the wood and the feel of the tools."

My father was broken in World War II and lived silently at the periphery of our family life. Like Jim, I pleased my mother and attended to my family as a pseudo-parent through my youth and adolescence, but did not depend on them for much. I turned to the woods and streams for solace and pleasure, building dams and tree forts alone, turning later to libraries, books, and ideas to feel alive and competent—by myself.

Here, Jim and I found a fundamental identification with one another. Jim told me in one of our conversations that he felt that the very early loss of his father had deprived him of the Oedipal struggle and its opportunity for full identification with his father and his own masculinity. As we grew to know each other, he said to me, "I am very womanly, in some ways sad and deformed, and still there is a richness I wouldn't have known if I was shaped by a father." Jim's early efforts to meet the Freudian ideal of the detached psychic surgeon were called out by his identification with a physician father (McLaughlin, 1961) whom he never knew but who had lived long in the family as a gravely idealized ghost. As Jim came to accept his more "feminine" (as he put it) traits, he was able to inhabit the stance of a "healer"—someone intimate, searching, and reparative at heart—the stance he sought to articulate in his book. As Jim aged, he came to see the analytic endeavor as affording a process of healing for patient and analyst each. He found that his patients far more often pushed him into areas of personal self-scrutiny and development than did his personal and collegial relations.

It was not easy for we two rather solitary characters to work so closely together, but we came to develop a deeply challenging and rewarding comradeship. He saw me, now partnered with a man, as far more masculine and aggressive than he, who had lived a heterosexual life. While I would argue with him that masculinity and femininity had little to do with sexual preference, his understanding of himself in this regard could not shift from the traditional analytic positions. He could not comprehend his "feminine" traits as something other than homosexual (see his discussion of Mr. F., 2005, p. 207–217). This was reflected in the title of his book, which he insisted upon over the objections of the publisher:

> I have come to refer to this discernable cluster of character traits as the *Healer's bent*. *Bent* underscores both the persistent internal shaping of character and behavior wrought by these reparative necessities and their external social thrust into the healer's world. It acknowledges also a slang reference to overt homosexuality. Together with *healer*, the word acknowledges some aspects of feminine identifications common to the homosexual and the healer . . . (italics in the original, 2005, p. 27–28)

Both Jim and I came to know and protect ourselves as children in quite fundamental ways through the unspoken and solitary activities of our bodies in relation to the physical (non-human) environment (Searles, 1960). We each, in our own ways, struggled to bring our solitary bodies into the realms of the interpersonal and intimate. While *The Healer's Bent* was Jim's insistent title, the subtitle of "solitude and dialogue in the clinical encounter" was mine. Jim's classical analytic orientation, which he was able to undo in many realms of his practice, created a kind of perfect storm of hard and blind spots with regard to the body. It was here that his theoretical training biases colluded with his personal, bodily isolation.

Rereading his papers on nonverbal behavior in the analytic process, I experienced anew this last frontier of his questioning and self-confrontation. Throughout his career, Jim endeavored to confront and overcome the iatrogenic damage he saw created to analysts and patients alike by the "strait-jacket" of classical analytic theory.

While we worked on his book, Jim read with great care and critique the papers I was writing on my own. He was adamant that I write more explicitly about my body-centered work to psychoanalytic audiences: What did I *do* with my patients? What did I *see* that informed my actions? He sensed that my neo-Reichian and body-centered trainings (rife with their own limitations and biases) afforded me a freedom to explore bodily experience and communication that he would not live long enough to unfold to his satisfaction. This particular work of exploring the life of the body was work he was leaving unfinished.

I am quite certain that Jim would find intense satisfaction in the growing psychoanalytic literature delineating analytic work within the realms of unspoken, subsymbolic realms of experience. He was a pioneer in this regard. Often underappreciated by his peers, Jim's pioneering explorations have inspired many of the generation of analytic practitioners that followed his. There is a sweet and poignant paradox in how much Jim loved words. He was a master of language, his writing so often evocative that it bordered on the poetic. There were frequent glimpses of how close Jim came to a true grasp of the enriching and intimate potentials of our bodily, unspoken domains of contact, as in this passage:

> Hour by hour, patient and analyst are awash in a steady flow of nonverbal information: body rumblings, postural stirrings, alterations in voice timbre and rhythm, the quality of the silence itself. (2005, p. 119)

Chapter 4

Hand to Hand: Touch Enactment or Touch Analysis?

The Centre Pompidou was filled with room after room of Louise Bourgeois' relentlessly disturbing sculptural representations of human bodies in beauty and anguish. The closing rooms of the 2008 retrospective exhibition, entitled *Tendres Compulions*, were devoted to works on paper. The final room was entirely devoted to a series of drawings in red ink of hands reaching to one another. It brought me to tears. Entitled "10 AM is when you come to me!!," these were drawings made each day of her experience of her hand reaching to the hands of Jerry Gorovoy, her devoted assistant and caretaker, coming each morning to get her out of bed. Every drawing was subtly different, each evoking a different relation of the one hand to the other. Ninety-five years old at the time of the drawings, she awoke each morning with the sense that this day would be impossible for her aged body. But every morning the reach and touch of Gorovoy's hands to hers made this new day possible:

> When you are at the bottom of the well, you look around and you say, who is going to get me out? In this case, Jerry comes and he presents a rope, and I hook myself onto the rope and he pulls me out. You see I can conceive of a way of getting out of the well. I'm just waiting for someone. (Louise Bourgeois, in Morris, 2007, p. 150)

The human hand. The human reach. The human touch. From the moment of birth we discover ourselves in and through the hands of others, in our vitality and vulnerability. Frail and close to death, Bourgeois discovered herself anew each day at the hands of her caretaker, in her vitality and vulnerability. We discover ourselves anew each time we turn to the hands and embrace of a lover, offering our own hands in return, in vitality and vulnerability.

In *The Hand*, Frank Wilson (1998) argues:

> . . . no serious account of human life can ignore the central importance of the human hand. . . . This message deserves vigorous renewal as an admonition to cognitive science. Indeed, I would go further: I would argue that any theory of human intelligence which ignores the interdependence of hand and

brain function, the historic origins of that relationship, or the impact of that history on developmental dynamics in modern humans, is grossly misleading and sterile. (p. 7)

And yet, so often, it is as though the hands of psychotherapists and psychoanalysts, as instruments of contact, exploration, and action, are to remain out of the reach of our patients. So, too, are the hands of our patients to remain at their sides, in the chair, on the couch, muted.

It was a brief experiment with hands that proved pivotal in the therapy with André. André had been in therapy most of his adult life. As we began our work together, he reviewed his previous therapies, each of which he found to be seriously lacking. Among the interventions he recalled with some feeling was that of being asked to draw his parents. André drew the backs of their bodies, hands in their pockets. He told his then therapist that all he ever knew of his parents were their backs: "They made it abundantly clear that my presence in their life was a nuisance." A childhood of bitter rejections fed André's adult life capacity to out-wait and wear down any offer of positive intent from those around him. In and out of therapy all his life, André's power was in his capacity to defeat others rather than to desire them. André sought me out because of my reputation of working with the body: "so maybe you'll have something more imaginative to offer," he said with a cynical edge that seemed to kill off any possibility of success. He filled the first session with bitter accounts of his childhood. I let his comment about working with the body pass for the moment. Now in his late 40s, he had two failed marriages and maintained reluctant contact with children from both marriages.

We had had only a few sessions, but I already had a sense that I, too, was sailing into the shoals of defeat. Then a session began with his commenting on his elbows, complaining that his elbows often ached, explaining that he used analgesic creams to alleviate the pain. "But you probably think it's psychosomatic," he said with the cynicism that was rapidly becoming all too familiar. He said his hands were tired of holding on, that his elbows ached from the tension of holding on. As he spoke, his shoulders curled slightly forward, his hands slumped in his lap. "Holding on? Holding in? Holding down? Holding back? Holding off?" I wondered out loud. "Hands can do lots of different kinds of holding." I reminded him that when we first met, he had expressed an interest in working with his body, so I suggested we could experiment with his hands and elbows.

I remembered his telling me of the drawing of his parents, backs to him, their hands in their pockets. Without reminding him of the drawing, I suggested that we stand, face each other, and that he bring his attention to his elbows and hands, noticing whatever sensations were there. He said it felt like there was a "log jam" between his elbows and his fingers. I asked if there were a movement of some sort that might move through the jam. He said he felt like grabbing my shoulders. I told him to go ahead. He gripped my shoulders quite roughly. I could feel the impulse in his arms to pull me closer, but his back braced and stiffened as his arms remained stiff and his fingers gripped. With the intention of bringing the tension in his back to his awareness, I brought my hands to his back, pressing my fingers into the tension there. As soon as I touched his back, his own hands went dead, and he announced, "I'm fed up with having to hold everything, and now you want me to do more." I explained that touching his back was to bring his attention to the "holding back" that seemed to be happening there and how it was affecting his arms. He asked that we do it again, and this time his arms and hands softened slightly. He said, "It's as though if I don't hold on tight, everyone goes away. It's always my job to hold on. I hate it and I resent it." I remarked that his resentment seemed to permeate all of his relationships, even with his children, continuing, "It is as though the only thing your hands are allowed is to hold on. It's as though there is nothing else your hands might want to do. Nothing else that your hands wish for, wish to express?" To my surprise, tears came to his eyes. He looked at his hands and then slowly, tentatively, brought the backs of his hands to the sides of my face. Tenderly. He wept. I was still, emotionally moved, imagining that he was realizing how much he held *back* as well as *on*. Our brief experiment with André's hands opened a wellspring of longing that countered his habitual, self-protective cynicism. Weeks of verbal exploration of his vulnerabilities and desires followed. André's hands served as our "consultant" when he found himself slipping back into his cynicism.

Perhaps the most marked dividing line between body-centered modalities and more traditional forms of psychotherapy and psychoanalysis is that somatic psychotherapists are trained to touch. The potential efficacy of touch in psychotherapy and psychoanalysis has been repeatedly lost in a swirl of professional fear, ignorance, and prohibition. In an essay examining the "preconceived prejudices" concerning touch in psychoanalysis, Nicola Diamond (2006) describes the communicative functions of touch as to be able "to feel the skin surface as affectively sentient [so as] to involve an open sense of the experience of difference, otherness, and relationship" (p. 79). She goes on to suggest that "touch can be considered a form of thinking, an affective 'know-how' tied to emotional memory; and touch operates in a way analogous to the function of language" (p. 80). Diamond concludes that, "It is not that touch is dumb, but that we have a legacy of debasing the sense, which has made us dumb about touch" (p. 96).

Over the course of McLaughlin's eloquent and challenging essays on psychoanalytic theory and technique, he coined the phrases "hard," "dumb," and "blind" spots, to capture the sense of the therapist's inabilities to adjust to the varying needs of a diverse clientele and the evolving timbres of the therapeutic process (2005, p.160). "Blind spots" refer to the residual unconscious limitations and rigidities created by the therapist's own unresolved personal issues. "Dumb spots" are created by the therapist's lack of experience in a given area of work, while "hard spots" are the rigidities of technique that result from unexamined theoretical biases. When it comes to the role of touch, its functions and potential efficacies, we encounter a nasty combination of hard and dumb spots: It is rather difficult to become thoughtfully informed about a subject that is met with the nearly universal "Don't do it!!" While there is some legitimacy in these cautions, a stance of *don't* does not allow the theoretical consideration of, professional training in, or practical exploration of the therapeutic functions of touch.

In the foreword to a recent collection of psychoanalytic papers discussing the role of touch in the psychoanalytic space (Galton, 2006), Orbach observes:

> Several assumptions dominate the discourse on touch in psychoanalysis. The first is that it is wrong, inappropriate, and unsafe: touch initiated by the therapist is invasive, potentially transgressive, and may bypass important psychic material. Another assumption is that when touch occurs it is because the patient has regressed and that a developmental deficit has brought it into therapy. Yet another assumption is to see touch as a one-off occurrence that was either unfortunate, that worked in this particular instance, or was a close shave. (2006b, p. xiii)

One can see a clear example of Orbach's comments in the work with André's hands, which simultaneously opened a place of developmental deficit *and* enabled the discovery of a powerful, forward intentionality.

One-off case examples of touch are occasionally presented in the analytic literature, with the typical conclusions that patient and analyst alike were able to escape alive and the therapy somehow survived. Orbach notes that as a result of these assumptions, there is a very sparse literature of any depth on the topic of touch in psychotherapy.

McLaughlin is one of the few psychoanalysts who not only acknowledged cases in which he touched, but wrestled theoretically with the analytic prohibitions against ever touching a patient. McLaughlin worried about the potential iatrogenic damage done by analytic intransigence.

Maroda is another analyst to openly discuss her conflicted thoughts and feelings about touching patients. She reflects:

> Up to now, all of my references to physical contact center on comforting a crying patient. Is that the only time I provide physical comfort? The answer is an unqualified yes . . . Physical contact is one of the most difficult issues for me. Though I no longer believe that some minimal, comforting contact is incompatible with the analytic process, knowing how and when to touch requires a great deal of sensitivity and a strong relationship between patient and therapist. (1994, p. 153)

I would suggest that training and supervision are also essential requirements. Over and over again when I present body-centered cases and papers to psychoanalytic audiences, I hear echoes of Maroda's struggles, invariably approached by analysts (over breaks, at lunch, almost always outside of the formal setting) confiding that they sometimes hug or comfort their patients with a touch or two.

Recent years have seen the publication of numerous discussions of touch in the psychotherapy literature from ethical frames of reference (Caldwell, 1997; Hunter & Struve, 1998; Smith, Clance, & Imes, 1998; Cornell, 1997, 2008d).

Authors grounded in Gestalt and neo-Reichian models offer differing frames of reference in regard to the use of touch (Smith, 1985; Kepner, 1987; Tune, 2005), but I don't think they adequately address the concerns and biases of the analytic and more traditional therapeutic communities. There is no systematic, informed clinical examination of touch in psychoanalysis, but attention to the clinical questions is emerging in the literature (Maroda, 1994; Casement, 1982, 2000; Ruderman, Shane, & Shane; 2000; White, 2004; Galton, 2006).

My operating premise is that the primary reason to touch a patient is to better inform both patient and therapist alike about the somatic, sensorimotor foundations of emotion and cognition (Fogel, 2009). The purposeful use of touch and movement in the therapeutic process is to enhance the understanding of *how* we know something, as well as *what* we know, to add experiential knowing to cognitive understanding. Sensate and sensorimotor experience is conceived as a crucial bridge between visceral experience and cognitive functions. We learn, at all stages of life, about the world and others through touch (Hertenstein & Weiss, 2011). Language and the symbolic capacities are obviously great developmental achievements, but we are continually shaping and shaped by our physical contact with the physical and human worlds.

Seen from an analytic perspective, with rare exception, virtually all of the clinical examples of touch in the psychoanalytic literature constitute poorly informed enactments on the part of the analyst, which were then more often than not handled thoughtfully after the fact. It is a central premise in my work that informed, consensual touch between analyst and patient can be an analytic instrument, in contrast to an enactment. I differentiate touch *analysis* from touch *enactment*, illustrating the analytic use of intentional touch and bodily movement to first evoke, then to explore and interpret, so as to facilitate understanding and containment.

Reich's extended case example in his work with a psychotic woman, "The Schizophrenic Split," (1949, pp. 399–503) offers an illustration of this physical exploration and interpretation of a profound disturbance. This treatment occurred during the early 1940s and although overwrought with Reich's "orgone biophysics" polemics of that era, presents an exceptionally detailed and sensitive rendering of his careful work with a deeply disturbed patient.

After several hospitalizations, this woman and her family, having read a good many of Reich's books, sought him out for intensive outpatient treatment. Bright, articulate, and sometimes highly functional, when faced with too much emotional stimulation she veered into pronounced psychotic ideations of "forces" that she told Reich she had fought against as far back as she could remember. While she insisted that the forces had "nothing whatsoever to do with her own inner urges," (p. 406) she said there were times she could hold on to reality only with great effort, feeling like she was hanging over an abyss most of the time and deeply confused by her simultaneous fear of the forces and her love for them. Reich wondered:

DO THE "FORCES" WHICH HAUNT HER AND WHICH SHE LOVES
DEVOTEDLY REPRESENT HER BODY SENSATIONS OF STREAMINGS

OF PLEASURE? IF THIS IS THE CASE, WHY IS SHE AFRAID OF THEM? (IT IS CLEAR SHE IS *devoted* TO THEM.) WHAT KIND OF MECHANISM IN HER BODY BLOCKS THE STREAMINGS OF PLEASURE? HOW DO THE BLOCKED-OFF PLASMATIC STREAMINGS TURN INTO "EVIL" FORCES? WHAT IS THE CONNECTION BETWEEN THIS BLOCK AND THE SCHIZOPHRENIC [psychotic] PROCESS? (1972, pp. 410–411, emphasis in the original)

I have placed "psychotic" in brackets within that quote as I believe from my reading of the case she would not be seen today as suffering from an organically based schizophrenia but from mechanisms of splitting and delusions typical of a psychotic structure (Sechehaye, 1956; Rosenfeld, 1992; Hinshelwood, 2004; De Masi, 2009).

From the beginning session, Reich is attentive to her descriptions and explanations of her experience (even as he considered them delusional) while carefully attending—through visual observation and exploratory physical contact—to her muscular tonus and respiratory patterns, linking together his clinical observations of her somatic processes to her verbal accounts. She was quite easily overwhelmed, and when overwhelmed the "forces" would emerge and menace her again and again. As Reich worked with this young woman, he received her self-understandings respectfully and would describe his observations and understandings of what was emerging in their work and her somatic/emotional experience alongside her own accounting of the forces.

In the tenth session, Reich reports that she came with a small cross cut into her chest at the sternum, saying she had done it "quite without any conscious motive," stating, "I must let off some steam or I am going to burst" (1972, p. 417). As Reich explored the meaning of this cut and her fear of exploding, she asked if he would permit her to choke his throat. "I confess that I felt, not embarrassed, but a bit frightened; however, I told her to go ahead and do it" (p. 419). This opened a 30-minute-long flood of contradictory, conflicted reactions and emotions. Reich continues:

> I knew that now her psychotic ideas would emerge with full force. When a certain degree of emotional upheaval was reached, I asked her quietly to try to stop the reaction. She responded instantly with full cooperation and began to slowly calm down. I had held her hand in my palm all through the breakthrough. . . . I asked her the meaning of the cross on her chest. I did not scold her nor did I threaten to commit her. This would have achieved nothing. (p. 419)

Reich sought to gradually facilitate her having undistorted experiences of her body sensations, that "would enable her to identify the true nature of the forces and would slowly destroy the delusion" (p. 423). He would ask her to voluntarily subdue her somatic and emotional reactions when they became too intense, and when she could not he would use his hands to coach her body in how to better contain and calm itself. He spoke with deep respect to her intelligence and her desire to get well, with great tolerance of and interest in her psychotic experiences, which he always accepted as meaningful and communicative, while constantly seeking to enhance her capacity to tolerate and understand her bodily and affective life.

Reich did not shy away from her violent eruptions and accompanying delusions, be they aimed at her own body or at him. He anticipated a three-task process that would be repeated over and over again to support her experience and gradual understanding that the forces which so disturbed her were actually coming from within her own body and psyche, not the external world or some supernatural realm. The tasks as described by Reich were:

a.   *To open the energetic valve of the organism:* SELF-SATISFACTION.
b.   *To brace her against breakdown* by a thorough working through of her hate against me.
c.   *To prevent,* if possible, *any attempt on her part to escape from the perception of her high-pitched organ sensations into delusions.* (p. 430, emphasis in original)

Reich was working to establish more aware and resilient sensorimotor functions as a substrate or infrastructure for her cognitive processes and affective tolerance.

Reich saw "rationality" as fundamentally, profoundly, situated in bodily experience and meaning. Reich was attempting to develop his patient's capacity for sustained emotional and sensate experience without psychotic splitting. He argued that self-awareness and self-perception precede self-consciousness, in which "its degree of clarity and oneness depends, to judge from observations in the schizophrenic processes, not so much on the strength or intensity of self-perception, as on the more or less complete *integration of the innumerable elements of self-perception into one single experience of the SELF*" (p. 442, emphasis in the original). Over and over again Reich would work with his patient to deepen her self-awareness to the edge of disintegration, psychotic splitting, and delusion, patiently calling together the pieces through work with his touching her body to focus her attention, while encouraging exploratory body movement to enhance her bodily awareness. He argues:

RATIONALITY, activity that is purposeful and meaningful in regard to the environment and one's own bio-energetic situation, now appears as a function of emotional and perceptual coordination. (p. 445)

Reich describes his intentions in the work as that of deepening the capacity for accurate, somatic self-perception rather than simple emotional catharsis. It is work that takes place in the here and now:

"Regression" is merely a psychological term describing the *actual*, present-day effectiveness of certain historical events. Childhood experiences could, however, not be effective twenty or thirty years later, had they not *actually damaged the process of the coordination of the biosystem.* . . . We are dealing with *actual, present-day functions of the organism,* AND NOT WITH HISTORICAL EVENTS. (pp. 446, emphasis in the original)

This focus of attention and intention is sustained throughout Reich's work with this psychotic woman. With further cuttings and even a knife attack and physical assault against him, he responded to her with respect and with an understanding of the deep disturbance within her body and psyche that was not yet able to tolerate all that it felt. Repeatedly, even in the face of the most delusional and violent reactions, Reich appealed to capacities for self-observation and understanding. With each psychotic reaction, Reich would bring her back to the sensations and emotional states in her body, bringing her own hands to areas of tension and disturbance in her musculature, using his own hands to focus and instruct her attention, offering descriptions and explanations (rarely interpretations), attempting to stimulate areas of her body that were cut off from awareness, all in the here and now. He stressed repeatedly that the capacity for meaning and purpose emerges from the organism's capacities for somatic (visceral and sensorimotor) integration.

Reich's very active level of intervention would be highly unusual for most psychoanalysts, but there was a method and clear intention to his activity. Repeatedly, subtly, sometimes dramatically, he used touch, movement, and sensation as instruments of the analytic process.

I offer another quite different case example to further illustrate the instructive and communicative functions of hands that may precede and inform verbal speech in a process that fosters an integration of subsymbolic knowing, nonverbal symbolic experience, and verbal symbolic articulation (Bucci, 2005, 2008, 2010).

At the point they entered couples therapy, Alan and Eric had been a loving, though often contentious, couple for nine years, eight of which had been mostly sexless. Both reported that in many ways their relationship worked very well, except for sex. Alan had had plenty of sex in his life, though little love or stability. He proclaimed himself quite content in their way of being together, which he described as very affectionate if not particularly passionate. Given that he and Eric were now in their 40s he didn't think this all that unusual. Eric, in contrast, was deeply hurt by their lack of sex. He would often provoke fights because Alan would then have some sort of sex as a way of making up. He, too, had had many short-term sexual relationships, but Alan was his first long-term partner, and he longed greater intimacy. Eric saw sex as essential for an intimate and passionate relationship and made it clear he was "not satisfied with cuddling." He imagined that Alan simply did not find him attractive any more. He was convinced that it was only a matter of time before Alan turned elsewhere. Alan, on the other hand, felt blamed and bullied. He was self-righteous in his argument that they had each already had far more sex than he thought most people—straight or gay—had in their lifetimes. Why couldn't Eric find a different satisfaction in their relationship?

In sessions, discussions of sexuality quickly descended into fights, with Alan expressing hurt and anger that Eric didn't value what they had, while Eric accused Alan of lying, given his very active sex life prior to their involvement. Eric felt undesired, unattractive, and increasingly bitter. I was more than bewildered and often felt relegated to the sidelines of their fights as a kind of referee to keep them from being too nasty. Neither could back away from the nearly instantaneous antagonism that accompanied efforts to talk about their sexual relationship. I could not get either man to reflect upon his own individual feelings, motivations, or fantasies in the presence of the other. I could not understand what was happening to them either as individuals or as a couple.

At the start of a session three months into our work, Alan was protesting that he was fed up with talking about sex as though it was the only important thing in their lives. He announced to me that he was considering quitting the couples therapy. He had told Eric earlier in the week, but this was the first time I'd heard it. Eric, close to tears, asked him to stick with the therapy in spite of his frustrations, and as he spoke, reached out to take Alan's hand. Alan snatched his hand out of reach, declaring, "Nice try! A little pat on the hand, and everything's supposed to be fine. You already tried that one in the car." I asked Alan what his comment about "tried that one in the car" meant. "Oh," he replied with a snarl, "Eric knew I didn't want to come to the session, so he reached across the seat to pat my arm, like the asshole thought that would make everything fine. I told him to keep his hands to himself." "That's not what I meant at all," Eric protested. "I knew you were having a hard time, that you didn't want to come to the session, and I wanted to show some gratitude. I was feeling tender toward you that you were making the effort, and I wanted some way to show it." "You could have just *said* so instead of trying to be cute," Alan snarled.

Now let's step back a bit from this interaction and consider the options for intervention, of which there were several. I might have (tried) to focus the session on Alan's frustration and wish to terminate. If Eric was able to hear Alan's frustration and respond to it, we might have laid some groundwork for further discussions of areas of conflict other than sex. I might have observed that Eric, rather uncharacteristically, was offering a gesture of reconciliation rather than argument and inquired of Eric what was happening for him that he was able to do that. I might have focused on Alan's abrupt "termination" of Eric's reachings and attempts at providing some tenderness, wondering what he feared if their fighting stopped. I was, of course, curious as to what was suddenly proving so unbearable to Alan, who had wanted to continue the relationship at all costs, to now be thinking of termination of the therapy (and perhaps the relationship?). So, too, was I struck by Eric's sudden tenderness in the face of Alan's wanting to quit. It was striking to me that it seemed Eric was able to sense that Alan was in some sort of unspoken trouble beyond their usual fights. Any of these interventions (among others that would undoubtedly come to the minds of other therapists) might have been productive.

This seemed like an unexpected, vital moment. I found myself reluctant to foster any verbal exploration of what was happening, as words had seemed so often treacherous in these sessions. I felt keenly that both Eric's gesture of reaching *and* Alan's gesture of snatching his arm away were extremely important and alive in the room in the moment. I chose a somatic intervention.

I asked Alan and Eric to go back to the car ride to my office for today's session. I asked them not to speak but simply recall, to fall back, into their thoughts, feelings, and fantasies in anticipation of the session. I asked Eric to feel again in his body what was happening as he reached for Alan's arm in the car and in my office. I asked Alan to feel again in his body what happened as he felt Eric's hand unexpectedly touching his arm. I asked that they say nothing but hold the experience in their bodies, noticing any feelings, sensations, fantasies about their own and their partner's bodies at the moments of touch and rupture. Both became quiet, though I could sense that much was stirring within each of them.

I then asked that once again Eric reach out and touch Alan's arm and that Alan recoil from the contact, each staying with the experience of their skin and muscles and any fantasies or memories that accompanied their bodily awareness, still without speaking. I asked that Eric again reach to Alan and this time that Alan not pull away. I encouraged Eric to allow his hand to respond in any way to Alan's arm staying within his grasp, for Alan to experience Eric's touch more fully, open to any surprises, feeling the impulses within his arm, still without speaking. As the touch continued, each began to feel a complex mix of reactions and impulses, which I encouraged them to explore, still without speaking. This time it was Alan who began to cry. Eric found his hand becoming more aggressive, insistent, as well as tender. Only after several minutes of nonverbal exploration of hand to arm did I ask them to begin to add words to their experience.

Alan was surprised to feel the conflict in his arm, simultaneously wanting to pull away and to stay. In staying, there was a sense of growing relief and some genital arousal. He was surprised and excited by the aggression and desire in Eric's touch. He realized that he welcomed the aggression but became anxious when he could sense Eric's tenderness. He was shocked to realize that what he now felt in Eric's hand was startlingly different from the meaning he had attributed to the initial, unexpected contact.

Eric could sense the initial shock in the reaction of Alan's arm—that he could feel how his touch was unexpected and unwelcomed. He said he began to wonder almost immediately why he hadn't noticed this before. He could feel the desire in his hand and the hesitation in Alan's arm. Though not about some sexual desire or demand, Eric could sense how familiar Alan's reaction was, and he began to wonder why he always took it personally rather than allowing Alan's reaction to be of interest and concern. "My body suddenly feels kind of patient," Eric reported.

Both Alan and Eric, as they described their own experiences and listened to the other's accounting, began to realize how intensely they each projected meanings onto the other's desires and motivations. Their speaking to each other began to emerge from their experience of their own bodies rather than interpretations and accusations of the other's intentions. They began to recognize that their impulses were complex and that their inhibitions were also meaningful rather than just some sort of stubborn refusal, power play, or punishment. This session was a turning point for several months of productive therapy. Each was gradually able to recognize and talk about family dynamics that fused and confused dependency, demand, and desire, often finding it difficult to distinguish one from another. Gradually each discovered his own sexual desires, deeply tied to their acceptance and curiosities about each other's areas of inhibition or withdrawal. They learned to talk (and argue) while in physical contact of some sort, so as Alan said, "We don't take our thoughts too seriously and can feel what's going on in the other guy's body is often different from what we imagine."

For Alan and Eric speaking was a means of defense, their language was embedded in profound and compelling projections. The complexities and vulnerabilities of their troubled relationship were masked, lost, overwhelmed by language that was wedded to self-protective furies. Here the languages of their bodies through touch and contact expressed something different, something fuller, evoking a subtle and deeply uncertain field of desire and vulnerability.

As in the case example from Reich, my activity level and directiveness could be seen as unusual from within an analytic frame. My intention was to create a space, a quiet space, for a deepening of sensate awareness and the noticing of accompanying fantasies and projections. Hands, touch, movement, sensation, and *flesh* provided the medium through which the analytic work could unfold.

Chapter 5

Alien Bodies: The Search for Desire

Elizabeth and I lay on our backs, side by side on the carpet of my office. We were in close proximity to each other, but our bodies did not quite touch. I asked Elizabeth to notice any impulses within her body in relation to mine and, if she wished, to explore any of those impulses through movement between her body and mine. This therapeutic invitation proved to be a complex, disturbing, and nearly impossible process of exploration.

Elizabeth's therapy did not start on my office floor. We began our work together seated in chairs talking to each other about the ways in which Elizabeth felt immobilized in her life. Successful in her career, with a wide circle of friends and warm relationships with her family, Elizabeth lived alone, never having been able to sustain an intimate relationship, never having had a sexual relationship.

She had been in psychotherapy before and had found much of it very useful. Many things in her life had changed in response to these therapies, but she was not able to establish an intimate, sexual relationship with anyone. While it was clear that something had gone quite terribly wrong in her emotional, interpersonal, and sexual development, it did not seem to be the result of some form of intrusive trauma. Elizabeth and her therapist agreed that "talk" therapy was not getting her the rest of the way she needed to go. Her therapist suggested that she work with a body-centered psychotherapist and referred her to me.

As we began to work, Elizabeth said, "I don't know what to *do*. I don't know what to *do with my body*. I can't tell if I'm attracted to someone. I just don't know how people know these things. It's like everybody knows something that I don't know, like I was looking the wrong way one day when they taught it in school." This was Elizabeth's experience and was at the heart of what brought her to a body-centered psychotherapy. It was something she wanted to learn. Re-establishing the capacity for sensate, muscular memory is a central task in body-centered work, working with and through the "flesh" of experience. Elizabeth's body was a cipher to her. "I don't know what to do with my body," became the central refrain in our work. Recognizing that we had entered the domain in which her previous therapy had become frozen, we decided to explore more directly her experience of her body not knowing what to *do* with itself.

An earlier version of this case was published in *Studies in Gender and Sexuality* (Cornell, 2009a) accompanied by a lively and challenging discussant paper by Shapiro (2009). Shapiro opens her discussion with a description of her own reactions as she read and reread my accounting of this shift to working on the floor and the direct attention to Elizabeth's body and my own:

> Upon every reading, I have a strong visceral response. The case opens shockingly: "Elizabeth and I lay next to each other on the floor." I feel anxious, tight as I read this. My body is scared, my breath held. Where do I feel it? Back, chest, arms, legs—in fact, everywhere. I feel like I'm slipping into being Elizabeth, my Elizabeth, this happens automatically for me, like the way I sometimes scream in movies even if I've seen them before. *I don't want to do this, why are you making me, I trust you but this feels weird and scary and I don't think I will feel any impulse, but what if I do, what do you want from me? What are you feeling in your body?* (p. 94, emphasis in the original)

As I discuss the somatic explorations between Elizabeth and me, I will return to Shapiro's responses to this case and my thoughts about her critique (Cornell, 2009b), expanding upon what I wrote at that time. I think Shapiro's critique mirrors the concerns and the anxieties that often occur for many analysts in the face of the possibility of therapeutic use of touch and/or movement.

In her personal introductory remarks Shapiro makes a personal statement, *"Oh shit, I can't do that. I can't remember how my body felt yesterday"* (p. 94), which is echoed again later in her discussion:

> I don't know about other readers of his essay, but I can't begin to remember what my body or another's body was like a week ago. Since, even after all these years of body-work, I lack a sophisticated language for registering those frequently non-conscious aspects of experience . . . I wonder how well others, analysts and patients and non-patients, might recall corporeal experience. (p. 99)

Shapiro's description here stands in considerable contrast to my own clinical experience of patients often spontaneously reporting that while they can't remember details of what was *said* in the previous session, they recall and report body sensations, feelings, or images. The capacity of many of my patients to remember and utilize somatic experience is likely a result of our frequent attention to sensate experiences during the sessions themselves. Perhaps Shapiro's contrasting clinical and personal experience is a result of the structure and process of the typical psychoanalytic session. In an article some 15 years earlier, Shapiro (1996) noted, "The analytic consulting room is now one of the more formal and physically constricting environments that analyst and patient inhabit. Traditional explanations of analyst and patient body movements presuppose a still body as the optimal presence." (p. 316)

Without memory there could be no psychoanalysis. "Analytic memory," traditionally, has been a predominantly narrative memory evoked and explored through such means as free association, dreams, transference, and enactments. In body-centered work there is a conscious effort to evoke unconscious experience through the body, the body becoming another vehicle of memory. Sometimes these are memories of childhood, the shadows of the deep past; other times, as with Elizabeth, these may be somatic memories of the previous week or, as with Alan and Eric, memory of the previous hour that are worked with in the immediacy of the session.

The experience Shapiro describes for herself does mirror that which brought Elizabeth into treatment and underscores the emergent treatment goals: that of developing the capacity for consensuality, sensate memory, and that of bodily agency. I'll speak here to the nature of consensuality and later in the chapter to bodily agency.

Segal (2009), drawing upon the work of Didier Anzieu (1989, 1990) and his theories of the skin ego, describes consensuality as "used by Anzieu for the fifth function of the skin-ego, which brings together the perception of all the senses in one place . . . and thus stands for the coherence, coincidence or co-presence of perceptions" (p. 5). "Intersensoriality," "common sense," "concordance," "correspondence," "convergence," "contiguity," and "consensus" are other words Anzieu used in his various writings to capture this felt sense of sensori-somatic coherence. Within this notion of consensuality are echoes of more contemporary terms as the referential process (Bucci, 2002, 2005), cross-modal and multimodal learning (Stern, 1985; Butterworth, 1993, 1995; Bahrick, 2004), modes of memory (Mancia, 2007), and Merleau-Ponty's description of flesh.

Frie (2007) notes that while "psychoanalysis is inconceivable without a conception of the human body, more often than not, however, the body is seen only as a way station to 'mentalized' experience" (p. 55). Recognizing that verbal, symbolic modes of experience and expression are not universal, particularly at those times when we are in crisis within ourselves, Danielle Quinodoz (2003) suggests altering the standard analytic frame:

> . . . instead of using the traditional formula "Say everything that comes into your mind", I say only "Say everything that comes . . . " I wish to avoid the risk of giving priority to the mind . . . what comes to mind certainly, but perhaps also what comes into his heart, senses, and body. It is for him to feel not only *what* comes but also *where* it comes. (emphasis in the original, p. 37)

Mancia reminds us that memory and unconscious experience are held in diverse forms, many of which are more visceral/somatic than cognitive/symbolic. It is a central therapeutic intention in most body-centered psychotherapies to utilize multiple forms of experimentation and expression to consciously facilitate multimodal forms of knowing, i.e., consensuality. Segal offers this translation of a statement from one of Anzieu's French texts: "Words have value and bear meaning through their weight of flesh. The unconscious is not language; it is the body . . . the intelligence of the body" (2000, p. 268).

Let us return to Elizabeth. She was 40 at the time she entered treatment with me. She first sought psychotherapy for depression in her senior year of high school, which she did not find helpful. Returning to home after the first semester of her college sophomore year, she again sought treatment for depression. This time it was twice a week on the couch with a psychoanalytically trained psychiatrist. She found this work extremely valuable. After termination and Elizabeth's moving to another city, her older brother came out as gay. Elizabeth wondered if perhaps she might be gay and that this could be behind her recurrent depressions. She returned home to discuss this with her former therapist, who "completely disabused me of that notion," and "having heard what I wanted to hear, I took that professional assessment to the bank and did not consider it again for many, many years."

In 1995, she decided she must be gay and returned to therapy—individual therapy with a female Gestalt therapist for five years and in a women's group with another female Gestalt therapist for five to six years. In the course of their work together, they considered the possibility of some sort of sexual trauma as an explanation for her sexual deadness but found no evidence of intrusive trauma. After years of social and political involvement in the lesbian community, sexual interest and involvement still eluded her. Sexuality remained out of reach. She rarely masturbated, as it brought little pleasure, considerable frustration, and painful reminders of her being alone. She couldn't tell if she was reaching orgasm. There was no medical basis for her sexual difficulties.

Elizabeth wanted a sex life and came to me to work with her body. As I began to incorporate direct work with exploratory movement between her body and mine, my intention was not to replace mind with body or to evoke primitive states, but to introduce an additional form of "thinking" and learning, that of sensorimotor exploration and re-organization. As sexuality is so deeply rooted in our fundamental, unconscious levels of affective and sensorimotor organization, I have found this style of intervention invaluable in working with chronic sexual difficulties.

As Elizabeth and I prepared to shift our way of working together to include direct work with her body, I asked Elizabeth when her previous therapist referred her to me for body-centered therapy, what had her fantasies been about what would happen in this yet-to-be-known therapy. She said she didn't think about it much, as she was tired of being stuck, wanted something to change somehow, and trusted her therapist's judgment. When pressed a bit to identify some sort of fantasy or anticipatory idea, she said she had imagined that I would be like a coach, teaching her what to do, showing her what to do. The image of a coach was an instructive one, suggesting a variety of associations—father, mentor, instructor, director, trainer—someone to teach, encourage, inspire, push, and pressure her. She explained that she was quite an accomplished athlete, so the notion of a coach to her body was a familiar (and positive) one. I inquired how she could be a skilled athlete on the one hand and have such a profound sense of her body not knowing what to do with itself at the same time. Elizabeth saw no contradiction. Her athletic endeavors were those of pushing herself, challenging her body to overcome fatigue and fear. She played *individual* sports—running, climbing, tennis. The impasse in her treatment was about how to bring her body *to someone else*, what to do *with* someone else. Here she felt totally inept.

When I first started listening to Elizabeth, I found myself often imagining her as an adolescent. I kept these imaginings to myself, trying to sense something about Elizabeth from my internal images and fantasies. I began to realize that I was wishing her a new adolescence. I wanted her to have that wonderful/awful period of adolescent development, in which most of us are so fueled by the frenzy of awakening hormones and bodily changes that we manage to blast through awkwardness and inhibition to figure out some way, somehow, however unskilled and unmannered we may be, to get our body and body parts to those of another. Grace and skill are not in the foreground for most adolescents, and I imagined myself as her coach in an emotional rather than athletic endeavor. It was becoming clear to me that while *my* mind (not Elizabeth's) was filled with images and urges of adolescence, the dilemmas of Elizabeth's body were rooted in much earlier phases of development. Elizabeth needed a chance to be awkward and de-skilled with her body in relation to another. I became that other.

Elizabeth's other image was that of my comforting her, holding her, hugging her, etc., but she was quite sure that wasn't what I would have in mind or that it would be particularly productive. She had experienced quite a lot of hugging in a previous therapy group and had not found it useful. I agreed that providing comfort was not the purpose of working at a body level. The work was meant to inform her body, not comfort it. I suggested Elizabeth begin by simply noticing during and between sessions whatever she could about her body in relation to mine. I encouraged her to notice between sessions how she remembered her body in my office, how she remembered my body between sessions. It soon became clear that she did not remember her sessions visually or with any felt sensation. She did remember and think about content but felt like a talking head. She reported feeling afraid that she would prove "too much" for me and that I wouldn't know what to do with her either.

This suggested to both of us that in some way she had a history of people not knowing "what to do with" her. She said she felt it would be "presumptuous" of her to expect something from someone else's body. The sense of a "presumptuous body" came to take on significant meaning as our body-level work evolved. Finally, after several weeks passed with no reports of body-level images or fantasies, Elizabeth said with great self-deprecation, "All I can imagine is like I'm going to be lying there on the floor next to you having no idea what to do, a lump." That, I suggested, was a place to start; this was her sense of our bodies in relation to each other. We moved from the chairs to the floor, so as to begin a different sort of therapeutic exploration.

As Elizabeth and I lay side by side that first time, her experience was one that we visited and revisited time and again: "I don't know what to do. I don't know what my body wants. It doesn't have any impulses." Her reactions were typical of her life-long experience of her body seeming dumb and alien. As we worked with this apparent lack of impulse, it became clear that Elizabeth experienced her body through what it *didn't* want. She began to realize that there *were* clear signals from her body about what "it" didn't want. She could, however, discover no sense of what "it" *did* want. I pointed out that her not-wanting was, in fact, an impulse in relation to my body. When she was free to explore this not-wanting, her body began to feel more alive in the room. Her body was becoming more connected to itself, more able to inform itself. In session we rarely touched. In her day-to-day life she began to notice how much she defined her experience thought not wanting rather than wanting ("I knew I didn't want to go to that restaurant/that movie, but I could never say what I did want. Somebody else always ended up making that choice").

Gradually she asked me if I would make suggestions as to what her body could do with mine, so that she could find out if she could tell what she liked, and what she did not like. The experiments were many: our arms lightly touching as we lay on our backs, lifting her head onto my shoulder, rolling onto my chest, sitting back to back pressing in and pulling away, pressing her head and shoulders into my back, spooning, wrapping our legs around each other playfully, aggressively, tenderly. She began to differentiate what she wanted and what she didn't. She began to notice that some of our experiments seemed to stay in her body between sessions, gradually developing a capacity for somatic memory. She began to have fantasies of her own about what she wanted her body to do with mine. She began to initiate the movement experiments between us, though often surprised at the results.

Shapiro frames this process between Elizabeth and me as "a rush to action," seeing my interventions as goal directed, staking out the analytic position, "And it is the work of psychoanalysis, in its refusal of goal-directed action, that allows this unknown to flourish and the patient to find herself" (2009, p. 102). Elizabeth and I didn't *do* something so as to achieve a certain outcome, we moved and touched in diverse ways—sometimes at my initiative, other times at her own—to find out what would happen, how it felt and what it might mean. Quite to the contrary of Shapiro's characterization, the intent was to create space for an unknowing body and to give Elizabeth exactly the freedom that Shapiro attributes to the psychoanalytic attitude.

I did not nurture her or soothe and comfort her. I paid attention. I waited attentively. Aalberse, a body psychotherapist, stresses the importance of not-knowing and of patient attention to the unfamiliar, the just-out-of-reach experiences:

> By concentrating on what is not yet clear, we find out that in that first and rather hazy feeling, a surprising intelligence is waiting to reveal itself. After a certain time deeper trust in this intrinsic intelligence and in the sensing body able to capture this intelligence can develop. (2001, p. 107)

In this regard, somatic exploration has a great deal in common with analytic listening. I wait and tentatively respond to the precarious emergence of impulses, using both my body to help give them force and form and my language to help give them meaning.

Typically, sessions began with some form of body-to-body interaction, often no more than five or ten minutes. The remainder of the session would be devoted to the verbal exploration and association of meanings to what we had experienced—sometimes evoking aspects of family history, sometimes of her feelings about her body, other times about our relationship or her relationships with others. As Elizabeth and I lay on my office floor, she began to use—and more importantly be *unable* to use—her body in relation to mine. This began to open for Elizabeth a lived history, a *domain of experience*, that she had not been able to access through conscious memory, thought, and language in her earlier treatment. She was able to begin experiencing and experimenting with her very literal experience of not knowing what to do with her body, the seeming impossibility of getting her body to the body of another. Elizabeth and I spent much of our time together in the space of the yet-to-be-known. Elizabeth was able to get to know her body in the presence of mine.

Stern (1985) offers an important account of the development of bodily agency, which he argues forms the basis for a coherent core self-experience:

> Agency, or authorship of action, can be broken down into three possible invariants of experience: (1) the sense of volition that precedes a motor act, (2) the proprioceptive feedback that does or *does not* occur during the act, and (3) the predictability of the consequences that follow the act. (p. 76, emphasis added)

This sequence of repeated somatic experience provides the foundation for a "motor plan" which creates for the sense of volition or will, such that, "Even when we are unaware of the motor plan, the sense of volition makes our actions seem to belong to us and be self-acts" (p. 77). Elizabeth lacked any sense of somatic volition of self-acts. The proprioceptive feedback during the process of one's own body and that of another are key to the integration of agency. This is the field of action and integration that Elizabeth and I gradually built together. These ideas will be further developed in Chapter 8.

Shapiro wonders how the direct somatic work may heighten (or precipitate an enactment) of countertransferential forces. My ongoing countertransference to Elizabeth was deeply paternal. Even as our work took us to the ground of the maternal, I felt like the father, not the mother. I felt anxious that she might not achieve what she wanted, and often (silently) shared her urgency. I was troubled by the depth of her despair and self-judgment. In the background, I had unsettling associations to a previous patient who had "never experienced my body as the object of anyone's desire." With that patient, I could not tolerate her despair, I kept a safe distance, and the therapy failed. I was determined not to distance myself this time. I experienced a welcoming in my body toward Elizabeth, satisfaction and excitement when she reported something in her body coming more alive in the session or with others outside session. I did, rather unexpectedly, feel a bit like the coach she had imagined I was going to be.

I often felt toward Elizabeth as I did toward my sons in their adolescences. In her discussion Shapiro (2009) suggests, "typically the father of an adolescent daughter has complex and conflicted feelings about her budding sexuality" (p. 98). She seems to suggest that I, too, must have had those feelings. I did not. As a father to adolescent sons whose home was often populated with adolescent girls and a charged sexual atmosphere, I did not find my own sexuality aroused by or confused with theirs. I did feel great pleasure and pride as I witnessed their coming into their own adult, sexual bodies in their relationships and their work.

As I worked with Elizabeth, I thought often of the extraordinary passage by Bolognini:

> I have an idea of my own, which I shall express by an image: *every good father should at least dance a waltz with his daughter* and show himself to be thereby moved and honored. . . . In the same way, every father must be capable of standing aside at the appropriate time, so as not to impede the gradual process of separation during youth, after having protected and encouraged growth—until he symbolically accompanies her to the altar to hand her over to her real adult sexual companion. (1994, p. 82)

Bolognini echoes my experience with Elizabeth and with my own sons. There is profound pleasure in the anticipation of handing over one's children, or one's patients, to the love and bodies of their own sexual partners.

Often the sessions had an unmistakable erotic vitality to them, experienced in the pleasure of discovery and mutual exploration, the moments of tenderness and excitement. Her body started to become a source of information for her mind not only in relation to me but, gradually, to others as well. She began to notice what it was in her body that let her know when she was attracted to someone and when someone was drawn to her. Through this somatic experimentation and interplay, Elizabeth and I entered the realm of the erotic.

Within erotic transference and countertransferences we can begin to recognize and understand what is becoming psychically and somatically possible for our patients. In his reflections on what he refers to as "innocent" sexuality, Slavin (2012) argues:

> It is this ensnared sexuality that emerges in the transference. The patient's capacity for an innocent sexuality has been "lost," as Leowald puts it. And it is in the engagement with the analyst that he or she must find it, initially *through the analyst's ability to envision it.* The urgency to frame the analyst's responsiveness in terms of personal countertransference, or an enactment engendered by the patient's pathogenic transference, may represent a flight from a direct and therapeutically necessary sexual experiencing and envisioning of the patient, just as the child needs the parents' appreciation and vision. (p. 63, italics in the original)

The emergence of erotic desires need to be returned to the patient. As we see in the work between Elizabeth and me, what Elizabeth experienced most keenly and tellingly with me were *the inhibitions to desire*. As she began to establish a more vital and informed relationship to her body, she gradually began to experience her body as a site of desire. Our relationship and somatic experimentations afforded an opportunity, *space*, for the exploration of desire, but I was not the *object* of her desires. When the therapist is cast (by either participant) as the actual object or the source of the patient's desire, the authorship of desire remains disowned.

There came a point when Elizabeth felt especially despairing about the progress of her therapy. She was now meeting women. She knew when she was attracted to someone in particular, but then the oft-repeated phrase returned as she struggled to allow a relationship to move forward: "I don't know what to do." She began to wonder if this was probably as far as she could go, that for reasons she might never understand her life was going to be one without a life partner. "It's not such a *bad* life after all," she said with quiet resignation. "Nobody gets everything they want out of life, do they?" I responded that, indeed, hers was not a bad life, but reminded her that her primary reason for working with me was to find her sexuality and establish a loving, sexual relationship. I continued (without giving much thought to what I was about to say), "I think you deserve more, and I'm rather determined to see that you get it. I can be quite stubborn with people I'm fond of." Elizabeth was stunned. "You're *fond* of me?" "I certainly am. I look forward to seeing you. I enjoy our work together," I replied, "Isn't that obvious?" It wasn't obvious to Elizabeth. In fact, the possibility had never occurred to her that I might feel affection for her or pleasure in working with her. It had simply been a given for her that I was doing my job, that I felt responsible to her. She knew and felt that I took our work seriously. She had never considered that there was pleasure for me in seeing her. Suddenly a window into her early childhood began to illuminate. She realized that her parents had always been responsible parents, seriously committed to their children, but she never felt herself to be a source of pleasure in their lives. Elizabeth realized that she never expected to be a source of pleasure or affection to her parents or anyone else.

Shapiro takes particular notice of this interchange: "As this treatment progressed I think it was the critical interpersonal exchange over Cornell's feelings for Elizabeth, rather than any body-based experience, that was mutative" (2009, p. 94). She does not say why she thought the treatment had progressed to this point, but toward the end of her discussion, she returns to this moment in treatment, arguing, "I think this moment is a critical turning point in the treatment of Elizabeth: it is the kind of rupture and repair that is familiar to all clinicians in deep work with patients" (p. 101). She highlights the moment that is the most familiar to her in her own frame of reference, dismissing the therapeutic utility of any of the body-based work. There is no doubt this was an important moment in our work, but it did not render the ongoing integration of our body-based exploration, development, and consolidation of new, enduring, organizing systems of movement, sensation, and sensorimotor processes irrelevant. I find it ironic that Shapiro identifies my un-thought-out disclosure of my affection for Elizabeth as "a key mutative moment," which I considered then (and still now) to be an error on my part, although one that we were able to take up very productively.

As we had been working together, Elizabeth had often expressed the worry of "being too much" for me. She could never really articulate what this phrase meant, but it seemed ever present. I would often suggest that she seemed ashamed of her body and any potential desire. She would insist that she did not feel shame, "that's not part of my repertoire," but she did worry that *I* would find her disgusting. Once we had stumbled into the reality of my pleasure in being with her, she was faced with her continuing fantasy that I found her disgusting, quite the opposite of what I actually felt. In the midst of this unexpected discovery, Elizabeth told me that she'd often had the fantasy of sitting on my lap, and with considerable hesitation, asked if she might try it. I agreed. I sat in the corner of the couch, and Elizabeth placed herself on my lap. I felt caring and tenderly toward her. To my shock, she became extremely upset, bolted from my lap, and declared herself far too heavy (she was not), crying that she had asked far too much of me. She declared that she had a "presumptuous body," and collapsed into shame. I struggled not to reassure her but to allow her experience to unfold.

After her leap from my lap, Elizabeth gradually began to realize that constant anxiety of being too much had come from her mother, that in many subtle ways her mother had always seemed ill at ease with Elizabeth and that Elizabeth had come to feel that she was disgusting. She had to keep herself subtly away from her mother so as to preserve a certain ease for her mother. Elizabeth's body knew well how to move subtly away; it did not know how to move close. She/we began to understand her body's relation to her mother's body. Elizabeth's body felt presumptuous, "too much," within the maternal field. It was fundamental to her experience of her body that "it did not, does not," evoke pleasure or desire in another (mother). "There was nothing to do," she realized. "No wonder I have this constant sense that I don't know what to do with my body."

Elizabeth began to see the signs of her mother's discomfort in their presentday relationship. She began to recognize her anger toward her mother, and with the recognition of her anger, Elizabeth began to develop a capacity for more aggression with her friends, for more conflict with me. She was able to see her mother (rather than herself) as physically and emotionally limited. She saw that she did not need her mother to change. *She* needed to change fundamentally in her ways of bringing herself, her body, and her desires to others.

This particular moment in the treatment was the one of greatest alarm for Shapiro:

> When, for example, an adult woman sits on an adult man's lap—as Elizabeth does in response to Cornell's agreement with her wish to do so—she knows that he has a penis, and obviously he knows it as well, and both know that the other knows this and what their sexual difference means, even if their infant selves, way at life's beginning, would not have known anything of the sort at all. . . . Cornell wants Elizabeth to have another adolescence. He wants her to have a sexual awakening, a sense of her body as desirable. How shocked he is when, in the midst of his caring and tender feelings for her, she leaps from his

lap with the intriguing self-accusation of a "presumptuous" body that is "too much," demands "too much." And as she leaps away from his penis to safety, so he leaps from the exploration of the many hetero-erotic aspects of her immediate experience to the safety of Elizabeth and her mother. (2009, p. 97)

I strongly differ with Shapiro's suggestion that Elizabeth's leap from my lap was a leap away from my penis. I think Shapiro makes an unwarranted leap of her own in her interpretation here. In that moment on my lap, Elizabeth's experience was of a sudden, shocking intrusion of her "presumptuous" (a term we had, as I have indicated, visited and revisited many times) body's wanting too much. My penis was not part of that particular clinical moment, though the theoretical penis is a frequent object of psychoanalytic interest. Our attention to the mother was the result of Elizabeth's associations, not my redirection of our attention.

At the same time, I find Shapiro's questions and arguments about the "confusion of tongues" within the erotic and sexual interplay between Elizabeth and me most compelling:

> However, even though the infant's sensory experiences clearly penetrate and inform later sexual experiences, this influence goes both ways. The adult sexual body and the adult's sexual history reciprocally inform any dyadic effort to enter and explore the pre-oedipal soma. Hence the increased risk of "confusion of tongues." (p. 96)

As I read Shapiro's discussion, I recalled a session in which Elizabeth was speaking of her fear of finding someone to whom she was attracted and then not knowing how to kiss. Once again the familiar anxiety of her body not knowing what to do. Could kissing be a part of our body explorations, she asked? I told her that would not be the case, and she asked why not. I said that kissing was outside the domain of a therapeutic relationship, "but even more important is that it would cheat you of a wonderful experience if your first kiss were to be with me. It's probably unimaginable to you now, but you will find the person you're attracted to and who is attracted to you, and that's where the first kiss belongs. And you'll find that it will give your partner great pleasure to teach you to kiss, to learn together about each other's bodies. Learn to caress. Learning together, teaching one another about your bodies, is all a part of the pleasure and excitement of sexuality." Elizabeth did not abandon her therapy to accept life as a single woman. My forecast proved to be true, as she was able to find a loving partner who accompanied her into exploring not only kissing but other domains of sexuality as well.

Although I felt a deep paternal connection and affection for Elizabeth, her actual father was rarely present in our work. He had been a subtle but consistent absence in her life, and I did feel induced to provide a paternal presence. Her actual father became unexpectedly visible and meaningful to Elizabeth when she was standing with him at his mother's bedside in the hospice as she lay dying. He cared deeply for his mother but stood at her side silent and motionless. Elizabeth realized silently, "Like me, like Mom, he doesn't know what to do either." "Dad," she suggested gently, "take your mom's hands." He did, and he wept. Elizabeth's grandmother died shortly thereafter. As Elizabeth and her parents left the hospice, she noticed again that they were leaving at the same time, and yet they were leaving separately. It did not occur to either her father or her mother to take each other's hands—or Elizabeth's. Elizabeth then felt the meaning of her father's absence, and he became a presence and a figure in our work.

By the time Elizabeth's attention turned to her father she had developed a close and sexual relationship with a woman. She realized that she now "knew" in her body what her father did not know in his. And by this time, as Elizabeth's body sustained a more consistently coherent sensate organization, it was no longer necessary that we work body to body. Her body now had the bodies of others in her company.

Shapiro wonders how I use relational psychoanalysis in my practice. By and large, I don't. I have certainly been influenced by my reading of the relational literature and my ongoing, collegial involvements with relational analysts. It is, interestingly, within the relational literature that discussions of the body (of both the analyst and the client) have most often emerged, often as discussions of somatic countertransference and reverie that have enriched the understanding of the analytic dyad. But as a body-trained psychotherapist, I have often found these presentations of the body limited and clinically unsatisfying in their development of any systematic approach to intentionally including direct work with somatic processes. Furthermore, at a more purely theoretical level, I question the rather relentless privileging of relational factors in the contemporary psychoanalytic zeitgeist (Cornell, 2008c). Lombardi, as an example, echoes my sentiments when he writes:

> I believe there is too much emphasis in contemporary psychoanalysis on object relations and the role of the other, and that this has contributed to a loss of contact with the deepest areas of the personality: those that have to do with life itself. In other words, we have underestimated the analysand's capacity to show good adaptation to external reality and interpersonal relations to the detriment of an actual connection with his or her most intimate sensations. (2011, p. 7)

My own style of practice has been most fundamentally shaped by the work of Bollas (1987, 1989, 1992) and McLaughlin (2005), whose modes of working were deeply immersed in the receptive and informative functions of their own somatic and countertransferential states. Neither would characterize themselves as representatives of a "relational" psychoanalysis, emphasizing the reality of distinct and separate subjectivities, "two-person separate" as Chodorow (2007) has recently characterized this position. While I am informed by my somatic and countertransference reactions (which is typically referred to in body-centered literature as "somatic resonance"), I rarely share them with the patient.

It is in the realm of touch between Elizabeth and me that Shapiro expressed her deepest concerns—concerns that I am certain are not hers alone but reflect those of many in the psychoanalytic communities:

> In my experience of engaging the body in psychoanalysis, then, you don't have to act on the patient's body in order to increase their awareness of their body. Many of the areas Cornell and Elizabeth investigate can be mined through encouraging a deep exploration and attunement to one's own in the presence of an other. Immediate and literal physical interactions with the analyst are rarely necessary and most of us are not trained in their use. (p. 100)

In her 1996 paper, Shapiro takes up the issues raised by the nonverbal realms of "multidimensional, multifaceted somatosensory experience" (p. 300), offering a discussion of the body-work practitioners whose modalities are outside of the analytic frame. But by the end of the article she concludes:

> It is the premise of this paper that what began as a liberating environment [Freudian psychoanalysis], in which one could at least talk dirty, has become a straitjacket for patient and analyst alike. Freedom of movement is restricted to kooks and fringe therapists, and borderline or child and adolescent patients. The mark of maturity is stillness. I don't yet have a solution to this. (p. 317).

The point of view argued by Shapiro reflects a position common among many psychoanalysts. It is worth noting that even Anzieu, with his abiding interest in the skin, strongly opposed any use of touch within the psychoanalytic process and was severely critical of humanistic and body-centered psychotherapies (1989, pp. 136–137; 1990, pp. 74–79). He argued, "It is up to the psychoanalyst, in his internal work of elaborating interpretation, to find words that are symbolic equivalents of what was missing in the tactile exchanges between the baby and his mother" (p. 73). He goes so far as to argue that it is the prohibition of touch in the later stages of childhood development of the psychic apparatus in the growing child. At the same time, in noting the rise of humanistic and body-centered modalities, Anzieu cautioned, "I am tempted to say that either psychoanalysis will survive by renewing itself and integrating everything to which these bodily therapies draw attention, in which case it will survive as it renews itself, or else in the year 2000 it will be shelved in the storehouse of obsolete accessories that are no longer talked about except in courses on the history of medicine and mentalities" (p. 69).

In fundamental ways, the vantage point that organized and informed my work with Elizabeth, in contrast to those of Shapiro, Anzieu, and many psychoanalysts, cannot be easily resolved. I'm not sure they should be. In these differences there is a great deal to be thought about. Most psychoanalysts and verbally based psychotherapists think and work from traditions (and biases) that are quite different from mine and those of somatically based psychotherapists. Had Reich and Ferenczi not been expelled from the psychoanalytic pantheon, and had the traditions they represented remained within the psychoanalytic tapestry and discourse, then perhaps our thinking now would not be so different. But different it is, and the resulting conversations need to be many and lively.

Among contemporary analysts exploring the place of the soma in psychoanalysis, Lombardi observes:

> The body not only reminds us of the importance of instincts and sexuality: it is also the concrete core of the personality, playing a role whose significance is equal to that of the mind, although the latter has generally monopolized attention in psychoanalysis. (2011, p. 20)

I would argue that the entire technical paradigm of psychoanalysis is, in and of itself, an action upon patients' bodies, which has not been sufficiently examined. The no-touch, no-action taboos of psychoanalysis need to be called into question. It is a common assumption in the analytic literature that touch and body contact collapses boundaries, unleashes unnecessary risks of sexualized transference or countertransference. If the practitioner has had no formal training in the uses of physical contact and doesn't know what he or she is doing, then this is likely to be the case. Body-centered psychotherapists are most often trained in a whole range of forms and functions of touch, many of which create and support boundaries, rather than transgress them.

Shapiro notes that psychoanalysts do not have the expertise to carefully monitor physical changes in the patient/patient's body and in their own, which is central in body-centered trainings. Recent psychoanalytic literature is beginning to introduce some glimmers of training models to the analytic communities (Bloom, 2006; Knoblauch, 2005, 2011; Krantz, 2012; Sletvold, 2012). Shapiro doesn't take up the limits and liabilities of this lack of knowledge and training within the psychoanalytic traditions. Instead, she urges, "if there is an agreed upon need for more work with the body, the patient can be referred to someone else for this work . . . " (p. 101). But she doesn't address the liabilities and potential problems of referring a patient in the midst of a deep psychoanalytic involvement to a body-work practitioner, who likely has had little or no training in transference and countertransference dynamics, unconscious processes, or other aspects of an analytic experience. It's not as easy a solution as she seems to suggest. I do, upon occasion, refer for conjoint work with body practitioners, but it is to a short list of carefully chosen professionals, and it necessitates careful attention to the changes that occur in the transference relationship.

Of course, the treatment with Elizabeth was not simply about touch, although our use of touch was central to the work. The careful, exploratory use of movement and touch between Eric and Alan and between Elizabeth and myself were deeply instructive. The contact was erotic, pleasurable, and enlivening. It allowed exploration of boundaries rather than a violation of them. New self-understanding and communication became possible, emerging from somatic experience that was vigorous enough to effectively challenge habitual behaviors and projections.

No regression was provoked or supported. While memories emerged and were addressed, the therapeutic processes of working directly with somatic explorations remained solidly within the here and now.

As will become clear in the chapters ahead, it is not necessary to touch our patients in order to work within somatic realms of organization. But the challenge of this and the previous chapter is to invite a reconsideration of how, with adequate theory and training, one can incorporate somatic work, including movement and touch, within psychoanalytic and other verbally based psychotherapies.

So why might we touch our patients? I would agree with the critics of touch that without a sound clinical theory and actual training in the therapeutic uses of touch, a therapist's or analyst's impulses to touch may by driven by countertransferentially derived expressions of power, nurturance, comfort, or sexual/erotic stimulation that are counter-therapeutic. But an outright condemnation of touch does not solve the problem. What are we seeking to discover through touch in our understanding of our patients' worldviews and life experiences? What are we hoping our patients can learn, perhaps undo and redo, through touch within the therapeutic process? In my view, the intentional use of touch in psychotherapy is to be *instructive* to both patient and therapist. Touch may, of course, at times be confrontive or comforting to a patient, with the intention to unbind enduring, typically unconscious, bodily patterns and open the body, and then the mind, to new possibilities. Informed and intentional touch within a therapeutic process can provide a somatically centered means of analysis and reflection, not simply a "rush to action" or enactment.

Chapter 6

Traces of the Other:
Encounters with Character

Liz had always had a rather clear, consistent and unquestioned view of herself. A pediatrician, now in her late 50s, she had been in and out of various forms of psychotherapy since finishing medical school. She had life-long interests in child development, psychotherapy, and psychoanalysis, particularly drawn to theories of attachment and empathy, with which she strongly identified in her role as mother and as physician. Other than her husband and children, most everyone else was held at a comfortable distance, including her various therapists over the years. Her therapeutic efforts were typically intense, but brief, focused on a problem to solve or a family crisis to resolve. Therapists were chosen primarily for their expertise in a given area, and she changed therapists with each new undertaking. She made it clear as she started with me that she was not in psychotherapy to develop a relationship or to become dependent upon someone, but to solve the problem at hand.

Liz entered twice-weekly psychotherapy, motivated this time by the loss of her family structure now that her children were grown and by her ambivalence in the face of a recent offer of new professional opportunities that would require additional training and significant travel. Both realms of life change were precipitating personal and marital crises, though Liz would never have used the word crisis herself. Liz and her husband were each accomplished professionals, she in medicine and preventative health care, he in business. Both had been primarily outwardly directed, deeply invested in their careers, relatively asocial beyond professional acquaintances. Both were deeply involved with their children, their involvements stretching well into the lives of their children now as adults.

Liz saw herself as deeply devoted to children within her family and her practice. She took pride in her determination and dedication in family and work. In the initial sessions she also presented herself as always having struggled with a slight degree of depression (though not at a level that would necessitate medication), a vulnerability to headaches, muscular and joint pain, and to increasing fatigue as she grew older. She told me that one reason for her seeking me out was my reputation for attending more directly to the body than most psychotherapists, but other than those initial references to depressiveness and pain, she made no references to her body as the sessions unfolded. As I sat with her in initial sessions, I often felt pulled between her self-presentation of endurance and devotion and of what I saw as a chronic sense of fragility, fatigue, and unhappiness (in my perception, not her words or self-perception).

Liz worried whether she "still had it in her" to learn more. Was this some sort of narcissistic ambition that this new training pursuit would represent? she wondered. What would be the consequences in her marriage now that her husband no longer had to work and was moving toward semi-retirement? Couldn't she, shouldn't she, be content to be a wife and now grandmother? Slight irritations with her husband would sometimes emerge, but they were quickly denied or minimized. Having looked forward to becoming a grandmother, she was surprised to find herself often bored and feeling taken for granted when asked to watch the grandchildren.

After a few weeks, I wondered aloud if this might not be a good time in her life to allow herself a sustained therapeutic relationship. I was hesitant to address the rather profound gap I experienced between her self-image and my visual/visceral reactions to her presence in my office. How could I speak to my experience without seeming judgmental, shaming, diminishing? Was this simply a countertransference reaction on my part? I felt cautious in what I could say to her. Gradually Liz was able to acknowledge her desire for an ongoing therapeutic experience, something deeper than she'd allowed herself before. She spoke of the possible need for a deeper therapeutic experience, though never defined as the need or wish for a deeper therapeutic relationship with me. When I would inquire of the possibility of a more sustained therapeutic relationship, she professed intense ambivalence. Was it truly a need? Or was it more of an immature, selfish wish-want-fantasy? She often expressed a reluctance to continue, and embarrassment at her being back in therapy "yet again." Why couldn't she be satisfied with her life as it was now? she often wondered.

Fleeting references to her childhood would emerge, only to quietly disappear with attention to more everyday, family-centered or work-centered concerns. An only child, she was born to parents who seemed to have little interest in her. The marriage was a second marriage for both of her parents, and Liz sometimes wondered if she had been wanted at all. Was she an obligatory baby, born to represent or cement a marriage that seemed more one of convenience and ambition than of passion or devotion? Her father was a well-known figure of authority in his field, passionately and narcissistically devoted to his work. Her mother seemed passionately devoted to status and economic security. Neither of her parents seemed to derive any particular pleasure or meaning from being parents. As a young child, Liz was frequently left in the care of her maternal grandmother, her mother professing at the time that her place was at her husband's side and that Grandmama was lonely and needed company. Liz's mother explained many years later that she was, in fact, terrified of losing her husband to another woman, as their relationship had begun as an affair. Liz's mother did not see loyalty as a strong suit for herself or her husband. Liz remembered her grandmother as a cold, demanding, and authoritarian woman, who, having raised "proper" children of her own without much apparent pleasure, was then entrusted with much of her granddaughter's upbringing. Liz was able to acknowledge both fear and hatred of her grandmother.

Liz frequently described herself as "enduring" in nature, and as our work continued over the months I often felt enduring in her presence. I found myself wondering
if we were co-creating a kind of masochist field within which we were both privately
and politely tolerating our discomforts and frustrations in the name of patience and
understanding. We seemed caught up in an idealized realm of waiting, seen by Liz
as evidence of her patience, forbearance, and thoughtfulness. I found myself wondering, "Waiting for *what*?," although *not* asking Liz, and *not* commenting on my
impatience in the face of her patience. I had stopped commenting on my experience
of our relationship or inquiring of hers. I would, however, frequently comment upon
how her hours with me seemed to fill my office with stories of the people in her life
but rarely of herself. I interpreted her dread of acknowledging within herself any
qualities that seemed to be like those she attributed to her parents—selfish, ambitious, oblivious to the wishes and needs of those around her should she decide to
pursue further professional goals. I observed how, in contradistinction to her parents, her life and her therapeutic hours seemed filled with the needs and wishes of
others, rather than her own. Where was *she* in her hours with me?

Curiously, I was hesitant to ask the rather obvious question of where was she in
her *relationship* with me. I could not hold myself within her field, just as she could
not maintain herself in the relational fields of those around her. We each disappeared from the other. I felt strangely quieted with Liz. I did manage to comment
on my caution with her. My carefulness, she explained to me, she took as a sign of
my empathy and caring for her, just as she was careful for others. I felt boxed in.
My carefulness did not feel to me to be particularly caring. I found myself bored
and irritated with increasing frequency. I censored confrontations that sounded
mean in my head, that I knew would more relieve my aggravation than enlighten
Liz. I was curious about my reserve, wondering how I could bring this sense of
my reserve into the work, to provide meaning. The sessions droned on with Liz's
preoccupations with professional and familial decisions, her ambivalence about
wanting more for herself and of life, her concerns for damaging her marriage and
family if she pursued these new professional opportunities. We had become mired
in an endless present of her life outside my office. References to the past were
fleeting; we could not seem to inhabit, feel, or explore her past. The future could
not emerge from her preoccupation with the present. My interpretations of her
fears of discovering herself to be like her parents—selfish, ambitious—did gradually begin to strike home and free her to think about herself with more autonomy.
Yet I remained dissatisfied, restless, irritated.

After sessions I would often experience affect that I could not reach in myself
during sessions. I increasingly felt dulled and used, related to more as hired help
than as an entrusted professional. My caution felt more like inhibition, but I
couldn't identify the inhibiting force. I felt physically restless during sessions
with an intense desire to *move* after her sessions. I was aware of a kind of "catch,"
an agitation, in the center of my chest, which I saw as a symptom of my growing
frustration with Liz. Increasingly my body seemed absent in sessions, seeming to
"report in" to me only after Liz left.

My eyes were often drawn to her body, though as had so often become the case with my way of being with her, I did not speak of what was drawing my attention. There were no accidents in Liz's appearance. Her hair, face, and clothing were lovely, colorful, graceful, and expensive without ever being ostentatious. Her attire was pleasing and yet unconvincing, as it seemed to decorate her body more than to express it. There was a flatness, a quality of resignation in her eyes. Her eyes seemed to search in silence, but they did not invite contact. Underneath the graceful drape of her clothes, she seemed too thin, frail. She rarely moved with any force or spontaneity. I began to realize that this subtle but deep bearing of her body was much of what quieted, inhibited me. I didn't feel the right to speak with too much force.

Her arms were typically folded across her chest, not tightly holding on to herself, but simply there, by themselves, draped as though another layer of fabric across her torso. I often looked at Liz without seeing anything in particular and began to realize that I was not supposed to see anything in particular.

As the time approached to make a decision to take the new position of professional advancement, with the training and travel it would require, Liz became even more deliberate in her deliberations than usual. But she had to make the decision or have the opportunity given over to a colleague. "Fuck!" she shouted suddenly in the midst of her familiar rut. "I wish just for once there was some exuberance in my life. Exuberance. Spunk. Trouble. I am so fucking careful about everything!" As she spoke, she flung her arms out in an arc, like a runner's arms spreading as she approaches the finish line. Just as suddenly her arms pulled back to her torso, her right arm bending at the elbow, bringing her hand (now in a fist) against her shoulder. Then both hands, fingers curled in, were drawn to the center of her chest. She became quiet, as though nothing had happened. This was a posture so familiar to me that I had ceased to see it. It was so familiar that it had become invisible, and in its invisibility had ceased to convey any meaning.

"Do that again with your arms, Liz. Notice your body. Fling your arms out again. Feel what happens." She looked startled at my suggestion, but she flung her arms outward again with a resounding, "*Fuck* them!" Spontaneously she pulled her arms in and then flung them outward, repeating the movements several times over. She began to cry.

I waited.

She gradually began to speak, reporting that as she flung her arms out the second time, now intentionally and consciously, her chest constricted, she panicked that she couldn't breathe, and she saw her grandmother, who was the most present figure of her childhood, filling in the gap of her often-absent parents. She heard her grandmother's "Don't get carried away with yourself, young lady." Liz realized that her grandmother's invective echoed through many years and scenes of her childhood, but in that initial moment of release she figured that the "young lady" who was the target of Grandmama's admonition was probably about three years old. Tears alternated with waves of subdued anger.

Her gesture of arms flung forcefully wide stayed with us for many weeks and became an anchoring point of reference for her ensuing psychotherapy, opening her past to habitation and exploration. As we worked with the gesture, her actual experience of it, and her associations to it, two central meanings emerged, accompanied by numerous affective and somatic memories of her self-inhibitions, collapsing herself in the face of distant parents and a disapproving, constricted grandmother. The first and most enduring meaning was of the sacrifice of exuberance in her childhood and adult life. In place of her exuberance, Liz developed her identity as self-sacrificing, enduring, and dedicated. She could begin to see her investment as a young girl in a pseudo-mature, precocious identification with mental activity, "bracing for disappointment" in the telling phrase of Shabad and Selinger (1995).

The second meaning, slower to emerge, was that of an embrace, the wish to embrace and be embraced, to be swept up in the arms of those she tried to love. Her body and our sessions were filled for weeks with memories of her unspoken wishes to be a source of joy in her parents' lives, for them to want her with them rather than sent off to Grandmother. From her earliest years, Liz had been excluded from any meaningful, emotional place in the lives of her parents. Pushed aside by their self-involvements, she in turn disavowed (consciously and unconsciously) virtually every trait or impulse within herself that reminded her of their selfish ways of being. At least with her grandmother, in the midst of her protection and moralistic control, young Liz had a place, and in that place she deeply internalized her grandmother's prohibitions. Her place with Grandmother may not have been one of delight and joy, but it was a place of belonging and security. This had had to be good enough.

I never touched Liz. Our work with her body (and mine) was through movement and her gradual discovery that the tensions and sensations in her body were *meaningful*, messages we might say from her unconscious. The emotional meanings of her past became alive in the present in our work together. She could experience the devastating memories of her childhood in her adult body. She could *feel* as well as intellectually understand the life-limiting decisions and adaptations she made as a child.

The opening up of her body and the revitalization of her childhood desires began to gradually open our relationship as well. It became possible for me to report my own experience of my body in relation to hers in a way that held meaning rather than complaint, correction, or demand. It became possible to discuss our mutual inhibition, dullness, and caution, our re-enactment of her childhood experiences in which everyone held their hands, arms, desire, and excitement back from one another. Liz had begun to experience my caution as disinterest rather than caring but was terrified to speak to it. We were able to acknowledge how much of our experience of one another we had been holding from each other in "protective," but increasingly angry silences. She was able to begin acknowledging her often confusing wishes that I would speak to her tenderly and also shake her up somehow. She decided to pursue the new professional opportunities and to bring her personal restlessness and desires to her husband in ways that look likely to enrich rather than destroy the marriage. Her mind and will increasingly function on behalf of her body rather than in place of it. There are still times when one or the other of us falls back into dulled deliberation and each of us has been known to fling our arms outward with an exuberant "Fuck!" to get the other's attention, re-open the emotional field between us.

The unfolding work with Liz illustrates a crucial, if unconscious, aspect of character as a powerful form of unconscious communication. Reich saw the function of character defenses as simultaneously inhibiting and deadening internal impulses that threatened one's sense of ego ideal and self-control while also protecting one from danger and disapproval in family and society at large. Our characterological modes also profoundly impact the feelings and behaviors of those around us—directing, inhibiting, and foreclosing the possibilities of relating. In the example with Liz, we see the induction of a kind of mutual, masochistic endurance and deadening, which may not have gelled to such a degree had I not had my own masochistic proclivities to dovetail with hers. We'll return to a further consideration of this work between Liz and me after a discussion of some aspects of character theory.

Reich changed psychoanalytic technique by moving his chair to the side of the couch, so that he could see the patient more fully and directly and be seen by the patient. Reich observed that from the moment a patient entered the room, *how* he or she entered the room was communicating something that was meaningful. Reich's emphasis was:

> What is specific of the character resistance is not *what* the patient says or does, but *how* he talks and acts; not *what* he gives away in a dream, but *how* he censors, distorts, etc. The character resistance remains the same in one and the same patient no matter what the material is against which it is directed. (1949, p. 47, emphasis in original)

Reich saw character expressed in *action and attitude*, arguing that character structure was a nonverbal, unconscious, ego-syntonic, and powerful shaper of one's interpersonal space.

Inaction as well as action can also be a powerful expression of character. One might say that it was Simon's *inaction* that most powerfully shaped his day-to-day life and our therapeutic space. One day I found myself saying out loud to Simon (without much forethought) what I'd often noted silently and rather sadly to myself: "You lie there like a corpse." Simon remained silent and unmoving. After a pause, I continued, "I used to barely notice how you lie there. It was just how you are, but now this stillness has become disturbing to me. I can't ignore it. It makes me sad. I can't stand it. I wonder how the hell you stand it? How do you stand this, Simon?" After a time, Simon replied, "I don't know any other way of being. How do I make you sad? What do other people do when they lie here? Is there something I'm supposed to do?"

The fact of Simon's asking questions startled me. Simon had been a cooperative patient—eager to report his dreams, his daytime fantasies, associating freely.

He lived with his aging parents, a kind of live-in caretaker after failing both at university and in his first and only love relationship. Now he took an occasional college course until he got bored or the schedule became inconvenient. He had no friends. His fantasies, as he reported them in session, were dominated by chance encounters with someone who would take an interest in him and suddenly alter the course of his life. Interpretations fell on deaf ears, as all possibilities of change were cast into a future that could exist only after his parents' deaths.

Simon was happy to get out of the house for his sessions with me. Content to lie on the couch talking of internal and external events, talking mostly to himself about himself, vaguely aware of my presence. Rarely did he address me directly. I rarely felt present to him. He seemed content to accept whatever I might have to offer by way of linking his dreams and fantasies, interpreting, confronting, quietly wishing for some life for him separate from his parents. His rare questions sought intellectual explanations for his feelings and fantasies. Suddenly, in response to my observation/outburst/enactment, Simon asked three very different sorts of questions. In these questions, there were suddenly two of us in the room. These questions sought action, not insight, asking *how* rather than *why*. These were questions of the body, not the mind. With these questions Simon had begun to struggle with *how* to bring his body and affect into the room.

I commented on how different these questions were from those he typically asked. Simon replied that it startled him and touched him to realize that I felt something for him and that I was *looking at* him as well as listening to him. He realized that he structured his life so that he was rarely seen by anyone, that he rarely saw anyone. He wanted to be able to see me. He wondered what else I saw about him? Silences grew. Not his typical silences of mental reverie but of noticing his experience of his body. I inquired as to how he might begin to *show* me his experience through movement, as well as tell me about it. I encouraged his noticing any potential movements, impulses, in his body and to let his body move on the couch.

Simon dreamed that in a session he rolled to his side, and I came over to sit at his back, my hip and thigh against his spine. We wondered together about the dream, Simon associating to it, I offering my associations and speculations, when suddenly Simon rolled to his side and asked me to move over to sit with him as in the dream. I did. Simon's body began to tremble, and he began to cry. He was stunned by the warmth of my body and his sense of the strength in it. He found himself thinking of his father's weak and withering body, which he found disgusting. He realized that he had always seen his father as weak, disgusting. He hated to have to look at his father, wished for a strong father and longed for his help. Simon began to feel as though his body had somehow absorbed the loneliness and weakness of his father's body. Every few sessions Simon would ask me to sit at his back as he talked and I listened. He began to separate his experience of his own body from that of his father's.

Reich realized that verbal interpretations were limited in their effectiveness in disrupting or shifting character organization. Significantly, Reich emphasizes the emergence of character within the transference dynamics. He recognized that he had to reach the body more directly. He experimented with describing the body styles to his patients, to imitating their ways of being in his own body. He tried to call attention to muscular postures and inhibitions as they were happening. He experimented with suggesting different postures and movements. He realized that his patients deeply, unconsciously identified with their character defenses, that these defenses were profoundly ego syntonic, reinforcing an ego ideal and often seeming necessary for acceptance and survival. Reich stressed:

> What is added in character analysis [to standard psychoanalytic interpretation] is merely that we isolate the character trait and confront the patient with it repeatedly until he begins to look at it objectively and to experience it as a painful symptom; thus, the character trait begins to be experienced as a foreign body which the patient wants to get rid of. (1949, p. 50)

As Reich sought ways, in an increasingly confrontive fashion, of making character traits conscious to his patients, he saw strong bodily reactions becoming more and more evident in the sessions. From these observations, he concluded that there were even deeper patterns of somatic, muscular armoring that provided the psycho-physiological underpinnings of character traits. With this observation, he then began to use his hands and direct physical contact to further identify and interrupt patterns of armoring. These interventions elicited intensely negative transference reactions and emotional abreactions. Reich became convinced that the expression of the negative transference and deep emotional discharge were necessary to re-establish healthy somatic and emotional functions. Later he understood this process as a surrender into the vegetative (autonomic) nervous system, relinquishing ego-centered, conscious control to more spontaneous emotional capacities.

Reich described the stages of character analytic treatment as:

1. The character analytic identification, confrontation, and loosening of the characterological mode (verbal intervention)
2. The eliciting of negative transference and breaking down of the interpersonal and muscular armoring (physical intervention)
3. The breakthrough to deeper layers of affect-charged material, memories, and associations, and often the reactivation of infantile wishes and trauma within the transference (shift from voluntary to involuntary muscular/emotional expression)
4. The working through of the abreacted material with less resistance and defense and release of pre-genital fixations (cognitive/analytic reflection)
5. The reactivation of infantile anxieties and re-emergence of early, somatic conflicts within the patient's sexual relations
6. The appearance of orgasm anxiety and the development of "orgastic potency."

For Reich, orgastic potency represented the capacity to tolerate anxiety and to establish patterns of trust and surrender in one's intimate, sexual relationship, which Reich believed ensured the continuation of healthy functioning and mini-mized the need for characterological levels of defense. Reich viewed the capacity for full sexual excitement, sexual intimacy, and the emotional/physical surrender in orgasm to be the hallmarks of health (and the enemy of Church, state, most families, and character structure). He understood, consistent with Freud and Abraham, that character represented pre-genital fixations, i.e., that trauma and disruptions at the oral, anal, or phallic stages became embodied as oral, impulsive, compulsive, mas-ochistic, hysterical, or phallic-narcissistic character types. Trauma, punishment, anxiety, and powerful superego prohibitions wove together to inhibit ego matura-tion and psychosexual development. For Reich, therefore, the capacity for mature love and pleasure in a sexual relationship ("orgastic potency") was the most telling indicator of emotional/somatic health. Reich believed that intimate sexual relations were the bulwark against the re-emergence of infantile, neurotic conflicts.

This was the theory of character I learned as a young psychotherapist, trained in transactional analysis and Radix, neo-Reichian education. It was illuminating in many ways, offering a way to see and comprehend systems in both bodily pat-terns and interpersonal interactions that often seemed to contradict or invalidate patients' stated treatment goals and verbal communications. There was something unique in the potential of characterological descriptions to evoke so much of the somatic, unspoken dimensions of a patient's way of being. Character theory provided a sense of an authoritative knowing, though I gradually came to see this as often misused in the hands of practitioners.

Of all of Reich's work, it is character theory that has been sustained in varying forms within the analytic lexicon. As with Reich's thinking, the models of charac-ter theory within psychoanalysis have tended to emphasize the defensive, psycho-pathological aspects of character (Akhtar, 1992; Kernberg, 1992; Josephs, 1992, 1995; Shapiro, 1981, 2000). It is rather telling, given the "cleansing" of Reich from much of psychoanalytic history, that most of these authors make little or no reference to Reich. Josephs' discussion of the clinical applications of character theory emphasizes the balancing of empathy and interpretation in the therapeutic work with character defenses while commenting:

> Reich, though, did seem to act as though his characterizations of the patient were authoritative and definitive rather than simply one way of characterizing a patient among many others that reflected his own preconceptions. It did not occur to Reich, who thought of himself as a neutral scientific observer, that his characterizations of the patient might also have reflected in part a repetitive transference enactment based on an induced countertransference . . . (1995, p. 35)

Johnson (1985, 1994), working within a bioenergetic perspective, retains Reich's emphasis on the body while both humanizing the model and emphasizing the devel-opmental and functional aspects of character styles. Sletvold (2014) makes a simi-lar critique of Reich's style and provides a fascinating accounting of Norwegian character analytic tradition. He draws upon his own training and supervision in

Norway and character analytic literature that has not been available in English. The Norwegian Psychoanalytic Society was banished from the IPA throughout World War II until 1975, largely due to their affiliation with Reich and character analysis. Most of the Norwegian and Danish analysts who studied with Reich during his period there ultimately could not follow him into his orgone-based theories. Typical of Reich's intolerance of dissent from his colleagues, these relationships were ruptured by Reich, but the character analytic tradition has continued through to this day.

Writing from an analytic perspective, Schafer (1983) presents a sustained critique and alternative clinical model for working with resistance and characterological defense, advocating a "nonadversarial approach to character analysis" (pp. 152–161). Consistent with Johnson's emphasis on the importance of empathy, Schafer argues:

> The chief technical point I want to make in this connection is the undesirability of the analyst's forcing the issue of characterological change. . . . inevitably, misguided therapeutic zeal increases the extent of the analysand's fright, alienation, and characterological rigidity . . . (1983, p. 154)

As I sought to alter my understanding of character and develop more flexible means of intervention, I found new directions in the writings of Winnicott and Bollas. I'll take up Winnicott's thinking in the next chapter, but here I'll discuss some of Bollas' innovations and contributions to character theory. Bollas' *Being a Character: Psychoanalysis and Self Experience* (1992) was a revelation to me. It provided a more fluid and imaginative framework that allowed me to see character differently: to grasp it in the context of the interplays of transference *and* countertransference, and as Bollas phrased it, "an intelligence of form" (p. 60). I began to see character as deeply formative and informative, as an unconscious structure of communication, "a bearer of an intelligent form that seeks objects to express its structure" (p. 64). Bollas writes of *being* a character, in contrast to *having* (or being had by) a character structure. This is not to deny the defensive functions of character with the capacity to foreclose aspects of experience and potentiality in the self and others, but Bollas' writing opened for me the phenomenology of character, the richness of its subjectivity, the compelling force of the individual's idiom (1989):

> To be a character is to gain a history of internal objects, inner presences that are the trace of our encounters, but not intelligible, or even clearly knowable: just intense ghosts who do not populate the machine, but inhabit the human mind. (Bollas, 1992, p. 59)

Bollas' moving and personal reflection on his work with a hysterical patient captures the impact of one's character style upon another:

> It is important to stress how the hysteric communicates through the **senses**, particularly if we understand the specific intersubjective communication

available in the clinical situation through the transference and countertrans-ference. What are these senses? **We see her**. . . . The body is aroused. **We hear her**. . . . The body receives. **We laugh with her**. . . . The body shakes. **We are angry with her**. . . . The body trembles. **We are moved to tears**. . . . The body aches. (1987, pp. 192–193, emphasis in the original)

The body to which Bollas refers is his own. Bollas' description of his own expe-rience can be seen to illustrate the impact of a patient's characterological style shaping the therapist's bodily and affective experience. The nonverbal force of character can be that of a fundamental, unconscious form of communication: look *here*, not *there*; notice *this*, not *that*; feel *this*, but not *that*; say *this*, but not *that*.

Bollas (1992) argues that character is not simply a defensive derivative:

Being a character means that one is a spirit, that one conveys something in one's being which is barely identifiable as it moves through objects to create personal effects, but which is more deeply graspable when one's spirit moves through the mental life of the other, to leave its trace. (p. 63)

He offers a radical revision of Reich's understanding. Bollas captures the paradox of character: that while character contains the intention to constrain and foreclose oth-erness, it also needs the other to come to life, to make its mark, to find its meaning.

A recent consultation illustrates the enactive, infective spirit of character that Bollas conveys. Andy, a graduate student in his early 30s, entered twice-weekly psychotherapy seeking relief from relentless depression, an inability to concen-trate in his studies, and a pervasive disinterest in life. Andy's therapist sought consultation because the therapy after two years was at an impasse, and both had become worried that Andy was on the verge of failure in his program. The therapist was wondering if it would be possible to work with Andy "more deeply, more analytically."

The therapist had referred Andy over a year ago to a psychiatrist who was pre-scribing two antidepressants, an anti-anxiety medication, sleeping pills, and most recently a mood stabilizer—an ever-shifting prescription cocktail which seemed to have little effect on Andy's mood or ability to study effectively. After a few weeks of consultation, it seemed to me likely that given the ineffectiveness of the medications, Andy's lack of affect and engagement seemed much more character-ological than biological.

Andy filled many sessions with complaints about his inability to break out of his unsatisfying relationship with a girlfriend. He reported that she was inter-ested in him, but he was not interested in her or anyone else, "I get involved with women who are interested in me, because I don't know who I am interested in. I don't really have any interest in anything. Why get out of bed? I don't even have interest in food. I feel obligated to eat, but I don't have any pleasure in it." Andy was preoccupied with his difficulties in sleeping, and then because of his lack of sleep, his difficulty in concentrating and "sequencing" his thoughts in his studies.

In one session he complained that his pants didn't fit any more because he was not eating, and he was not eating because when he does his stomach "gets upset and swells." "My brain is congested. The neurons aren't firing, it's like I've lost my higher brain functions." When the therapist inquires about how all of this "feels," his inquiries are met with blank "I don't know"s.

In a subsequent session, Andy complained of being very tired and physically cold: "maybe I'm just more tired than depressed." The therapist referred him for sleep studies, but this resulted in arguments between Andy and his therapist. Andy was skilled in steering his therapist, who was rather desperate to provide relief to his client, into parental positions, which Andy was thoroughly skilled at then defeating. He went on to describe seeing his "fat" belly in the mirror and hating "that guy." He reported going to a party at his girlfriend's insistence, where she told him, "I miss you even when you're in the same room with me. Why don't you talk to people?" He exploded, "*Never* do that. Do not push me to be someone I am not." The therapist registered the transference elements in this story but did not see a way clear to speak to the transference. The thickness and persistence of what I saw as a characterological enactment was having an unspoken impact on his therapist. His countertransference was one of growing impatience and ineffectiveness. The focus of my consultations at this point were on the transference/countertransference dynamics and how to bring these dynamics and their meaning into the work. But it seemed nearly impossible to get Andy to attend to anything happening within the treatment session. His insistent attention was to his body and events outside of the therapeutic process.

Andy's experience of his body dominated session after session in one way or another. He spoke of his mother's getting angry at him when he was little and sick: "I was so frightened when I was sick that she would yell at me. I sucked it up and didn't fight back." He told a story of enduring intense stomach pain that got worse and worse until his mother took him to the emergency room. His appendix had burst, and he nearly died. When the therapist inquired about "feelings," Andy again reported that he didn't have any, that he has already talked about "all that stuff" in his therapy during his teenage years, insisting that it was just that his body and his brain don't work right.

Andy's concreteness and lack of emotional awareness unsettled the therapist, who kept falling back into a problem-solving mode that yielded little result. It had become clear to me that Andy's experience of himself was very consistently in concrete, physical terms: He had a body whose distress had no meaning and a brain with congested neurons but no mind. The task here it seemed to me was to begin relating to Andy's body and its disturbances directly. This therapist had no desire be a "body psychotherapist," but he needed to become a therapist who would attend to Andy's troubled body.

The next session began, again, with Andy complaining that he was exhausted but found no relief in sleep. He was now considering getting an extension of his graduate studies and postponing his thesis. The therapist panicked and moved into an argumentative mode: "It's difficult for you to pursue your health care needs. I make referrals and you don't follow through. You hit a roadblock, and you just give up. You seem ready to give up here, too. You just say something is wrong but that nothing is going to work." Andy replied, "I feel like life is an ongoing fight, just to get out of bed, to be on time for things, to get any work done." The therapist, growing increasingly desperate, confronted this statement as passive self-sabotage. The session devolved into an extended argument.

It seemed to me that the therapy was on the verge of collapse like everything else in Andy's life, so I spoke with the therapist of the need to significantly change the focus of the therapy. We spoke about the possible meanings of Andy's anxious preoccupation with his body and how to address it. What was he needing his therapist to understand? I imagined that he had unconsciously recruited his therapist into enacting his parents, highly driven professionals who found their beleaguered son rather tiresome, being either angry with him or sending him off to someone else to fix him. Now here was his beleaguered therapist sending him off yet again, this time for medication, sleep studies, and other doctors, as if to say, "too much for me . . . take him off my hands . . . somebody else fix this guy," as I imagined Andy's unspoken transferential fantasies of his therapist's referrals for additional interventions outside the psychotherapy.

I suggested to the therapist that he needed to *accompany* Andy's exhausted body from session to session, week after week: "Ask Andy to take you with him through his day in his depressed and listless body, his congested brain. What is happening in his body when he goes to bed? What allows his body to go to sleep? What happens when he wakes up in the night: physical sensations, dreams, fears, bodily anxiety, fantasies, night thoughts? What is it like when the alarm goes off and he lies in bed: what is happening in his body, how does his stomach feel, where is the tiredness, does he hurt, what are his fantasies, his awakening thoughts? What does he imagine he looks like to others during the day? What does his body wish for from others? What, if anything, feels good to his body? Are there moments when his brain seems clear? Live this exhausted body and congested brain with him—don't fix it, experience it. Help him develop a different way of relating to his troubled body. Don't leave him alone with it. I think you need to stop sending him and his body off to various repair shops." All of these noticings, taken up week after week, have the potential for the development and sustenance of the referential process described by Bucci (2002, 2008) as inherent in successful analytic therapies.

For the therapist to become truly interested in and engaged with Andy's suffering body and his muddled brain would be a fundamental change from the neglectful and punitive treatment Andy and his body had known all of their life. What had been most apparent through the weeks of our consultation was the deadening impact of Andy's character on his therapist. And yet, at the same time, while this character style infected, affected, and nearly immobilized Andy's therapist, pushing him into attitudes and behaviors that mimicked Andy's parents, at the same time it was a silent, unconscious call for something different.

This process would require many repetitions in order for it to begin to feel real and reliable to Andy, such that he could internalize it at both conscious and somatic levels.

The work with Liz and Simon illustrates aspects of both Reich's theory of defensive deadening and of Bollas' perspective of an essential spirit of being seeking to infect and inform the other. In Reich's model, Liz would be seen as living out a masochist character structure with her severe inhibition of aggression, long transformed and subdued into a capacity for endurance and sacrifice, tinged with bitterness (Reich, 1949, pp. 210–247). Her aggression found secondary expression in her control of those around her. Her expressions of love were not marked so much by pleasure, delight, and sexual passion as by loyalty and devotion, which she both offered to and demanded of her family members. Though she suffered from her masochistic stance, it was a characteristic that she valued in herself, and was often admired (or taken advantage of) by those around her. In the face of her character style, I, too, became subdued, echoing Grandmother's stern and shaming admonition, "Don't get carried away with yourself."

From her earliest years, Liz had been excluded from any meaningful, emotional place in the lives of her parents. Pushed aside by their self-involvements, she in turn disavowed (consciously and unconsciously) virtually every trait or impulse within herself that reminded her of their selfish ways of being. At least with her grandmother, in the midst of her protection and moralistic control, young Liz had a place, and in the place she deeply internalized her grandmother's prohibitions. Her place with Grandmother may not have been one of delight and joy, but it was a place of belonging and security. This was good enough. These patterns of care and place became the primary object world that she offered to herself and her loved ones. A deep sense of decency and devotion to others was expressed through her "masochism."

The ghosts of parental absences were harder for Liz to see and tolerate within herself. These were the "inner presences" of her rejecting and rejected parents and her much needed and steadfast grandmother that she brought to me, transferring them onto me, to which I was receptive out of my own masochistic tendencies. This was the internal world and interpersonal system that we inhabited together, unconsciously, for quite some time. Within this world, we each quietly and caringly endured our frustrations, until Liz finally swung out her arms and uttered that glorious—if uncharacteristic—declaration of being "fucking" fed up. Then space opened up between us and within each of us—space for emotion, for new understanding, and for new ways of relating to each other.

Simon would most likely be understood in a Reichian characterological frame as exhibiting the cold, intellectualized detachment of the schizoid character, content (and comforted) by his internal fantasy world. While I could barely tolerate the psychic deadening of the space between us, which precipitated my outburst, Simon was unconsciously warding off rejection and maintaining a protective loyalty to his ailing and profoundly inhibited parents. His suffering was largely silent and unrecognized by those few around him. He was quite literally doing the best he could, barely even able on his own to long for more. It was the impulsive outburst of my own frustrated vitality that created a disturbance in the field between us and unexpectedly gave him a whiff of life. Simon did not kill it off but slowly took it in and made it his own. His corpse-like body, newly seen and unsettled, emerged in his dreams, opening new horizons of possibility.

Through my reading of Bollas, I learned to be receptive to the form, the impact, the compelling subjectivity, the subtle traces of history and desire laden in character as a structure of unconscious communication. I have developed the capacity to be *moved* by those somatic, affective patterns that I had previously been taught to categorize, analyze, and then break down. Characterological patterns contain a constant, living tension between unconscious restraint of self and others on the one hand and the spirit of unconscious communication to the other, which seeks to permeate the mental lives of one another, hoping to make their mark, come to be understood, and thereby find new freedoms of experience and expression.

Chapter 7

The Silent Call: Reich, Winnicott, and the Interrupted Gesture

Wilhelm Reich and Donald Winnicott were contemporaries who offered radical challenges to the theories and techniques of classical psychoanalysis and to the child-rearing practices of their times. They shared deep and abiding interests in the world of the mother/infant dyad and the fundamental interrelatedness of mind and body. In spite of numerous theoretical parallels, their writings show no evidence of familiarity with each other's work. This chapter will explore how the work of each is enriched by the perspective of the other.

While born just a year apart, each to rather prosperous families, Winnicott's and Reich's formative years and professional careers afford an extraordinary contrast. Winnicott was born the youngest child, and only son, in a proper English family of Methodist background, a family that can readily be described as "secure." Winnicott grew up in a maternal world, surrounded by women—two older sisters, a nanny, a governess, in addition to his mother—isolated from other children until attending boarding school at age 14, and quite removed from his father. Winnicott characterized his early years as growing up "in a sense . . . an only child with multiple mothers and a father extremely preoccupied in my younger years with town as well as business matters" (Phillips, 1988, p. 23).

Reich, in contrast, was born in Austria to Jewish parents who kept their Judaism hidden, a well-to-do, aristocratic family dominated by a cruel and domineering father. Reich's family life could best be described as isolated, conflicted, quite incestuous, and ultimately tragic. In a frank autobiographical account of his youth, Reich wrote that he both hated and feared his father's authoritarian ruling of the family:

> For the slightest mistake or lapse of attention he struck me, made me eat in the kitchen or stand in a corner. . . . My mother always protected me from his blows by standing between us, and I finally begged that only she give me instruction. (1988, p. 8)

It is impossible to imagine such a scene in Winnicott's straitlaced English upbringing.

Winnicott completed two psychoanalyses, while Reich never completed one. Winnicott had two wives and no children. Reich had four long-term love relationships (three of them formalized by marriage), numerous affairs, and three children. Winnicott nurtured and nourished contact and creativity with patients and colleagues alike, joining colleagues, while standing always slightly to the side and nudging the existing order. Reich fomented conflict at every stage of his life and career, eventually coming to blows with almost every significant emotional figure in his life.

It can be tempting to examine the work of these psychoanalytic pioneers through the lenses of personal history and character. It is certainly apparent how the lives and characters of these men both fueled and limited the visions of their work, but what is far more amazing is the brilliance that emerged from each, a testimony more to strength of character than its limits.

When I was a young clinician, Reich's descriptions of character and muscular armor as the unconscious mechanisms of defense helped me begin to understand why and how it was so difficult for people to change. Reich understood character as a system of defense against threatening internal impulses and needs and as patterns of resistance to be named, analyzed, confronted, and broken through. This was my early training. It was both invaluable *and* insufficient.

There is probably no contributor to the evolution of psychoanalysis who has written more eloquently about infants and mothers than Winnicott. His observations and speculations about infancy as both pediatrician and psychoanalyst have humanized British object relations theory and have inspired (along with Bowlby and Mahler) the current research into mother/infant relationships and the psychological world of the infant. He wrote simply, as often to parents, teachers, and physicians as to psychoanalysts, with language that is emotionally and somatically evocative. Winnicott's language has been absorbed into our vocabulary. His central concepts and wonderful language—the good-enough mother, primary maternal preoccupation, ruthless love, regression to dependence, holding environment, facilitating environment, the spontaneous gesture—are rich in bodily reference and invariably convey an experience of relatedness.

Winnicott was clearly conscious of the centrality of bodily experiences between mothers and their infants and in developmental learning; he was fascinated by the body, but he never seemed to figure out what to *do* with the bodies of his patients on the couch. He wrote: "One can look at the developing body or the developing psyche. I suppose the word psyche here means the *imaginative elaboration of somatic parts, feelings, and functions*, that is, of physical aliveness. . . . At a later stage the live body, with its limits, and with an inside and an outside, is *felt by the individual* to form the core for the imaginative self" (1949/1992, p. 244, italics in the original). He conceived of the "spontaneous gesture" of the infant as primary, bodily expression that formed the foundation for "true self" experience. In his discussion of the development of an infant's "personalization" (in contrast to depersonalization), Winnicott observed, "The beginning of that part of the baby's development which I am calling personalization, or which can be described as an indwelling of the psyche in the soma, is to be found in the mother's ability to join up her emotional involvement, which originally is physical and physiological" (1989, p. 264).

In Reich's language, this is a description of the mother's capacity for "orgonotic contact." In Winnicott's thinking, this capacity for contact is first demonstrated in the emotional resonance of the "holding environment" and then subsequently in the mother's "handling," i.e., "the environmental provision that corresponds loosely with the establishment of a psycho-somatic partnership" (1965, p. 62). In their overview of Winnicott's work, Davis and Wallbridge (1981) summarized his views of this early developmental embodiment in this way: "Through adequate handling, the infant comes to accept the body as part of the self, and to feel that the self dwells in and throughout the body" (p. 102). Winnicott clearly noticed the bodies of his analytic patients, but his writing and conceptualizations with regard to the body remained awkward and undeveloped, especially in contrast to writings on relatedness. He had a way of writing *about* the body, but from his written work one gets the impression that he rarely worked *with* the body as part of the therapeutic process in a systematic way. There were exceptions, but these exceptions seemed reserved for periods of psychotic regression.

However, it may well be that what he wrote is not entirely consistent with what he did. According to Bollas:

> DW Winnicott had physical contact with many, if not most, of his analysands. One senior training analyst told me that for her this was the most important part of their work. She would enter the room, he would be seated in a solid chair with a cup often on a side table, and without saying anything she would sit on the floor, her back supported by his legs, and enter into a therapeutic regression. This took place over months. He would also reach over from his chair and hold a patient's head in his hands, not like Freud did in the early days (i.e., "concentrate"!) but because he felt the mind needed a physical holding environment and contact was made in this way. All the people with whom I have discussed his technique refer to these two devices, so I think it was common but very restricted, in that he did not move over to the patient or sit on the couch, there was no other form of physical contact, and so both patient and analyst could engage body-to-body but in a very specific way. (Personal communication, 2011)

I know of no account in Winnicott's own writing of this physical positioning and contact with his patients. Perhaps, like McLaughlin, he feared the outright rejection of his analytic colleagues, so this aspect of his work in his intentional promotion of regression was kept private. In a personal account of her experience as Winnicott's patient, Little (1990) wrote, "Literally, through many long hours he held my two hands clasped between his, almost like an umbilical cord, while I lay, often hidden beneath the blanket, silent, inert, withdrawn, in panic, rage, or tears, asleep and sometimes dreaming" (p. 44).

Adam Phillips has written, *"The mind turns up when it is already too late"* (1995, p. 238). Reich knew this with every fiber of his being, and this knowing is at the core of his therapeutic work. Winnicott seemed to know this as well, but he seemed to never quite figure out what to do about it. It seems that he never challenged the psychoanalytic ideal of words over action, the "psychoanalytic wish," as characterized by Phillips, "that words can lure the body back to words" (1995, p. 36).

At the end of his biography of Winnicott, Phillips cautioned Winnicott's followers that they will "have to recover from Winnicott's flight into infancy, his flight from the erotic" (1988, p. 152). The lack of attention to sexuality in Winnicott's writings is quite stunning. In his classic collection of papers, *The Maturational Processes and the Facilitating Environment: Studies in the Theory of Emotional Development* (1965), there is virtually no reference to sexuality. He wrote frequently and eloquently of regression, aggression, love and play, but rarely of sexuality. His fleeting discussions of sexuality have been in the context of his papers and books about child development and the life of the family (1987, 2001).

In a 1967 talk on "The Concept of a Healthy Individual," sex has a very peripheral place. In discussing adolescence, Winnicott states:

> They [adolescents] need to be able to ride the instincts rather than be torn to pieces by them. Maturity or health in terms of the achievement of full genitality takes on a special form when the adolescent changes over into an adult who may become a parent. The test is: can this sexual experience join up with liking and the wider meanings of the word "love"? (1986, pp. 25–26)

He ends the talk with a reflection on "life's purpose," suggesting, "we can agree that it is more nearly about BEING than about sex" (p. 35, emphasis in the original), going on to quote the character Lorelei from *Gentlemen Prefer Blondes*: "Kissing is all very well but a diamond bracelet lasts for ever." So in this wry and rather sardonic twist of British humor, Winnicott dismisses the importance of sexual intimacy that was at the very heart of Reich's clinical and political work. I have found no case studies in which Winnicott discussed working with a patient's sexual difficulties.

In a talk given to the Progressive League in 1970, "Living Creatively," Winnicott makes a more positive statement of the place of sexual satisfaction in adult relations, though his ambivalence remains apparent:

> It would be quite a good axiom, I suggest, that it is not common to find married people who feel that in their sexual life they each live creatively. . . . It is not possible for the psychoanalyst to maintain the illusion that people get married and live happily after, at any rate in their sexual life. When two people are in love and they are young there can be a time, and it can be a prolonged one, in which their sexual relationship is a creative experience for each. I think it is very wrong if we advertise to young people that it is common for such a state of affairs to last for a long period after marriage. . . . One has to say that mutual sexuality is healthy and a great help, but it would be wrong to assume that the only solution to life's problems is in mutual sex. (1986, pp. 46–47)

As a neo-Reichian trained psychotherapist, I would characterize two generations of Reichian and neo-Reichian therapists as struggling with a rather opposite problem: that of recovering from Reich's flight *into* the sexual and his flight *away from* relatedness and the relational aspects of psychotherapy. Reich wrote compellingly about the social, political, emotional, and somatic ramifications of sexuality. Genital satisfaction in adult love relationships was central in his conceptualization of health and a primary therapeutic marker. At the same time, he created a model of psychotherapy that, while deeply emotionally charged, was remarkably non-relational. This has been a deeply held, problematic legacy of Reich. The second generation of neo-Reichian theorists has maintained this bias, most managing to simultaneously enshrine and embalm Reich's work. Now, with the belated influence of feminist and queer theorists and the emergence of a third generation of more open-minded, less worshipful neo-Reichian practitioners, the relational aspects of body-centered psychotherapy are receiving long-overdue attention.

Winnicott tended to conceive of the parental/familial environment, even in failure, in rather gentle terms, speaking of environmental impingement, environmental failure, the good-enough mother, the antisocial tendency, and the tolerance of destructiveness leading to the development of concern. A fiercely independent and free thinker, virtually every major theoretical paper he wrote had an embedded, though typically indirect, critique of Melanie Klein or Anna Freud and others. He challenged without provoking conflict, with remarkable success; he was the embodiment of tact.

Reich, in contrast, tended to conceive of the family and social environments as being at war with human nature, with the needs and essential goodness of the infant. His language evokes conflict and the forces of antagonistic powers, evidenced in accounts of characterological and muscular armor, socio-political oppression, the emotional plague, black and red fascism, and (the ultimate) Deadly Orgone Energy. Reich was at private war with virtually every social and governmental structure he lived within; he courted confrontational conflict and misunderstanding in every phase of his career, a true "fury on earth," as so compellingly characterized by biographer Myron Sharaf (1983).

It is disquieting for me, now a far more experienced clinician, to recall that it was exactly Reich's passion and fury that first drew me to his work. Having first read them while still in college, I still remember the impact of Reich's words in his interview with Kurt Eissler for the Freud Archives:

> What they [infants] do is shrink. They contract, get away into the inside, away from that ugly world. I express it very crudely, but you understand what I mean. . . . So what does that infant do? How does it respond to that [environmental disruption and coldness]? How does it have to respond to that bioenergetically? It can't come to you and tell you, "Oh listen, I'm suffering so much, so much." It doesn't say "no" in words, you understand, but that is the emotional situation. And we orgonomists know it. We get it out of our patients. We get it out of their emotional structure, out of their behavior, not

out of their words. Words can't express it. Here in the very beginning, the spite develops. Here, the "no" develops, the big "NO" of humanity. And then you ask why the world is in a mess. (Reich, 1967, p. 29)

Reich (1983) foreshadowed the contemporary interest in infant/parent research by several decades, publishing articles on patterns of parent/infant contact from the late 1920s through the early 1950s. His Last Will & Testament (reprinted in 2012, pp. 256–261) established the Wilhelm Reich Infant Trust, through which he had intended that "80% of all income, profits or proceeds due me and the Trust from royalties and tools originating in my discoveries shall be devoted to the care of infants everywhere, towards legal security for infants, children and adolescents in emotional, social, parental, medical, legal, educational, professional or other distress." Reich named his daughter, Eva, as Trustee for his Last Will and Testament. Unfortunately, she was so traumatized by his imprisonment and sudden death, that she could not fulfill her duties, and Reich's estate fell under the control of Mary Boyd Higgins, a patient of an orgonomic colleague of Reich's. Higgins has chosen to use the estate to carry out her own interpretation of the opening statement of Reich's will, i.e., "the foremost task to be fulfilled was to safeguard the truth about my life and work against distortion and slander after my death." Reich's family lost control of his estate and his archives.

Reich, like Winnicott, had a life-long fascination with infants and the mother/infant relationship. Unlike Winnicott, he failed to bring his passions and insights about infancy and infant health into his therapeutic process. He did not bring his studies of sexuality, on one hand, with his studies of infancy, on the other, into a theoretical coherence. His understanding of sexuality remained rooted in classical Freudian drive theory. In his earliest researches on sexuality he wrote that, "pre-genital drives are autoerotic by nature and thus asocial" (1980, p. 200). He never grasped the pre-genital longings and striving for the other, the fundamental sense of object seeking and object relatedness that infuses Winnicott's work.

The primary failure of Reich's clinical work was his failure to incorporate his understanding of infancy into a broader vision of human erotic desires or into his therapeutic theory and technique. Winnicott remained stuck in a dependence on language and relationship, too far removed from—avoidant of—passion and the body, the realms of the erotic. Reich remained locked in a classically Freudian drive and libidinal (ultimately, orgone) theory, too far removed from the relational, vulnerable, tender, and transferential aspects of adult life as it emerges in the therapeutic relationship.

Crucial to Reich's evolution and central to the work of body psychotherapists was his "breakthrough into the vegetative realm" (1961, pp. 234 ff.). With this theoretical breakthrough, Reich began to create a new psychotherapy, one grounded in precognitive neural and somatic processes, leaving for ever his identification as a psychoanalyst. He opened a new realm of understanding and technique to the therapeutic process. His clinical focus shifted from the interpersonal expressions of character resistance to the interruptions of the vitality of the organism itself;

increasingly Reich's preoccupation became that of the body in relationship to itself rather than of the patient in relationship to others.

What Reich failed to grasp, however, was that the breakthrough into what he called the "vegetative realm" (the realm of sensation and affect, of the limbic and autonomic nervous systems) was often a simultaneous breakthrough into the infantile realm. This phase of therapy, the shift to non-cognitive and prelinguistic realms, is accompanied often by intense anxiety and disorganization. Winnicott wrote of the fear of breakdown; Reich wrote of falling anxiety. Reich saw his patients as being afraid of their own impulses; he did not seem to register the intense fear of the *absence of the other* at points of extreme disorganization and infantile vulnerability.

Emotional availability, empathy, quiet waiting, tenderness—qualities so needed from the other in entering these early vulnerabilities—were rarely a part of Reich's character or his therapeutic repertoire. In his clinical work, Reich had a supreme confidence—perhaps a supreme *wish*—in the innate "self-regulating" capacities of the organism. In the standard Reichian approach to treatment, the therapist focuses on characterological and somatic patterns of resistance. The therapist attempts to describe, confront, and break through the defensive armor, so as to remove blocks to the "orgasm reflex," so as to deepen and enliven the emotional, energetic, and sexual capacities of the patient. For Reich, if the armor could be dissolved *in session*, the patient/organism becomes more self-regulating through his own, innate somatic and energetic processes. The body comes more alive through the deepening of its somatic and orgastic capacities. The relational change comes through the genital embrace with a loved and loving partner. The relational "work," as such, occurs outside of the psychotherapy session.

Clearly, the first such somatic/emotional partnership is that of mother and child; it is a physical partnership and (hopefully) a passionate and tender one as well. While Winnicott characterized the mother/infant relationship as a psychosomatic partnership, there is little sense in Winnicott's writings of the mother/infant relationship being an *erotic* relationship.

What happens when we conceive of therapy as a somatic partnership, of therapist and patient learning to move together with the conscious, intentional utilization of somatic and cognitive processes? Phillips has written of patients who strive to live as though "there is no such thing as a body with needs" (1995, p. 230). But he observes that these efforts are doomed to failure, as "the body is misleading because it leads one into relationship, and so towards the perils and ecstasies of dependence and surrender . . . it reminds us, that is to say, of the existence of other people" (p. 230). Can we develop a therapeutic model and process that unites the somatic and the relational, action and word, passion and tenderness?

When we touch our patients or work directly with their bodies, we simultaneously evoke their histories, desires, anxieties, and resistances to desire in the immediacies of the here and now. We evoke lived experience rather than a cognitively recalled history. We ask that they try again in domains of experience and effort in which they have failed and been failed repeatedly.

Therapists and patients alike are faced with the task of awakening, enlivening, and sustaining an intimate field in which emerging desires may be wedded to anxiety, shame, guilt, and/or fury. It is a world that Romanyshyn (1998) has described most eloquently:

> What the patient brings into the field of therapy is a body haunted by an absent other, a body whose gestures find no witness, no reciprocal, for their appeal. Addressed to the therapist . . . an absence which galvanizes the field between patient and therapist, establishing a magnetic tension between them, a field in which each infects the other with desire and longing, impregnates the other with hope and with fear. . . . The therapist, working on the knife edge of disappointment, allows the ghosts who haunt the symptoms their release. . . . We practice a way of speaking which is responsive to the gestural field as a haunting presence. (pp. 52–53)

This is not work for the faint of heart. Romanyshyn captures the magnetic, erotic force of transference that is the heart of depth psychotherapy, the evocative and often disorganizing forces which I think send many psychotherapists retreating into more simplified, depersonalized therapeutic routines. When I first read Romanyshyn's essay, it had a profound impact on me, underscoring the risks we invite our patients to take when we enter the urgent and fragile terrain of transferential desire.

While Reich spoke of breaking through character and muscular armor to free up libidinal and erotic drives, Winnicott spoke of the analyst's "provision of a setting that gives confidence" and "an unfreezing of environmental failure" (1992, p. 287). Winnicott saw the therapist's primary responsibility as that of providing management and responsiveness rather than confrontation and interpretation:

> Eventually the false self hands over to the analyst. This is a time of great dependence, and true risk, and the patient is naturally in a deeply regressed state. (By regression here I mean regression to dependence and to the early developmental processes.) This is also a highly painful state because the patient is aware, as the infant in the original situation is not aware, of the risks entailed. (1992, p. 297)

In contrast to the typical structure and process of a Reichian session, Winnicott emphasized: 1) the quality of the therapeutic setting—its quiet and freedom from impingement upon the patient; 2) the provision by the analyst of what is needed by the patient—absention from intrusion, a holding environment that heightens/amplifies the patient's experience, a sensitive body-presence in the analyst's person and way of being, and "letting the patient move around, just be, do what he needs to do" (Khan, 1992, p. xxvi); 3) a relational attentiveness, aliveness.

In Reich's descriptions of the mother/infant relation, he understood the fundamental importance of the infant's bodily experience of being a source of pleasure to the mother. In Reich's work we also find a powerful accounting of oedipal, genital strivings and of the drive of the body to become fully alive and passionate. In Winnicott's work we find an eloquent evocation of pre-oedipal, pre-genital damage and desires and of the analyst's function to soothe, manage and facilitate the patient's maturational forces. The vision and genius of both of these two men is essential to a balanced psychotherapy.

For Winnicott, an essential feature in healthy parenting is the parent's capacity to be aware of and responsive to the spontaneous gestures of the infant and young child, which he saw as the earliest expressions of the "True Self" rooted in bodily experience. For Reich, the parent's capacity for "orgonotic contact" allowed the infant to feel vital in its own bodily process and to become self-regulating. It was Reich who brought the body fully into psychotherapy. It was Reich who foreshadowed the contemporary understanding of the centrality of limbic and autonomic processes in affective and mental life. It was Reich who compellingly described the developing body forced by familial/cultural failure and hostility to be at war with its own innate and natural impulses. In Reich's thinking and therapeutic methodologies, however, there is little sense of Winnicott's gesture to the other. Winnicott offered the metaphor of mother/infant and analyst/patient relationships as psychosomatic partnerships. He described the therapeutic process as a *space* within which patients could play, imagine, attack, experiment, fall apart, and explore.

The responsiveness of these first interpersonal environments with primary caretakers supported the development of an active, embodied sense of a "true self." For Winnicott, environmental failure, i.e., parental unresponsiveness or intrusiveness, promoted the evolution of a "false" and a disembodied sense of self:

> The spontaneous gesture is the True Self in action. . . . The True Self appears as soon as there is any mental organization of the individual at all, and it means little more than the summation of sensori-motor aliveness. . . . Every new period of living in which the True Self has not been seriously interrupted results in a strengthening of the sense of being real. (Winnicott, 1960/1965, pp. 148–149)

It becomes possible to reconceptualize Reich's (1949) descriptions of resistance and armor as traces of *interrupted* gestures between self and other. I have come to understand "armoring" as the interruption of the "spontaneous gestures" of both the somatic and interpersonal activities of the developing child—a child intent on both attachment and differentiation. I have come to see a primary therapeutic task in body-centered psychotherapy as the identification and facilitation of the patient's "interrupted gestures." I have learned to wait, to listen, to watch, to be less active, to attend to my own somatic and counter transference responses. How does a patient need to move: toward their own bodies, toward deeper states of affect, toward others, toward the world, toward me? How can I in thought, voice, and movement enliven and support the emergent gestural field? This is the realm of hope and dread so beautifully articulated by Mitchell (1993).

A crucial therapeutic function in psychoanalysis and psychotherapy, therefore, is not so much the interpretation and confrontation of resistances as of the re-establishment of an attentive and responsive gestural field between patient and therapist. When open and attentive to the realms of our somatic resonances, both patient and therapist enter the world of nonverbal gestures, our somatic, un-languaged movements *toward* and *away from* the other. The transferential worlds that patients so often bring into psychoanalysis and psychotherapy are those of thwarted gestures interrupted by indifference, neglect, punishment, shame, violence, trauma, and failures within our foundational love relationships.

Chapter 8

Rough and Tumble: Sensing, Playing, and Maturation

Zach began his session as he did most every session, proclaiming the past week "the same" as the previous week and the week previous to that, "the same, ya know," declared with a listless voice. "Can you tell me more?" I asked. "Not really. I mean, what is there to say?" While the immediate impact of his reply (or I might say non-reply) was to evoke an impatience in me with his "resistance," I wondered if perhaps I had asked a question framed and directed to Zach at the wrong level of awareness. I sat quietly trying to find a sense of "the same" within my own body. I allowed a fantasy of my week being the same as my last week, anticipating the next week being the same as well. I felt a deepening flatness in my body and a subtle edge of bitter futility. I wondered if Zach experienced something like this.

"The same," I said. "The same," I repeated. I waited. "Can you feel this sameness in your body as you sit here? Where does it live in your body?" I waited (body time tends to be slower than cognitive time).

"I don't know," came a tentative reply, but now with an edge of energy in his voice.

"Take your time, maybe close your eyes. It's like you can take those familiar words—the same—into your body. Your body may know something about being 'the same.' Give it time." I am here intentionally using language to separate Zach's bodily experience, "it," from his more familiar, cognitive experience of himself.

"I don't like this," Zach said suddenly and rather urgently after several minutes of silence.

"This?"

"Yeah, it's like my skin is too thick, stuff can't get in. Lonely. No, more kind of pissed really. It's like I can't let anything matter. The same. The same. It's like nothing. Fuck. More hungry than lonely, maybe."

"Hungry?"

Zach: "Ya know, like when you go out to eat, you look at the menu, but you can't tell what you want. It's all the same. I can't let anything be that important."

"What happens in your body when something becomes important?"

"Fuck it. Better safe than sorry."

"Safe. Same. It can't make a difference? Safe, same."

"Yeah, safe, same, thick, nothing . . . "

"Nothing?"

"Fuck. Fucked. Shit. Nothing. Oh, I *really* don't like this. I don't like where this is going."

"Where is it going? Can you tell?"

"Nowhere fast. Fuck. I keep playing it safe. Safe, same. Shit. Dull. Dumb. What the fuck! I kill everything off."

"And if you didn't?"

"That's enough for now. If I didn't? I don't think the news would be good, but let's wait on that one."

"I don't want you to wait, Zach. I wonder if stopping here now, waiting, is a killing off. You have so often disappeared into this sameness. What's the risk? What's the bad news? Would you stay with your body a little longer?"

"Alright." [silence] "Alright. My chest is constricted and there's a pain in my stomach. Like there's something that's gotten into me that's not good for me. Sick to my stomach."

"Thick skinned. Hungry. Sick to your stomach. It's like your body doesn't know what to do with itself. Should it keep everything out? Can it let stuff in? What if it lets something in and then has to puke it out?"

"Yeah. What you're saying makes sense and no sense at the same time. But it is like that somehow. I hold myself back all the time. My body is thick, like it doesn't want anything to bother it. It's like it imagines that everything out there is going to be bad news. So nothing gets in, everything goes flat. The same. OK, that is definitely enough for now! I've got a lot to think about. Maybe this next week won't be quite the same."

I consistently spoke of and to Zach's body in the third person—"it" as distinct from "you"—to create the potential for a kind of non-cognitive, sensate space. My hope was to open up an exploratory space in which Zach could deepen and then "play" with his sensate experience. Zach, with my assistance, was able to sustain a quiet, persistent, and ultimately unsettling attention to the *sensations of sameness*. Gradually his bodily experience began to disrupt a habitual pattern of a sameness of being, generate associations, and take on the edge of new meaning and potentials:

> Insufficient or lifeless play is a common experience of children with depressed, withdrawn, apathetic, and drugged mothers. . . . Parents may put toddlers in swings or pools and push them beyond their comfort zones into fear states, all the while shaming them for crying or protesting. A common effect of these violations of mutual regulation in play is that the infant's self-regulation is sacrificed. (Lichtenberg & Meares, 1996, p. 9)

"Does this make sense?" "Am I making any sense?" How many times sitting with patients have I heard these questions in many variations reflecting one's anxieties about "making sense." What these questions usually mean is something like:

"Am I being reasonable, clear? Is this sensible, rational? Is this sane? Does this make sense to you? Am I understandable?" Questions about "making sense" usually reflect anxiety about being irrational, nutty, confused. It's an appeal to order and rationality. Zach and I sought a different kind of making sense—a sense of enlivening play, of exploration and self-experiencing,

From a body-centered perspective, however, making sense has quite a different meaning. *Sensing*, the conscious use of one's senses, while not exactly rational, can be deeply sensible; that is, organizing, orienting, informative. We can use our senses, our body sensations at the surface of our skin, in our muscles, and within our viscera to learn, to disorganize ourselves, and reorganize ourselves. In the earliest stages of life sensorimotor functions and activities are a primary means by which the maturing infant or child begins to make sense *of* the world, make sense *in* the world, find and explore structure in the physical environment, and make sense of oneself in the world (Thelan, 1995; Gallese & Sinigaglia, 2011). Sensorimotor learning is not limited to early childhood, however, as our sensorial and motoric capacities remain plastic and vital throughout our lives. The life of the body is never fully replaced by the life of the mind. Mind and body remain in constant dialogue, often in a dialectal tension.

Body psychotherapists have a broad repertoire of modes and activities to encourage sensing and sensorimotor exploration, in keeping with what Winnicott referred to as "play." This focus of attention shifts our primary mode of conscious experience of ourselves from cognitive realms to sensorimotor and visceral/sensual realms of noticing, knowing, and organizing.

Play is central to Winnicott's theories of child development and of the psychoanalytic process itself. Play for Winnicott found expression in two rather different but interconnected realms of mental development: play as an imaginative and interpersonal ("transitional") space, and play as the child's physical/bodily exploration of his/her own body and the physical environment. In his most formal treatise on the topic, *Playing and Reality* (1971), we find a complex exploration of the forms and meanings of "play" in the exploration, discovery, and emergent meanings of "reality."

Winnicott's use of language was often quite idiosyncratic as he sought to find an unusual word or turn of phrase that might capture a *sense* of something, using terms rather intentionally ambiguous so as to evoke multiple layers of unconscious meaning, often more suggestive, evocative, or paradoxical, than definitive.

In his discussions of movement and play, Winnicott drew a distinction between *mobility* and *motility*. "Mobility" has to do with movement from one place to another and the use of one's muscles and movement to get something. "Motility" refers to the literal experience of movement in and of itself, the experience of what Winnicott called "muscle pleasure." What is central in motility is not the goal of the action, but the pleasure in the movement itself. It is a body sense, a body pleasure, a body learning, a body knowing, which can remain quite distinct from verbal, cognitive, symbolic forms of knowledge or lay the foundation for subsequent symbolization.

Winnicott saw movement (motility) as fundamentally linked to aggression, as in one's capacity to explore one's environment (both impersonal and interpersonal), and inherent in the pleasures of play. Lichtenberg (1989), from a developmental perspective, and Panksepp (1998), from his neuroscience research, expand on Winnicott's observations of play, linking play and the evolution of sensorimotor competencies as essential to the healthy development of language, symbolic capacities, and socialization.

In "The Role of Play in Things Human," Lichtenberg and Meares observe:

> In every caregiving cycle moments occur during which the awake baby is fed and diapered, has been played with and talked to and has been put down on the floor or play enclosure. During these moments of disengagement, the infants will actively explore their surroundings—grabbing, grasping, looking, listening, mouthing any object available, and will assert a preference for one object or mode of exploration over another. Significantly *the motivation for exploratory-assertive play does not derive from the caregiver, that is, from attachment,* but from the infant's innate repertoire of responses. . . . The exploratory-assertive system is the fundamental source of the motivation for play, the exercise of educative skills, and work. (1996, p. 8, italics added)

They emphasize that the exploratory-assertive motivations arise from the infant's *interest*, and that in the pursuit of these interesting phenomena, the infant (child or adult) develops efficiency and competence.

Building on decades of neuroscientific research with animals and humans, Panksepp and Biven (2012) observe:

> The PLAY urge is both robust and fragile. It is fragile because a great number of environmental manipulations can reduce play—including all events that evoke negative emotional states, such as anger, fear, pain, and separation distress . . . This is a general principle: Play only occurs when one is safe, secure, and feeling good, which makes play an exceptionally sensitive measure for all things bad. (p. 355)

Winnicott (1950/1992) delineates three patterns of motility. In the first, which he defines as a state of health, "the environment is constantly discovered and rediscovered because of motility" (p. 211). The environment to which he is referring is both the human and the nonhuman physical world. When all goes well, "the summation of motility contributes to the individual's ability to start to exist" (pp. 213–214), i.e., to experience one's self as a separate source of interest, initiative, and agency. In this aspect of motility the infant or individual has what Winnicott characterizes as "*an experience of the individual*" (p. 211, italics in original). This is a manifestation of the healthy narcissistic gratification of being able to impinge upon and create something in relation to an aspect of the environment, human or nonhuman. Often, for infants and toddlers, this involves the manipulation of the physical environment or the experimentation with one's own body independent of interactions with other people. This is the experience of "muscle pleasure." This is not so much an expression of psychological meaning or intent per se, but more a purely somatic, self-organizing experience.

One's relationship to the nonhuman environment is a rather underdeveloped arena in psychoanalytic theory. Searles (1960), writing in a personal voice, says, "As far back as I can recall, I have felt life's meaning resided not only in my relatedness with my mother and father and sister and other persons, but in relatedness with the land itself—the verdant or autumn-tapestried or stark and snow-covered hills, the uncounted lakes, the rivers" (p. ix). He continues in a more theoretical voice to underscore, "The thesis of this volume is that the nonhuman environment, far from being of little or no account to human personality development, constitutes one of the most basically important ingredients in human psychological existence" (pp. 5–6). Our bodily capacities to move, to seek, and to explore the physicalities of the non-personal world around us, are fundamental to our sense of having an alive self.

And then there are the physicalities of one human body toward and against another. Now many years ago, my colleague, Mark Ludwig, and I were leading a series of body-centered workshops for men. We designed a "warm-up" exercise to get the participants interacting and moving physically with one another. We divided the large room in which we were working into four "wrestling rings," within which two of the participants would play wrestle like father and son, with a third man as "referee." Mark and I were both fathers to young sons and were well accustomed to various forms of rough and tumble play, especially wrestling matches in which we always managed—at the very last, exciting moment—to be overpowered by and lose to our boys. Unfortunately, in our enthusiasm (or perhaps our disavowal or dissociation), we neglected to factor in the reality that our own childhood relationships with our fathers were less than robust and playful.

We also failed to consider the likelihood that the histories of most of the men in the group with their fathers were very similar to those of ours, so the result of our warm-up exercise was complicated, to say the least. What we had envisioned to be a simple, fun, interactive "warm-up" proved to be frightening, infuriating, and/or humiliating to most of the men in the group. These men had not had this kind of experience with their own fathers, or if they did, it was the father rather than the child who always won the match. Almost all associated this kind of physical play not with pleasure but with fighting, competing, and intimidation. It also uncovered intense longing for male-to-male play, physical contact, pleasure, and intimacy. Our opening "warm-up" heated up the group in ways we hadn't even considered, providing the context for all of the work that weekend. While I had grown up largely alone with creeks and woods, I had always envied what I imagined other boys had with their fathers and friends. It was something I had been determined to correct as a father to my sons. I learned that weekend that I was not alone in my experience of feeling both isolated from and intimidated by other guys as a boy, an adolescent, and young adult. That weekend Mark and I had the challenge and the pleasure of watching twelve men struggle with bringing their physical bodies one to another in "rough and tumble" action, gradually discovering the joy and intimacy of this kind of contact.

Winnicott described patterns of motility within the interpersonal environment, the crucial ways in which an infant's exploratory, often "unintegrated" movements are perceived, received, and given meaning within a primary relationship—which may involve parents, friends, lovers, or therapists among the central cast of characters. Winnicott emphasized the child's (or patient's) delight and relief in having someone to come up against with aggression (as distinct from hostility), so as to feel the force and boundaries of one's own body against the body of another that can welcome the contact, stay put, and keep its own form. "In health . . . the individual can enjoy going around looking for appropriate opposition" (1950/1992, p. 212), the kind of playful, oppositional experience that Mark and I had been looking for in our wrestling matches in the men's body therapy group. It is within this realm of body-to-body interaction and meaning-making that Winnicott wrote that, "The true self is bound up with bodily aliveness. It comes from the aliveness of the body tissues and the working of the body functions. . . . The spontaneous gesture is the true self in action"(1960/1965, p. 147). Absent from Winnicott's accounts, as was so often the case in his writing, was the description or acknowledgment of the erotic qualities of these aggressive, bodily interactions.

Healthy development and healthy relationships embody a life-long dialectic between the capacity to shift from somatic and self experiences that have nothing to do with others, to the desire and capacity to be deeply *received by* and *responsive to* others. It was Winnicott's conviction that for the psyche to be truly vital it needed to become fundamentally rooted in the soma, and that for the actions of the "spontaneous gestures" to be sustained as a source of self-agency, these bodily movements, patterns of motility, need to be recognized as healthy and meaningful in the caretaking environment.

The second pattern of motility delineated by Winnicott is what he describes as *"reactions to impingement"* of the environment upon the individual (1950/1992, p. 212), be it intrusive, unresponsive, shaming, abusive, seductive, needy, controlling, etc. Winnicott tended to frame these interactions within the context of the mother/infant relationship. However, play often occurs in myriad interpersonal environments (think of schools) that are less than receptive to curiosity, excitement, experimentation, and learning by trial and error. In our men's group wrestling match, we witnessed the lasting impact of reactions to impingements within the father/son relations, evoking shame, avoidance, anger, and/or collapse.

According to Winnicott, after a series of such impingements, the organism's motility is likely to be organized in some pattern of neurotic withdrawal from the environment and others, so as to preserve some sense of individual existence.

Here the child does not have a "good-enough mother" or an adequately responsive "facilitating environment" (1965, pp. 238–239). In coping with chronic environmental impingement and/or neglect, the activities of the child's developing body become invested in the creation of what Winnicott came to call the false self (what Reich would have characterized as the beginnings of character armor) as the underpinning of a neurotic character structure. In Winnicott's description we see a preservation of the "true" self in withdrawal and solitude with the protective, social shield of the adapted "false" self. While there is a suggestion of movement and muscularity underlying neurotic structure, Winnicott does not elaborate these somatic patterns in any systematic fashion, as Reich endeavored to do.

"In the third pattern," writes Winnicott, "which is extreme, this is exaggerated to such a degree that there is not even a resting place for individual experience, and the result is a failure in the primary narcissistic state to evolve an individual" (1950/1992, p. 212). Here Winnicott's description is quite chilling:

> The "individual" then develops as an extension of the shell rather than the core, as an extension of the impinging environment. What is left of a core is hidden away and is difficult to find even in the most far-reaching analysis. The individual then *exists by not being found.* (p. 212)

Here we find Winnicott's clinical description uncannily mirroring that of Reich's account of muscular and character armor, although Winnicott never writes, to my knowledge, in characterological terms. The motility of the body becomes the force, the means of immobilizing the body's freedom for narcissistic exploration, turned instead to hiding and warding off the interpersonal world.

What is significant here, from a body-centered perspective, is Winnicott's comprehension of bodily action/movement as central in both the development and the defense of the self. His brief article is punctuated by moments of brilliant recognitions in the midst of ideas-in-becoming, more unformed than informed, struggling to recognize and articulate something and figure out what to do with it as a psychoanalyst. I think he gained an appreciation of the place of the body and its actions through his work with children, which often involved physical play. This informed his understanding of adult psychopathology and I imagine fostered some of his more radical experiments with deeply disturbed patients of literal accompaniment, holding, physical contact, and physical proximities between patient and analyst.

Over the years of reading and teaching Winnicott, I have found it rather sadly amusing how he has been transformed, iconized even, as the paragon of The Maternal presence. The full scope of his thinking is in fact often paradoxical, welcoming of aggression and conflict, quite dark and solitary. Such ideas as the holding environment have great seductive power, evoking the fulfillment of our longings for comfort and being known by others, for the relentless, unsoiled empathy and attunement, captured in the image of the Mary Cassatt mother and infant painting on the cover of Stern's *Interpersonal World of the Infant* (1985).

But what happens if we take up the sense of "holding" from a somatic/movement perspective? There is holding, as in an embrace within the arms of another (mother). Winnicott's emphasis was on the holding provided by the mother (or the analyst). But children hold as well as their parents. Patients, too, can hold. Holding in its very nature is not just comforting, it is also aggressive. I think of the classic marital vow, "To have and to hold from this day forward." There is holding tight. Holding off. Holding out. Holding back. Holding on. Holding in. Holding up. Holding down. Each of these holdings contains a very different sense of the body—of the body in relation to itself, of the body in action (or inaction), of the body in relation to the physical environment, of the body in relation to other bodies. Each reflects a differing and individual manifestation of patterns of motility. A sensorimotor exploration of "holding" could take one of many different directions, as it did in my exploration with Fred of his hands and holdings or of Winnicott's holding of Little's hands through thick and thin.

The quality of movements to be explored within the field of "play" in a session can be very subtle and deeply informative. To illustrate, these are notes from a recent consultation with a body-centered psychotherapist seeking a new perspective on work with a patient that was going well but had become a little too predictable. The consultation consisted of my direct observation of an actual session, with my observations to be shared directly to both therapist and patient. I went into the session knowing no history of the patient, being asked to observe and comment upon the work as it developed in the here and now.

In the notes that follow, I provide a summary of the verbal dialogue between the therapist, Paul, and his patient, Guy. Descriptions of the nonverbal interactions are provided in square brackets. My thoughts to myself are included in italics. The session begins with Paul and Guy sitting in chairs facing each other.

GUY: "It's good to be here with you. I've been looking forward to seeing you."

[Deep, rapidly passing smile. Eyes lively, moving forward in his chair toward Paul, arms extending. Hands reach his knees, hesitate, stop in mid-air. Fingers curl inward. Arms drop to legs, pulls back into the chair, shoulders slump forward, chest collapsing. Face still.]

He seems to be pulling back from Paul, as though he's moved back into a cage. Hands first open, then seem anxious.

[Paul holds Guy's gaze, remains silent. Paul's body is moving, mirroring Guy's movements, intensifying them slightly.] *Looks like an intentional, nonverbal amplification of Guy's movements. Hoping to bring Guy's attention to his body activity?*

GUY: Describes feeling shy, saying he is too often isolated in his life and that he knows he isolates himself but can't seem to stop it.
PAUL: "And how are you feeling now here with me?" [Shifting back slightly in his chair.]

GUY: "Cagey." [Paul's "trial" movements become more pronounced, body shifting back noticeably.] *I have the strong impulse to move behind Guy, put my arms alongside his and move his arms forward toward Paul. I feel intensely fatherly.*

GUY: "There are a couple of issues I'd like to address today. Maybe." [Laughing, fleeting smile.]

PAUL: "Yes?" [Body moving forward in his chair.]

GUY: "My relationships . . . It's like I put a capsule around myself. I want to get OUT more in the world . . . " [Hands keeping opening, moving toward Paul, always stopping at his knees, fingers then curling back in to themselves.] *Not like forming a fist, but more like wanting to grasp but can't allow it. Caged.* "It's like when I go out, I feel open, good, and then all the old habits come back quickly. I feel ashamed of myself." *Shame. Is it too early in the session to focus on the shame? Too much exposure?* "I come back into my capsule, and I isolate. Shame. I want to be seen but then I go into hiding. I read the New York Times, see all the catastrophic threats, and retreat." [Hands moving back and forth, opening and closing.] *Profound ambivalence. What's it about? Focus here. Hold the ambivalence. Speak to it. Go into the ambivalence, not the shame.*

PAUL: [Also moving back and forth, slightly more so than Guy.] "Can I?" [Extending his hands toward Guy. Guy does not take them, sitting still, face goes blank.] *"Leave me alone!" Perhaps this is the message. Does Paul notice? Killing off.*

GUY: "I want to spring into action." [Voice intense, body shifting forward.] "To live in the world. To live in the woods! To sleep in the woods, hearing a bear, knife at my side. Eager for a fight. I get ready, energized, and then I don't take action. I am disappointed in myself." [Face goes flat.] *Despair? Deeper than disappointment. Collapse. Stay with it! Drop into it, this disappointment with himself, a kind of abandonment of himself. Why?*

PAUL: "So much easier to just numb out?" *Not numbing out—more forceful than that!—killing off!*

GUY: "I want to dissociate from my nervousness, this anxiety . . . My mother, she's always anxious. I spend a lot of time with her because she needs help." *My fatherly urges grow. Where is his FATHER? Where is the paternal presence in this work? PATERNAL.*

PAUL: "I know something about that kind of mother, that little kid . . . " *Paul offers a kind of identification here. Why? Intentional? What is he hoping for here? Paul knows history here that I don't?*

[Guy looks anxious. Face mask-like, deadening.] *Killing off.* [Silence.]

PAUL: "What interests you here so far?"

[Silence.] *Guy is retreating. The capsule/cage. Enactment.*

PAUL: "Can I tell you what interests me so far?" [Gesturing forward toward Guy, gesturing to Guy to move toward him.] *Paul keeps trying to pull Guy forward. I would speak to Guy's withdrawal, the repeated deadening of the space between them. It doesn't look intentional or even conscious. I would be paternal, move toward him rather than inviting him to move toward me. I would speak, describe. Stop asking questions and permission. Is Paul being too "maternal"? Guy will defeat him.*

PAUL: "Whatever you might like to go with your hands . . . " [Guy's face goes dead, a heaviness coming over it.]

PAUL: "Me, too." [Gesturing with his own hands, as though inviting/demonstrating/encouraging.]

[Guy's face drops.] *He looks like he's aging. Spooky. Aging, weary. This is not an invitation, but a pressure. Guy looks nailed to his chair. I think there's relief when he cuts contact. And sometimes there's a little, fleeting smile. A smile of victory? A tiny triumph. Cutting off, killing. The knife and the bear. INHIBITION. WHERE IS THE FATHER? What is the threat? Repeated depersonalization.*

PAUL: "I was imagining some way we might connect." *I wouldn't connect. I would focus on the disconnect, Guy's depersonalization of their interactions. Follow his retreat. Here is his sense of agency. What does this mean?* "How might we connect physically? I was thinking about our feet, your putting your feet on top of mine . . . "

GUY: *Appears to agree, fleeting smile, moving chairs closer. Placing his feet on top of Paul's.* "I just did that in a Breama session last week." [Face goes flat.] *OUCH. Depersonalization. Breama is a form of bodywork.*

PAUL: "I can take more of your feet. More pressure."

GUY: "It's a little like spooning." [Warmth comes over Guy's face, a softening, a smile of genuine affection.] *I think it's genuine. Now an area of intimacy, erotic. Can see real affection between them.* "I feel a little more connected now . . . and a little more exposed." *Explore this sense of exposure!* "My heels come up. I feel real critical of others when I see them sitting with their heels up off the floor, like they're not really there . . . "

PAUL: "I want to be the ground underneath your feet. Put more pressure on my feet. I can take more. I want to be the ground underneath your feet."

GUY: [Guy stands, feet full on Paul's feet.] "Not quite spooning any more." [Face goes flat, sits back in chair, feet still touching Paul's. Chest sinks.] *I might say, "Don't like to stay too long."*

PAUL: "You are brilliant at this!" *Is he referring to Guy's repeated cutting of contact? I'm feeling suddenly very sad, close to tears, fiercely protective of Guy. What am I wanting to protect him from? The mother? "The wind beneath your wings?" Yuck. Where is the father?*

GUY: "Gone . . . You're gonna have to raise the bar now."

PAUL: "Oh! You shouldn't have said something like that to someone like me!" *YAY! Finally some real aggression.* [Guy suddenly stands up on top of Paul's feet.]

GUY: "I want to *crush* you." [Face alive, eyes intense, then pulling back.]

PAUL: "*Crush* me?!"

GUY: "Well, not exactly crushing . . . "

PAUL: "So crushing isn't quite the right word. What's the right word?" *It is EXACTLY the right word. Go with it. Don't let him take it back. Hold the aggression. The paternal has arrived.*

GUY: "This takes me way back. An ancient echo. I can remember stepping on my dad's feet and walking around with him, me on top of his feet. More like an ancient echo, not sure it's a real memory, maybe more of a wish." [Sadness and pleasure in Guy's face.]

PAUL: [Looking sad.] "Oh, I feel that in my chest." [Brings his hand to his chest, eyes open, very direct eye contact with Guy. Guy sits down, pulls back into his chair.]

GUY: "I felt my energy shift. A little less excited . . . a little less big." [Looks a bit disoriented, sad, hesitant.]

PAUL: "What are you going to take with you from what we've done?"

GUY: "Going inside more." [Silent pause.] "Where is my grief? My Dad's death . . . " *I want to hear more. When did he die? How did he die? How old was Guy? Maybe Paul already knows.* "Where is my grief? It doesn't come up. I can't find it. I can feel it here just a little bit." [Hand to chest.]

PAUL: "It's like, 'I just got too scared to pause and feel my grief.'"

GUY: "It's ancient history." *Distancing. The history is alive in this room in this moment. It's been here all through this work. The presence of the father, the dead father. Who will be my live father to protect me from my alive, anxious mother?*

PAUL: [Looking very sad and tender.] "The biggest loss of my life was my father's death." [Quiet pause, each in contact with the other, quiet sadness, a kind of acknowledgment of something understood.] "I hope you will remember my feet underneath yours."

GUY: "I will. Thanks."

The three of us sat quietly for a while, allowing each to absorb his experience of this "play" space between Paul and Guy. After a while, I asked if either had any particular questions they wanted me to address. Guy said no, but he said he could feel my attention to what was happening while he was working with Paul. Paul asked that I comment on different choice points in the process, what I saw, what I might have done differently.

My initial reflections to Paul and Guy were to comment on what I saw as Paul's repeated offerings of and seeking greater contact with/from Guy—efforts that Guy with equal consistency turned away. I told them that as I watched Guy, I found myself thinking of Winnicott's accounts of "reactions to impingement," imagining that Paul's offerings were not perceived by Guy as invitations, but as impingements. And, as Winnicott observed, the individual then comes to exist by not being found. I could sense a profound ambivalence in Guy, an ambivalence that infused his gestural field, beckoning to Paul and simultaneously rebuffing him.

I told them that as I watched, I had interpreted Paul's mode of relating as that of offering a maternal presence, while what was evoked in me was much more of a paternal pattern. I was struck by Guy's repeated extending of his hands, stopping at his knees, fingers curling inward as though a grasping movement was cut off. I wondered if Paul was aware of Guy's repeated "deadenings" of the contact between them, and if so how he had been processing it. I described my repeated thoughts and wonderings about the absence of Guy's father and my being moved by the father's sudden appearance in the ancient echo. I appreciated the quiet reception Paul offered at that point and the space for Guy to stay at the sad edge of memory, wish, and loss of his father.

Paul replied that he was well aware of Guy's shifts away from contact. His comment, "You're brilliant at that!," was intended as an acknowledgment, and a bit of a provocation, of Guy's cutting of contact. Paul was monitoring the patterns of Guy's movements, side to side and forward to back, movements in a horizontal plane. Paul was intentionally mirroring and intensifying the horizontal movements with his own body to see if that facilitated contact between them. When Paul realized that it did not, he shifted his attention to the vertical, imagining some way to move Guy into a vertical position, probably standing up and getting him more grounded through his legs and feet. Paul was not framing his interventions as maternal as I was imagining in my associations to his interventions. His hope was to interrupt Guy's breaking of contact in the horizontal plane by bringing him into the vertical, offering his own feet as a kind of "shared ground" on which Guy could stand and feel grounded with and through another, no longer all by himself. He was not intent on interpreting the "meanings" of Guy's movements, but rather trying to engage Guy through working directly with his patterns of movement.

In my discussion with Paul and Guy, I said that my own inclination would have been to follow Guy's repeated withdrawals from contact in a kind of "killing off" that I thought gave Guy a sense of "little triumphs." Guy acknowledged that this was true and that it was satisfying to him that I had seen it. I thought that there was a sense of agency for Guy in his various forms of refusal and withdrawal, so I would have followed those patterns rather than try to correct them. I probably would not have intervened with direct physical touch but would have worked with the movements occurring at the various points of withdrawal, then verbalizing the associations that came up as we worked with the movements. I commented on the difference in our styles, in which I saw my preferences as emphasizing self-awareness and agency, while Paul tended to emphasize direct, interpersonal contact. Certainly as the work between Paul and Guy continues to unfold, there will be time and room for all of these possibilities to emerge and be explored. I was not, and am not, sure if these differences were reflections of our own character styles, theoretical bents, induced unconscious enactments, countertransferences, or some combination of all these variables.

After writing up this consultation, I shared the written version with Paul and Guy. Guy said that he particularly appreciated my accounting of his aggression, his killing off, which has often been a source of shame for him. He found an acceptance and meaning in my description of his "killings off."

Paul thought of the work as an exploration of the "arc of contact," a process of repetition and extension: "Can you stay with that a little longer?" Paul sought to support Guy's sense of agency, but had to monitor his own tendencies to do more, so as to overcome Guy's deflections. Paul told me that Guy's father was a military man, very controlling, so Guy has profound bodily links with aggression and loss. It was a delicate process of hanging back and then coming to meet, hanging back and then coming to meet. "I wanted to demonstrate a clear respect for the distant boy, who needed his distance, but I also wanted to offer, insist a bit, on an alternative."

My notes make it clear that as consultant I am as vulnerable to countertransference as is the therapist. It is always an interesting supervisory question to wonder whether if I were the one in the face-to-face presence with the patient, how might my countertransference change? As supervisor I must process and utilize my own somatic experience and impulses, as I would as therapist. Cast strongly, from the beginning, into a paternal countertransference, I projected a maternal meaning onto many of Paul's interventions. His was not a processing of the maternal and paternal, but of the horizontal and vertical (La Barre, 2001, 2005). Neither perspective was superior, each was informative and potentially useful. My inclination as consultant (and I presume would have been had I been the therapist) was to speak to and hold Guy's ambivalence, which was demonstrated consistently and unconsciously in his body movements. Perhaps because I had no previous history with Guy, I had no inclination for interventions involving movement or touch. I would have used verbal observation and description to heighten and explore the physicality of the session. It was my consultative fantasy that if Guy's ambivalence had been held in sharper awareness, he might then have felt his "killing off" gestures and reactions. It was satisfying to my consultative fantasies that Guy appreciated my verbalizing of his "killings off," which were a source of the shame I had observed.

This brief example of our consultative triad illustrates not only the multiple levels of observation and thinking typical of attending and working therapeutically with bodily processes, but also the multiplicity of meanings and possible therapeutic interventions.

An appreciation of the meanings of sensation and movement is beginning to emerge in the contemporary psychoanalytic literature. The recent book edited by Francis Anderson, *Bodies in Treatment: The Unspoken Dimension* (2008), is a collection of articles by psychoanalytically informed clinicians, several of whom have experienced or experimented with various forms of body-centered treatments for their own personal growth. Frances La Barre (2001, 2005) and Katya Bloom (2006), both of whom have been trained in systems of movement analysis and therapies, influenced by the work of Kestenberg-Amighti et al. (1999), Laban (1960), and their followers, offer coherent accounts of working with bodily movement within psychoanalytic frames.

Katya Bloom (2006) came to psychoanalysis and the perspectives of Winnicott, Klein, and other British object relations theorists from a background in dance, choreography, and movement therapy. Her understanding of movement is based in practices of movement and dance therapies. As a movement-centered therapist, her consulting room is quite different from the traditional setting: hers is a small, light studio with a wooden floor, empty but for folded blankets at one end of the room for her and her patients to sit on, such that "each patient makes use of the space and the blanket in his/her own way, and this can be see to have implications for exploring patients' internal object worlds" (pp. 155–156).

The explorations are through physical movements in each session as well as verbal interaction. Bloom's primary task as therapist is to provide "embodied attentiveness" to both bodies in the room. Her attitude is typical of an analyst working well—attentive, receptive, curious, reflective—and these capacities are communicated through her own exploratory movements as well as words. Movement is an essential means of communication and understanding.

Bloom's case descriptions capture the experience of the gradual surrender of familiar movement patterns to the exploration of novel patterns, often precipitating a period of "unintegration" (which is quite distinct from regression) that provides the ground for new movement and integration of a more fluid and varied sense of self.

La Barre has developed the concept of "kinetic temperament," bringing a body-centered understanding to the work of Stella Chess and Alexander Thomas on temperament (Chess & Thomas, 1984). According to La Barre:

> *Kinetic variations of temperament are intrinsic foundational physical modes of operating beginning in utero and present at birth that initially shape a baby's actions and affect, and thus contribute heavily to patterns of behavior that are mutually created by baby and parents.*
>
> *The kinetic temperament* can be summarized in three main parts: (a) the body attitude, which is formed over time by (b) favored intensity dynamics and (c) dimensional [relationship to three-dimensional space] preferences. (2008, p. 415, italics in original)

There is a keen kinship between Winnicott's notion of motility and muscle pleasure and La Barre's sense of kinesthetic temperament. Both infant and parent *move*, and each has his or her preferred modes of movement, which may match, complement, contradict, or override the other. In lovemaking, both partners move, in preferred modes, differing tempos and intensities. In psychotherapy and psychoanalysis, differing kinetic temperaments register at a somatic and often unconscious (or at least unarticulated) level that shapes the nature of the therapeutic couple. One's temperament may be variable and fluid, it may be rigid and pressuring, it may be under-defined and tentative, each of which will influence the quality of contact and engagement within the dyad.

I find Bloom's and La Barre's work exciting, offering bridges between the realms of the sensate body and the "analytic" body. Bodywork and body psychotherapy are at their best when they afford a patient or student the opportunity to discover, to *find out* through moving from the embodied known into movements, sensations, or interactions that are unfamiliar. This is learning through experience rather than from analysis or interpretation. Symbolization and cognition may follow, but here they do not lead. There is, of course, over the course of a psychotherapy or learning experience of any depth or intimacy, a constant to-and-fro between somatic/subsymbolic realms of organization and the cognitive/symbolic. And yet in most traditions of psychotherapy and psychoanalysis, cognition is privileged over somatic and sensate learning.

Just as this book was going to press, *The Embodied Analyst: From Freud and Reich to Relationality* by Jon Sletvold (2014) was published. In addition to his involvement with relational psychoanalysis, Sletvold has experienced character analytic work within the Norwegian tradition following Reich, as both patient and trainee. Like the work of Bloom and La Barre, this book provides a deeply informed and exciting bridge between disciplines. It is not possible for me to take up an in-depth discussion of Sletvold's writing here. His book represents another step in re-presenting Reich's work for serious reappraisal. Sletvold states that his book "is not primarily about the body" but "about *the mind*, specifically *the body in the mind, the embodied mind*, about how the mind is shaped by the feeling and sensing of our own and other peoples' moving bodies" (p. xiv, italics in original). In contrast to some of what I have written in this volume, he does not present "external body techniques" (p. 37). Rather, borrowing a phrase from Shapiro (1996), his emphasis is that "given a growing recognition of movement as foundational in psychoanalysis and psychotherapy, a new common ground with body therapies can emerge centered on 'a body that is moving itself'" (p. 37).

Chapter 9

TAKE ME: Erotic Vitality and Disturbance

Erotic passions have come to a precarious place in the history and values of psychotherapy and psychoanalysis (Efron, 1985; Green, 1996, 2000; Shalev & Yerushalmi, 2009). Sexuality and passion were at the very heart of Reich's work, which first drew my attention to Reich's work as an adolescent. Reich was someone who wrote *of* passion *with* passion. His writings excited me. He was relentlessly disturbing. While Reich's grandiosity and paranoia also tended to be woven throughout his life and work, his was a passionate madness. And there were truths strewn throughout it, often uncomfortable truths. He confronted colleagues, patients, social structures, and sacred beliefs. He provoked excitement, anxiety, and hatred—three primary emotions so often linked in love and sex.

Throughout his lifetime, Reich returned again and again to the nature and problems of sexuality. Why, he wondered, is such an essential pleasure such a source of personal anxiety and social sanction? Reich was relentless in his confrontation of the social control and repression of sexuality. Reich asserted that the capacity for sexual vitality was essential for emotional health and the achievement of mature relationships. Reich's early clinical observations of pleasure anxiety, falling anxiety, and orgastic surrender were rich with possibilities for a fuller understanding of emotional and erotic life.

This chapter is a reconsideration of the place of passion, sexuality, and the erotic unconscious within contemporary psychoanalytic and body-centered psychotherapies. Many of the trends in contemporary therapeutic cultures foster the disappearance of sexuality from the heart of our emotional, relational, and therapeutic landscape. It is as though sexual passions and conflicts have quietly vanished from the therapeutic landscape, to be replaced by theories of attachment needs, traumatic intrusions (in lieu of traumatizing desires?), relational and empathic injuries, and spiritual quests of one stripe or another.

How do we speak more richly of the erotic body, to the passionate body? How do we develop a language for our passionate and erotic attachments? Anita Phillips (1998) challenges our psychotherapeutic sensibilities:

> The idea that sex should be gentle, loving and caring is not only generally approved but even generally prescribed. . . . All I can offer is the view that

sex can be such a strong experience that it seems to need taming so as not to overwhelm. The shattering quality of sex needs to be diluted for those who cannot fully handle it, and it does seem that these people still vastly outnumber those who *can* handle a wide-ranging field of erotic experience. . . . The former category make a kind of civic virtue from their own necessity to retreat from the challenge of a full-blooded encounter. (p. 123)

More than three decades ago Dorothy Dinnerstein was challenging the impact of traditional gender arrangements in child care, which she argued were maiming the emotional health of our children and straining and often crippling our erotic capacities as adult lovers. Her language, shot through with the life/resonance/ memory of the body, conveys a sense of passion, power, and disturbance often lacking in the attachment and infant research literature:

Our most fleeting and local sensations are shot through with thoughts and feelings in which a long past and a long future, and a deep wide now, are represented. . . . But our sexuality [as humans] is also characterized by another peculiarity, one that is central for the project of changing or gender arrangements: *It resonates, more literally than any other part of our experience, with the massive orienting passions that first take shape in pre-verbal, pre-rational human infancy.* (1976, pp. 14–15, emphasis in the original)

Dinnerstein was writing intuitively and passionately long before the emergence of attachment theories, infant research, or our current understanding of implicit relational knowing or subsymbolic processes. She captured these realms of experience in the compelling language of massive orienting passions.

"*A deep wide now*": drenched in fantasy, enthralled in the moment, flung back into past, only to be thrust forward into future, wrenched with hope, desire, vulnerability. Essential to both the disturbance *and* the excitement of our erotic desires is the simultaneous evocation of the infantile underpinnings of our somatic/emotional experiences as well as the force and complexity of adult love and passion. One's adult *sexual* body involves far more than a replay of infantile erotics (Efron, 1985).

Dinnerstein's writing offers a startling and enlivening contrast to the de-eroticized and sanitized language of so much of our contemporary therapeutic theories. She captures the heat and the anxiety, as well as the warmth and caring, in the passions of our life-long attachments and longings, in our massive orienting passions. I am reminded of Dimen's question with regard to some of her psychoanalytic colleagues' writings on sexuality: "What happened to the heat?" (1999, p. 419).

One of the things that has happened to "the heat" is the growing dominance of attachment models in psychotherapy and psychoanalysis. Attachment patterns have first and foremost to do with the establishment or disruption of security, the provision of a secure base, in Bowlby's now famous phrase, of one person's reliability and emotional responsiveness to another. Most attachment and mother/ infant researchers stop short of communicating the force of unconscious relations, of the erotic and passionate forces of desire. Reading the attachment and infant research literature, one witnesses a neutered mother/infant relationship, too often absent of any sense of the erotic/sexual elements between parent and infant or even between adults (Bowlby, 1969, 1979; Karen, 1994; Holmes, 1996; Clulow, 2001; Fonagy, 2001; Beebe & Lachmann, 2002; Schore, 2003; Hart, 2011; Eagle, 2013).

Bowlby emphasizes the biological aspects of sexual behavior, devoid of any mention of passion or eroticism. His brief references to sex embed his discussion of the functions of sex among birds and mammals. Reading Bowlby in this regard reminds me rather of a nervous father retreating to tales of the birds and the bees, ne'er a trace of the jarring realities of lips and tongues, hands to breasts, teeth to skin, hands to cock, vaginas, anuses. In Bowlby's book, *The Making and Breaking of Affectional Bonds*, there is remarkably almost no reference to sexuality, and when there is, it is as a critique of the psychoanalytic emphasis on feeding and sex in early object relations and attachment.

Reading Bowlby on sex doesn't take very long and is rather reminiscent of the scant references to sexuality in Winnicott's entire oeuvre. But at least with Winnicott one can readily translate his writings on the infant's ruthlessness, object usage, and aggression into realms of sexual relations to which Winnicott was perhaps too much the British gentleman to speak too directly. Fonagy (2001) observes:

> In neither the attachment nor relational context is sexuality seen as primarily a push from within even if it is experienced so, rather it is better conceived of as a response, within a relational field, to an external or even internal object. . . . Neither sexuality nor aggression are seen by either attachment theory or relational theorists as driving forces of either development or adaptation. (pp. 128–129)

For the most part here I think Fonagy offers a fair generalization of the field, though I presume that the relationalists to whom he refers are primarily those writing from the perspectives of mother/infant research. Certainly there are relational theorists—Muriel Dimen, Jessica Benjamin, Jody Messler Davies, and Ruth Stein among them—who ground their work in vigorous, complex models of sexuality. If one privileges attachment and security as the highest value in human relations, then one is likely to be quite ambivalent about the place of sexuality, given its potential for intense and destabilizing affects, in human relations.

Some attachment theorists (White, 2005; Diamond, Blatt, & Lichtenberg, 2007; Eagle, 2013) have begun to explore the links between sexuality and attachment. Holmes (2007) conveys this essential sense of the attachment perspective:

> Although the experience for mother and infant of lusty breastfeeding may be in some ways only *analogous* to . . . enjoyable lovemaking, pleasure is inescapably the appropriate word to apply to kissing, cuddling, tickling, holding, mutual gazing, stroking, playing, patting, and all that goes on to cement a

secure attachment bond between parents and their infants and small children. What makes for a secure base is in large measure its physicality: the warmth, holding, feeding, reassuring heartbeat, soothing words, and gentle touch that proximity to parent gives to the infant, and that is something *desired* by both child and parent. (p. 142, emphasis in the original)

Absent here, as in most of the attachment literature, is the ruthlessness of the infant emphasized by Winnicott, the essential eroticism described by Bollas (2000), or the disturbing, unconscious erotic elements of the parent/infant relations emphasized by the French psychoanalysts (McDougall, 1995; Green, 1996; Laplanche, 1999; Widlocher, 2002; Stein, 1998a, 1998b, 2007). More recently we are seeing theoretical and clinical discussions taking up the relationship and possible antitheses between attachment forces and those of genitality in adult sexuality (Mitchell, 2002; Widlocher, 2002; Caldwell, 2005; Diamond, Blatt, & Linchtenberg, 2007; Eagle, 2013).

Green bemoans the desexualization of sexuality in the object relations theories of Fairbairn and Klein as well as of Stern and other mother/infant researchers. For Green, the function of sexuality must not, cannot, be reduced to some enactment of the mother/infant attachment patterns and early object relations. While he would not dismiss the psychic and unconscious relevance of infantile experiences infiltrating our sexual unconscious, he argues quite passionately that "the role of a sexual relationship is not to feed and nurture but to reach ecstasy in mutual enjoyment" (1996, p. 877). A vital sexuality can nourish and sustain the willingness and capacity to withstand the frequently debilitating stresses and disappointments of life.

Parental delight, love, and anxiety can intermingle in our reactions to young, emerging bodies. This erotic delight is not to take possession of our children. Such parental delight throws them forward, outward into life, outward into the arms of others. As therapists in passionate involvement with our patients, we engage, wonder, uncover, confront, protect, encourage, accompany, delight, and then let go.

These are the early erotics that carry the child beyond the cocoon of infant/parent comfort and nurturance to lay the foundation for all of the intensities of adult relations. Oxenhandler (2001) argues passionately:

The task of parents is to bear the ambivalence they feel about their child's sexuality—whatever the mix of embarrassment, protectiveness, amusement, pride, hope, anxiety, or envy that might be—in a way that stays focused on the child's needs. For adults to protect their children, it is not necessary to render them sexless, but rather to ensure that their sexuality unfolds without interference from adult needs. (p. 224)

Just as the parents of an infant or growing child serve, amplify, and delight in the vitality of emerging sexuality, so too is the therapeutic relationship a means of creating and strengthening the capacity for vital and aggressive affects, as well as for the mitigation of distress and negative affect. In order to protect our clients, we need not render them sexless.

Security, among other things, is undoubtedly a fundamental need in infancy and childhood, but as a foundational model for adult psychotherapy it introduces a number of biases that I find questionable. My comments are not to dismiss the attachment model as irrelevant to psychotherapy, but to speak to the limits and subtle biases this model has introduced when applied to psychotherapy and analysis with adults. I would argue that while adult patients need a secure base to some extent, they also need (and I think hunger for) a challenging, enlivening relationship with a therapist, lover, and others. I seek to provide the sense of a *vital* base (Cornell, 2001), of a deeply engaged relationship which contains room for conflict, aggression, fantasy, insecurity, and uncertainty in addition to security and empathic attunement.

When we see our patients through the lens of attachment theory, we tend to see infants and children. When we see our patients through a lens of sexuality and erotic desire, when we allow ourselves and our patients to discuss sexual desires and fantasies, we tend to see our patients as adults. The adult body is more complex and competent than that of an infant or a child.

Dimen laments that in much of the current psychotherapeutic and object relations literature, "Sexuality has become a relation, not a force" (1999, p. 418). In this chapter I want to communicate a sense of the *force* of the body, the *force* of sexuality, the *force* of desire. Passion suggests a union of love, aggression, and sexuality within a wish to create states of mutual ecstasy, with an intensity that approaches the edge of madness in the arms of another. At their best, these are indeed moments of madness—the madness of union and reunion, desire imbued with both aggression and vulnerability, fugues of past and present realms of my body with that of another.

Green argues that the "sexual revolution" of the 1960s has not cured sexual malaise. Quite to the contrary, he notes, "Our patients still complain about disturbances in their sexual lives with more or less complete impotence, frigidity, lack of satisfaction in sexual life, conflicts related to bisexuality or to the fusion and defusion of sexuality and aggression, to say the least" (1996, p. 872).

I think of how often my patients struggle with disappointments in an idealized fantasy of tender, romantic, and selfless love. I see a version of this ideal in Judith Jordan's perspective on adult sexual love:

> Women are often attuned to and want sensitivity to feeling, while men tend to focus more on action. . . . Often mutuality comes more easily for women in woman-to-woman relationships, which can provide wonderfully sustaining mutual empathy and care . . . in sexual engagement there is such a rich potential for expression of exquisite attunement and the possibility to give one's attention in equibalance to self and other. There can be mutual surrender to a shared reality. It is the interaction, the exchange, the sensitivity to the other's inner experience, the wish to please and to be pleased, the showing

of one's pleasure and vulnerability that that implies which distinguish the mature, full sexual interaction from the simple release of sexual tension. (1991, pp. 89–90)

This is a heady and subtly judgmental, one might even say coercive, perspective. Who, we might ask, can argue with a goal, a vision, of "exquisite attunement"? To my ears, however, it has the ring of an idealized, rather sentimentalized vision of maternal tenderness and resonance. Where, I wonder, are the selfish, conflictual, aggressive components of sexual passions and relations—the capacity to excite and disturb, the desire to get to and under a lover's skin, to get into the other in such a way that you will not be forgotten, to be taken over by one's lover, to impose oneself upon the other, to penetrate and be penetrated? Oxenhandler offers a refreshing contrast to Jordan's perspective in adult sexuality:

> Erotic love—at whatever end of its continuum—always involves an element of transgression, the overflowing of ordinary boundaries. At the very least, transgression is present as a possibility, as what we refrain from, as what we play with and balance on the edge of: the way a kiss can so easily become a bite, or a "squeeze" become a painful constriction. The very permission that is granted to physical love in certain contexts, as in the marriage bed, occurs over against the backdrop of prohibition. (2001, p. 205)

As I sought out darker, more complex (and more realistic) portrayals of adult sexuality, I have found them in the writings of women analysts, particularly McDougall, Dimen, Stein, and Benjamin. Benjamin, for example, offers a more complex and dark representation of erotic attachments: "The other becomes the person who can give *or* withhold recognition, who can see what is hidden, can reach, conceivably even violate the 'core' of the other. The attribution of this power in erotic attachment may evoke awe, dread, admiration, or adoration, as well as humiliating or exhilarating submission" (1995, p. 149).

We give the other, in our erotic bonds and sexual intensities, the opportunity, the power to *know* us in the most essential ways, and in that knowing to unsettle, disappoint, and sometimes hurt us. We struggle to come to know the other as different from us and in that differentness find an object of excitement. Desire, vulnerability, aggression, tenderness, surrender, and conflict are continually intertwined.

In her essay on lust, Dimen (1999) exults in the "messiness" of intimacy both in the psychoanalytic process and in sex: "intimacy, relatedness, and warmth as well as complexity, confusion, and the half-lights of bodies and minds growing into and out of each other—a viny, complicated mess" (p. 430). Dimen continues, "Way down deep, *Lust* means not the conclusion of discharge but the penultimate moment of peak excitement when being excited is both enough and not enough, when each rise in excitement is, paradoxically, satisfying" (p. 431).

In a similarly evocative essay on eroticism, Stein (1998a) wrote that "eroticism in its vehemence and irrationality may seem monstrous, or at least unintelligible"

(p. 257), describing eroticism as a means "for carrying us beyond the toll of our separate individuality: it 'undoes' us" (p. 255).

To be "undone," as Stein voiced it, was the absolute opposite of Tony's determined stance in his life. Tony was someone who refused to be undone. He held life at a skeptical distance, yet had entered therapy with me, despairing of his ability to join his affectionate life with his sexual activities. The re-emergence of sexuality during the therapeutic process is not always welcomed. It is often accompanied by the memories and experiences of failure, anxiety, shame, or embittered withdrawal. My work with Tony was typical of my experiences of many men.

Tony was referred to me by his mother's therapist, who called me herself, rather than having Tony make the initial call for himself. An interesting beginning, I thought silently. She justified her call by explaining that she only knew of me by reputation and felt the need to do some personal assessment of my treatment philosophy before giving my name to her patient's 40-year-old son. She further explained that she had seen Tony herself several times within the context of his mother's treatment. She was troubled by Tony's treatment of his mother, which she found distant and cruel. She was further worried that he would be less than honest with me, so she wished to provide background. I told her that I did not want her perspective, pointing out that most patients are less than honest with their therapists and that I would welcome whatever facts, lies, or defenses Tony brought to me.

It was clear from the initial phone contact with Tony that he was a fellow quite willing and able to make his own phone calls. It was also clear that he was serious about entering psychotherapy. From the very beginning of our contact Tony maintained an exquisite contradiction in his presentation of self: Internationally known in his field, he felt the object of everyone's disdain, haunted by a relentless sense of failure. He managed a wondrous melding of obvious competence with a chronic, self-deprecating submissiveness. Quick to claim all responsibility for evidence of his neurotic, avoidant functioning, he constantly thanked me for my patience and understanding with him.

Patterns of submissiveness also characterized his love life. Although he had frequent "lascivious" fantasies toward women on the street, Tony did not approach women. He was certain that to do so was to be selfish and demanding. He waited to be approached. Good looking, well dressed, well behaved, and reasonably well off, he didn't wait too long. Divorced once, he had occupied himself with a series of frequently thrilling but constantly chaotic relationships. He had been well trained. His mother's life, from his earliest childhood, was rich with disappointment, crises, eruptions, and collapses of one sort or another. His father having abandoned the family early on, Tony was the salve for his mother's woundedness, even now as he entered his 40s and she her 70s.

Tony's waking life was dominated by women, including his mother, each of whom seemed to constantly want of him but never seemed to be satisfied with what they got. His dream life was dominated by hyper-masculine men who took away his women, threatened or assaulted him, but whom he found mesmerizing. These guys knew, at least, "how to be men." The men of his dreams reminded him of aggressive, narcissistic colleagues whom he both detested and envied. The men of his dreams were like his mother's often-told tales of his self-indulgent father who left the family when Tony was a baby and who cared for no one but himself (according to her).

As he got to know his father in adult life, he saw his father as more of an inept, child-like bully than an all-powerful bastard. He experienced his dream life as a humiliating reminder of his failures as a man, his inability to stand up for himself or hold on to what he wanted. He was terrified that these might be homoerotic manifestations of some sort. It was difficult for him to see the identificatory core of these dreams. He also sensed in some vague way that he wanted me to be a version of these men in his own actual life, that he needed to stop seeing the dream men as reprehensible and frightening.

Tony and I have worked several years now. Myriad factors have interwoven to support his development of a more forceful and vigorous self. I would place at the heart of his changing, my consistent confrontation of his submissive, demeaning presentations of self, especially within our relationship. We have created a therapeutic space of relative disinterest in the interests of those around him, as we have painstakingly built a space of interest in his self-interest. He's learned that lust is not such an ugly motivation, that it does not deaden his heart or destroy his sense of the other. He is discovering he can be engaged by differentness, excited even, rather than sacrificing himself in the face of the other's experience and desire. He is no longer apologetic for his sexual appetites.

Tenderness may well infuse our lovemaking at times, sometimes to the point of becoming unbearable, but by no means is all sex, or the intention of sexuality, tender. Fundamental to the force of sexuality is the impersonal relationship (commitment, one might say) to one's own body and genitality, which may make use of another as an object quite devoid of their own unique subjectivity and desires.

Sexuality, as I have come to understand it, is deeply woven into *both* our capacities for true object love *and* the ruthless pursuit of self-interest and pleasures of autoeroticism. We could say that while sex is often a rich and gratifying component of love, love is not inherently a component of sex. Anita Phillips (1998) captures the ruthless aspects of sexuality in unapologetic terms:

> Love does not ask for excitement, but sexuality depends on it. Love involves a hospitality towards another person, it means bringing them within your own boundaries; sexual desire demands that these boundaries be broken down. . . . The tension between the two groups of demands is not easily resolved—and this is what many couples discover, to their chagrin. (pp. 123–124)

In the undoing and overstepping within erotic relations, in being "naked" to another, we are continually invited to undo ourselves and to revisit, undo, and (hopefully) redo the history of our loves, desires, dependencies, and moments of madness and fury. These undoings and fragile redoings are the source of profound hope and anxiety.

Within the therapeutic relationship, entering the erotic field is not always a delight. The experience of erotic transference and countertransference can create a disquieting undoing of the comfort of therapeutic distance, the force and forms of adult desires emerging from the shadow of disowned, disavowed, and disorganizing longings.

When we enter the realms of the erotic with our patients, do we court disaster or invite possibility? Do we dance on a knife-blade edge between the two? Do we allow the forces of erotic desire and fantasy to push against the familiar, established order of therapeutic limits? What is the nature of erotic transference? What is there to be gained for the patient? The erotic is inherently contagious. It creates the confusions of desire: "Whose feelings are these? Who started it? Who are you to me? Who am I to you? Where are the boundaries between desire and action?" The erotic moves not only the patient but also the therapist into realms of ambiguity, ambivalence, excitement, anxiety, and disgust. How can this be good for anyone? How do I contain and use my erotic countertransference as a source of information rather than a means of contagion?

In this regard, I have learned a great deal from Davies' articulation of function of the "post-oedipal parent," described as "a parent whose object functions and self-experience are more grounded in the mutual recognition of experienced sexuality and intimate exchange and who must nourish and then set free the child's emergent sexuality" (1998, p. 753). The therapeutic relationship, even in the midst of intensity and turbulence of erotic transference and countertransference, is not an end unto itself, but provides the means to finding love and sexuality elsewhere. Davies continues, "Perhaps it is openly in our role as parents, or, in this case, as analysts, that we finally come to terms with what we can and cannot have—the haunting residues of our own oedipal longing that we nourish in our children and then set free for someone else, some more appropriate lover, to enjoy" (p. 764).

Davies observes that "psychoanalysts have contorted themselves, their patients, and their understanding of the psychoanalytic process in an attempt to minimize, disavow, project and pathologize the sexual feelings that emerge between the analytic couple in the course of their emotionally powerful and most intimate encounter with each other" (1998, p. 747). She sees this anxiety as rooted in the fears and prohibitions of sexual acting out between therapist and patient and as fostered by the lack of any intelligently articulated theory of the "nature of normal adult sexuality and its manifestations in clinical practice" (p. 751). She argues that a sexual aliveness is inherent and healthy in the later stages of an in-depth therapy and that these concomitant feelings of aliveness and attraction are not to be avoided, lived in silence, or eliminated through clinical consultation, but are to be welcomed and examined.

There is a fundamental difference between *erotic* transference and an *eroticized* transference (Gorkin, 1985; Bolognini, 1994; Mann, 1997; Bonasia, 2001). To speak of an eroticized transference is to speak of the defensive use of sexuality and the erotic. In an eroticized transference, the feelings do not *emerge* from within the developing and deepening of the relationship: They are *imposed* upon it in an unconscious defense. The eroticized transference is typically an idealized transference that forecloses deepening and seeks to defensively ward off conflict and loss. There is typically an overt or covert demand for the therapist to validate and reciprocate these feelings. The eroticized transference is one sided, from the patient to the therapist, and while a therapist may become enmeshed in this kind of transferential conundrum, this is not a transference that evokes delight and affection in the therapist. An eroticized countertransference is equally one sided, now serving the narcissistic needs of the therapist and imposed upon the patient (Dimen, 2010).

In working within the erotic transference/countertransference matrix, I am not advocating for the therapist's direct disclosure of sexual or erotic feelings to the patient. I have found consistently (I think without exception) that direct disclosure of my personal feelings of sexual interest or disinterest has trivialized the erotic space, foreclosing (at least temporarily) more complex and ambiguous territories of exploration. I am arguing for the therapist's making use of the erotic countertransference to recognize and understand what is becoming psychically and emotionally possible for the patient within the therapeutic relationship.

The erotic transference/countertransference matrix is by no means all sweetness and light. The light of the erotic to which Mann refers as being shone into the deepest recesses of the psyche must often penetrate dark shadows and conflictual spaces within both patient and therapist. Patient and therapist are both likely to experience emotional and bodily turbulence, uncertainty and conflict. As Billow observes, "The analyst's passion, the capacity to feel both primitive and mature, like the patient's, cannot be legislated into existence or produced on command" (2000, p. 418).

The elements of an erotic countertransference may include the therapist's deadness, disinterest, or disgust as well as attraction, tenderness, or arousal. All of these reactions are signals that something is becoming possible within the patient's erotic, somatic, and psychic life. In my clinical experience, it is rarely helpful for the therapist to simply disclose such feelings to the patient. The therapist needs to sit with these feelings, metabolize them, discover their meaning, so as to offer the patient a kind of translation service for erotic vitality. The therapist's simply disclosing (not to mention acting out) erotic feelings likely forecloses exploration and understanding, derails the patient's opportunity to take ownership of emergent desires. Bonasia states succinctly that "the analyst must 'sink into' the erotic fantasy without 'drowning' in it" (2001, p. 260), also, I would add, without drowning the patient in it either. For the erotic to remain open and alive, it is essential that the patient not be an object of the therapist's ongoing desire and attraction, but of ongoing attention, curiosity, and affection in the midst of the pleasures and passions of the therapeutic process.

I am not suggesting that we need to *lead* our patients into realms of the erotic. Our bodies, given time and attention, will take us there perforce. Instead, we need to examine the many subtle and not-so-subtle ways that we may facilitate our patients avoiding these realms, perhaps even leading them away. We need to create an evocative and reflective space for our patients, a kind of erotically charged space, to hold for our patients as they investigate realms of passion in psycho-therapy and out in the world. Our willingness to enter erotic realms of anguish, desire, and delight with our patients offers the opportunity to reclaim the body in its full vitality from the deadness and distortion of parent/infant eroticism gone awry or the fears of passionate attachments and adult intimacies.

What happens when we do not celebrate the bodies of our patients, when we turn away from erotic fantasy and interplay? We do a disservice to our patients when we avert our gaze, our minds, our language, and the attention of our patients from the realms of the sexual, be it to the manifestations of the erotic imagination or attention to the depths and pleasures of their sexual relationships and desires. How often, I wonder, do we offer our patients empathic relatedness, holding environments, and spiritual quests so as to avoid the intensity, uncertainty, and disturbance of sexual passion?

Joseph Olshan, in his novel *Nightswimmer*, provides an eloquent description of the deepening of erotic desire, this intertwining of one's body/self with that of another, and the ever-present possibility of irrevocable loss:

> That first feast of another man's body is both joyful and confusing. I want to fill myself with everything, every nipple and biceps and every inch of cock, but I want to savor it and that demands more than one occasion. When I know a man for a while, when the parts of his body become more familiar to me, as his own scent that I carry on my clothes, on my forearms, when he ceases to become just a name and becomes a familiar man, that's when the real sex begins. By then he's told me private things, and I know something of his story; and when I reach over to touch him in a bed that we've both slept in night after night, nothing casual, no matter how galvanic, can rival the power of that touch. For that touch is now encoded with the knowledge that I can lose everything, and movement by movement, as I make love, I'm more completely aware of what I stand to lose. (1994, p. 64)

As adults we seek to learn that it is possible to sustain desire without the promise or certainty of gratification. We can sustain erotic desire and sexual arousal either in the arms of or in the absence of another. But we cannot avoid loss. Can we sustain or regain passionate desire after the loss of a loved one, be it through separation, divorce, conflict, or death? Meadow describes her own struggle:

> I know that now, as a single woman who has lost a partner of many years, I must, to avoid the deadness, direct my longings to another human being with passion and love, and find a person who will return these longings to me. I am confronted with finding a person who wants the same kind of sex at the same time. For me this feels like a traumatic undertaking. (2000, p. 175)

I think of my own struggle after leaving a 25-year marriage to find myself capable of resuming a life of passion, to open myself to another again. Sex was relatively easy to re-establish. Passion and intimacy were not. Opening to someone new was not. Such re-opening inevitably evoked the pains, failures, and anxieties of the disintegration of my marriage, not to mention the losses of my childhood that lay in dark shadows only to be torn into the light of day by my decision to end the marriage. It is the force of our sexual and erotic drives that can provide an essential somatic and emotional infrastructure to navigate traumatic losses and re-establish an engagement with life.

It is in the nature of impassioned relations to excite, to disturb, to transgress. Sexual passion has to do with the capacity, the willingness, to be fully alive in one's own body and with the body of another. Love and lust, at our best moments, when we don't turn away from the heat of passions, come together to move us more fully to each other and into life. Within our erotic passions are a multitude of desires—pleasant and unpleasant, regressive and progressive, soothing and demanding. Here is both the hard work and the excitement of love and of love-making. In the heat of our erotic passions we need the other, we want the other, we wish to be wanted, desired, to be taken up, to be tender, to be unrelenting. We face the other, we face ourselves, we hate the other, we hate ourselves, we overcome the other, we are overcome by the other, familiar gender roles and orientations begin to blur. We are thrown backward and forward in time. We are excited and disturbed. We lust and we love.

Chapter 10

Why Have Sex? Character, Perversion, and Free Choice

It was nearly 15 years ago that my son, Caleb, then 15, asked me to see a documentary film, *Sick*, about Bob Flanagan (Dick, 1998), with him. I agreed, having no idea what I was getting myself (or Caleb) into. Flanagan had appeared in a Nine Inch Nails music video, which caught Caleb's interest. I had heard something of Flanagan as a performance artist with a sadomasochistic bent, and I knew Caleb was busy exploring some of the nastier sides of human nature, so off we went. The movie, the full title being *Sick: The Life and Death of Bob Flanagan Super-Masochist* (Dick, 1998) was in fact a documentary made by Flanagan himself before his death at 43 to cystic fibrosis and completed by Sheree Rose, his long-time dominatrix and life partner.

I was shocked by what began to unfold. There were explicit scenes of Flanagan impaling his body, and his genitals in particular, with clothespins, needles, and nails. I am watching this with my 15-year-old son. There were graphic scenes of sadomasochistic enactments with his dominatrix partner, Sheree. I was watching this with my adolescent son! There were interviews with Flanagan's family members, his reflections of how his masochistic patterns began to develop in childhood, scenes of him singing campfire songs at summer camp for children with cystic fibrosis, films of his performance art pieces, which all involved his torturing his naked body in some way before live audiences, and comic self-commentaries. He talked with great insight and compassion about his ill body and the evolution of his masochistic relationship to his body as he struggled to master the pain of his illness and the torment inflicted by the medical treatments. I was horrified, entranced, disgusted, disorganized, and deeply moved. I was trying to imagine what Caleb was thinking and feeling. How were we going to talk about this afterward? Should I get him out of the theater before the film was finished? Get myself out? Enough already! Over the course of the film, Flanagan's impending death was a constant presence. It became clear that even his death was going to be recorded for this documentary. Death to cystic fibrosis is truly horrendous. It was almost more than I could bear, far worse than the scenes of S&M. As the film came to an end, I was filled with tenderness, compassion, and respect for Flanagan. I left deeply disturbed and full of questions. Caleb was as moved as I was, equally touched by the humanity and complexity of the documentary.

Sexuality evokes profound states of somatic intensity that simultaneously sweep one into oneself, below the familiar surfaces of one's being, while propelling one toward the body of another in passionate embrace and, perhaps, the state of mutual ecstasy that Green defined as the point of it all. Our sexualities may provide a wondrous and healthy antidote to the stale and steadfast lives that many come to inhabit in adulthood, so often these days buffered by the very latest, heavily advertised mood-altering medications.

Unfortunately, sex is not always simple, and ecstasy is not the only outcome of sexual relations. Sex merges past and present, body and mind, actuality and fantasy, hope and loss, conscious and unconscious, action and emotion, and one's own body with that of others in a "viny, complicated mess" (Dimen, 2003, p. 169). Perhaps nowhere else in our adult lives are the complexities of vitality so fully evoked as in our sexual and erotic arrangements. Joyce McDougall characterizes sexuality "as a somatopsychic universe" (2000, p. 155), in which "eroticism is a powerful way of overcoming early psychic trauma and allows Eros to triumph over Thanatos" (p. 163). McDougall's writings convey the relentless force of sexuality but may be a bit optimistic here, as we so often see that for some, early psychic trauma continues to infuse and define their adult sexual experience. I think it is the very persistence of sexual desires—so often persevering in the face of familial, social, religious, and legal injunctions—that makes sex both liberating and frightening. Sex just won't quit, in spite of innumerable maneuvers to domesticate, avoid, or repress it.

By almost any psychotherapeutic standard Bob Flanagan's sexual behavior would be considered profoundly sadomasochistic and perverse. I had always thought of sexual perversion in the ways that seemed part of the common wisdom, i.e., defensive strategies to ritualize sexuality, so as to make it more predictable, manage excitement, control the other, and depersonalize the intimate potential of sexual relations. My understanding of masochism in particular was grounded in Reich's (1949) analysis of the masochistic character. I have found Reich's perspective on masochism clinically wise and useful. His commentary on masochism was in part a challenge to Freud's concept of a death instinct and at the same time a deeply sympathetic understanding of the functions of masochistic defenses.

Reich depicted the defensive subduing of aggressive impulses into the capacity to endure and the transformation of love into submissive (though demanding) loyalty to be at the core of the masochistic character. At the same time, he observed:

> There is always some kind of wish for activity at the skin or at least phantasies of it: to be pinched, brushed, whipped, fettered, to make the skin bleed, etc. . . . All these wishes have in common that the patient wishes to feel the *warmth of the skin*, not pain. (1949, p. 227, italics in the original)

Reich's understanding of masochism was fundamentally relational, emphasizing the defensive compromises that maintained some means of contact with others based on patterns of submission to preserve a relationship, as an alternative to the threat of outright abandonment or humiliation and punishment. Reich made it clear that the etiology of masochism was in the actual mistreatment of the infant and young child, the humiliation and punishment of the child's spontaneous love and aggression, rather than an expression of the death instinct. Reich's observations have been repeatedly confirmed in my work with patients who have variations of masochistic character styles.

But what I saw in *Sick* was to my mind at that time a masochistic *perversion*, and here there seemed to be something quite different from the characterological defenses Reich described. It was not so much the availability of parental and love relations that seemed at risk, but it was the integrity and viability of his body that seemed the object of his masochist patterns. Flanagan's family seemed almost bizarrely normal in the context of his sadomasochistic treatment of his body. His parents were clearly overwhelmed with the care of three children with cystic fibrosis, but deeply committed to the wellbeing of their children. In an interview discussing his family and childhood, Flanagan (2000) said:

> I was a good student, never did anything wrong in school and didn't give my parents any trouble (except by being sick a lot). I was the oldest, so I was "in charge of the house." I did a lot of cleaning, I cooked dinner, and took care of the rest of the kids. My parents could depend on me from a really early age, because they both worked two jobs. So while I was doing all these weird things, I was also the one in charge. (p. 17)

I began to understand that Flanagan's masochistic perversion was anchored in relation to his own body, its illness and frailty. In Flanagan's words:

> My mother said that when I was a baby and really sick in the hospital, they had to stick needles in my chest to draw fluid out. . . . the doctors tied my hands and feet to the bed so I wouldn't hurt myself. And it's still one of my favorite positions to be in: flat on the bed, tied up. Because of my early, really horrible stomach-aches, I would rub against the sheets and the pillows to soothe my stomach and this became more and more erotic—I started to masturbate this way; slowly it all blended together. (p. 12)

> I didn't even relate my secret activities to sex or pornography; if I were caught I thought people would think I was crazy more than some kind of sex fiend. (p. 19)

I realized that there was something very important for me to learn about my work with the body in psychotherapy through a deeper understanding of sexual perversion. In beginning first to further explore literature on masochism, Anita Phillips' *A Defense of Masochism* (1998), Emmanuel Ghent's "Masochism, Submission, Surrender: Masochism as a Perversion of Surrender" (1990), Robert Stoller's psychoanalytic and ethnographic studies of sexual excitements and perversions (1975, 1979, 1985, 1991a, 1991b), and the provocative, complex studies of Joyce

McDougall (1991, 2000), Muriel Dimen (2001, 2003, 2005) and Ruth Stein (1998a, 1998b, 2005) all deepened my understanding of what I had witnessed in *Sick*.

Stein offered a systematic exploration of the excessive and enigmatic qualities of sexuality. In a very important and unsettling voice, she drew deeply from the traditions of French psychoanalysis and literature, noting in a bit of understatement that ideas pertaining to sexuality and eroticism "are dealt with in their extreme forms more in French thinking than in British or American conceptualizations of the psychical" (1998b, p. 257). She observed that "eroticism in its vehemence and irrationality may seem monstrous, or at least unintelligible" (p. 257), describing eroticism as a means "for carrying us beyond the toll of our separate individuality: it 'undoes' us" (p. 255), and which "responds to and expresses the need for magic, for overstepping one's boundaries, for endowing one's sensuality and profound corporeality with meaning, a meaning that is both clarifying and mystifying . . . " (p. 266).

Forms of sexual arousal and expression experienced as compelling to the individual may be seen as compulsive, addictive, or perverse to the clinical observer, especially when they seem to deaden or eliminate the differentness of the other. Stein emphasizes that "sexual experience has an 'otherness' about it that distinguishes it from daily, habitual modes of experiencing and relating" (1998a, p. 594). Stein conveys a compelling sense of an erotic/sensual/unconscious "tension arc" between one's own body and that of an "other" in our sexual relations:

> A tension arc is created between bodily sensations and the enigmatic other carrying over into adult life and constituting a bedrock for the sense of enigma and unfathomableness and the sense of profound revelation that sometimes accompanies sexual experience. (1998a, p. 594)

I see that this tension arc is two-fold, sometimes energizing the terrain between self and other, but also energizing the realms of body and self. I think that what we have come to label "perverse" sexuality is grounded in this second tension arc. In my own clinical work and reading outside of the clinical arena, I have found that arousal states that are often defined as perverse are enduring sensate/somatic solutions to maintain "a tension arc" (Stein, 1998a) between one's sense of a coherent and cohering self and one's own bodily aliveness when the "tension arc between bodily sensations and the enigmatic other" has never formed or has been traumatically disrupted.

As Dimen (2001) deconstructs and depathologizes the concept of perversion, she asks the reader to wonder with her, "why do we still talk about it?" (p. 827). Dimen delineates the pairing of ever-changing definitions of perversity against ever-changing definitions of normal, sanctioned expressions of sexuality. She concludes, "the label of perversion is as clinically superfluous as we now understand the label of homosexuality to be" (p. 853). Dimen's challenging essay underscores the difficulty of any definition of perversion that is not held in contradistinction to a culturally sanctioned norm. She confronts the labeling of perversions in the creation of stigma and shame, following Foucault's admonition that the power to name is the power to blame. Over his many years of research, Stoller became even more outspoken:

> I believe it is immoral for psychoanalysts to hide their moralizing in jargon-soaked theory. . . . Because I am no longer a covert enemy of my patients and informants, I can let them open themselves up to the search for an understanding of the origins and dynamics of their erotic practices. And with that flood of new information, I can enjoy giving up previous positions and no longer burn with the fevers of righteousness. (Stoller, 1991b, pp. 21 and 48)

Can we name without creating blame? I would suggest so and further suggest that the concept of perversion persists in the clinical literature in an effort to comprehend a crucial aspect of sexuality anchored in primary sensate and sensorimotor organization within the "tension arc" that arises between one's own bodily sensations, one's development of somatic competence and coherence, and one's relatedness to others.

As first observed by Freud and further articulated by Laplanche (1995, 1997), sexual desires are at once and the same profoundly impersonal and fundamentally relational. As psychotherapists and psychoanalysts, we tend to tilt in favor of the relational, valorizing our relational capacities as evidence of health and maturity (Dimen, 2001). In so doing, we are in danger of joining with the forces of cultures, states, and religions to sanction certain forms of sexual expression while pathologizing (condemning) others. I would argue that the essential force and nature of perversions challenge us to question the relational tilt, and to reposition our sexual body at its core.

Perversion has been edged out of the diagnostic lexicon, often now to be replaced by the language of sexual compulsion and addiction. Jacobson (2003) argues that addiction is "by definition passive" (p. 107), while the concept of perversion conveys a meaning that is "more active, and the ominous elements are in the person, not in some external master" (p. 107). The model of sexual addiction collapses the sense of the individual's interiority and intentionality. The addict is viewed as a victim of disease, while the pervert is the carrier of an internal force, the author of desire.

Perhaps more than anyone else in the psychoanalytic literature, Stoller has undertaken the most systematic study of sexuality and perversion inside and outside of the consulting room. Stoller was never one to mince words. He saw no need to turn away from the term "perversion"; quite to the contrary, he embraced it emphatically:

> Paraphilia: how clean, how neat, disinfected, sanitized, and tidy. Science triumphant. Change the sign on the door and the activities inside change.
> *Nonetheless*, I want to retain the term perversion just because of its nasty connotations. *Perversion* is a sturdy word, throbbing with assumptions, while

paraphilia is a wet noodle. In trying to say nothing, it says nothing. It is not neutral; it is neutered, pithed. It does not contain the quality I believe the person we would call perverse finds essential. (1985, p. 6, emphasis in the original)

In the psychoanalytic literature on perversion, Stoller's 1975 text, *Perversion: The Erotic Form of Hatred*, is often referenced and quoted. Interestingly, that was his first book on the subject, but by the last in 1991, *Pain & Passion: A Psychoanalyst Explores the World of S&M* (1991b), his views had changed significantly, though this book is rarely quoted.

Stoller, unlike most psychoanalysts and psychotherapists, left his consulting room to talk with people of varied sexual persuasions and practices in their actual sexual habitats. There is much to learn not only from Stoller's hypotheses and conclusions but also from his means of study and his demonstrations of respect for those whose behavior often left him quite unsettled and judgmental.

In *Pain & Passion* there is an almost uncanny echoing of Bob Flanagan's film and words. In talking with a group of sadomasochists, Stoller found that "they had consciously forced themselves to master what at first, in infancy and childhood, was uncontrollable physical agony and terror by taking the pain and working with it in their heads, eventually via daydreams, altered states of consciousness, or genital masturbation, until it was converted into pain-that-is-pleasure: voluptuous pain . . . their triumph is their perversion" (1991b, p. 25). Stoller observes that "no sadomasochists like all kinds of pain" (1991b, p. 16), or as Flanagan says it, "Even people who are into SM are not turned on by getting their hand slammed in a car door" (2000, p. 35). Stoller continues:

Consensual sadomasochism is theater—an amusement park—not only in its pornography but in its playgrounds in the real world. . . . Erotic excitement is a vibration, an oscillating between two possibilities—one positive, the other negative—such as pleasure–unpleasure, relief–trauma, success–failure, and danger–safety. . . . Every detail counts in increasing the excitement and preventing true danger or boredom. (1991b, pp. 17–18)

Again, mirrored in Flanagan's words:

If the pain is too heavy, or if it escalates too quickly, it'll psychologically destroy whatever illusion you're working up to, or whatever feelings are being increased. . . . You have to get on a wavelength with a person, plus you have to get on a wavelength with your own body. And you build up the pain threshold, you don't just immediately get together with somebody and start flailing away at them . . . But in general most people want a scene to be an erotic, sensual experience, not a *brutal* experience. (2000, p. 35)

Throughout his studies of sexual excitement and perversion, Stoller saw the anchoring of patterns of sexual desire and expression in early childhood experience, motivated more often than not by the need to master and transform early somatic pain and trauma. He concludes that elements of sadomasochism and perversion are perhaps present in all forms of sexual fantasies and behavior.

In a personal and moving case of "working with a patient over a period of 10 years, a man seemingly unable to forge an intimate relationship and who used sex to create distance" (2013, p. 49), Frank offers an accounting of his own facing of his patient's behaviors, "uncomfortable though they may be—that need to be explored and understood, not dismissed as perverse" (p. 49). David had been in psychotherapy or psychoanalysis most of his adult life. Gym buffed, gay hustler, David's primary sexual outlet was in bisexual *ménages a trois*, usually with married couples, which "allowed him to connect sexually, to disconnect emotionally, to avoid intimacy and to deny his homosexuality" (p. 53). Over time his sexual encounters became increasingly ritualized, instrumentalized (leather, masks, dildos), and gay. The work was not easy for either analyst or patient, but gradually an intimacy and honesty developed, and David was finally able to confide, "I eat shit." Frank asked a simple question: "Why?" Frank's openness to understanding, rather than disgust and pathologizing, opened the way for Frank and David to understand David's most fundamental, visceral need/horror that had permeated his sexual self.

Frank argues, "There is a long tradition of psychoanalytic thinking that associates non-normative sexual behavior with dehumanization and perversion, but can't these often nonconventional acts that seemingly treat the other as an object, when viewed in their specific, meaningful context, reveal unexpected meanings such as ties of mutual recognition and connectedness?" (p. 57). In previous therapies, David had made the effort to reveal and understand his scatological behaviors, to be met with silence, disgust, or judgment. He told Frank, "Now, I felt like shit. . . . I wanted to scream at him, 'What I do may disgust you, but it's who I am that disgusts me. I can't connect to another human being. I don't know how to love another human being. Isn't that worse?'" (p. 58). Frank's reply was, "Yes, David, that *is* worse" (p. 58).

Downing (1996) stresses the importance of the infant's development of "affect-motor schemas" and "affect-motor beliefs" that are an elaboration and integration of the infant's sensorimotor development within the relational and affective patterns with the caregivers. These patterns are not encoded in language but in literal affective and motoric experiences; that is, in the somatic infrastructure. Downing conceptualizes these affect-motor schemas as forming prelinguistic, sensorimotor belief systems for connectedness, differentiation, and bodily effectiveness. He hypothesizes "that certain physical parent–infant bodily interactions . . . leave a trace . . . that this trace can be understood as a shaping, an influencing, of the infant's motor representational world . . . that the vestige of these early motor beliefs will later affect adult behavior and awareness" (p. 150). He stresses the importance of the parent/infant relationship fostering for the infant a sense of embodied agency, that "the infant's ability to impinge upon the other must equally be unfolded" and that the infant "must build up a motoric representation of the other as engagable, and of himself as able to engage" (1996, p. 169, quotes taken from unpublished English language manuscript).

When there is profound and chronic failure of this sensorimotor engagement, I think we see the "traces" of affect-motor schemas lived out in the sexual realm as "perversion," an attempt, I believe, to keep one's body erotically alive, to maintain the "tension arc" of sensate life. The motoric representation of the other as engagable, a crucial link in McDougall's "somatopsychic universe," may never have adequately developed in the first place or may have been traumatically severed at some later stage. I think that perverse sexualities often reflect an unconscious effort to maintain an experience of the intactness of one's own body in relation to remnants (or fantasies) of an available, penetrable other.

The rich clinical literature evolving from the work of Frances Tustin (1986, 1990) and Esther Bick (1986) in exploring psychogenic autism offers important insights into the somatic underpinnings of perversion. Bick described the primitive, "adhesive" attachment to sensation as an object, creating a defensive "second skin" (1968, p. 484) as a defensive reaction to a disturbance of the primal skin function. The interpersonal membranes of skin to skin (flesh to flesh) interchange are replaced with a protective, depersonalized "second muscular skin" (Anzieu, 1989, pp. 192–199). Tustin (1990) states that in the formation of "adhesive pseudo-object relations" the physical sensations of one's physical existence replace that of a less stable, and likely threatening, experience of relatedness to others.

The sensory descriptions of Bick, Tustin, and their colleagues offer rich insight into the experience of perverse sexualities. When the early object relational realm goes consistently awry, the forming body may be thrown back upon itself. While the parental other is too often out of reach (the depressed parent), too disorganizing a force (the manic parent), too disgusted (the hysteric parent), or too frightening (the psychotic parent), the sensate world of the body/self is always within reach in a solipsistic tension arc. Perversions are an effort to maintain life in the face of an endangered body (as we see with Bob Flanagan) or perhaps in relation to sexually deadened (or actually dead) parents. Jimenez (2004) characterizes perversion as "the compulsive and futile effort to extract life from a dead couple" (p. 72), or, as described by Ogden (1996), "an important method of attempting to infuse the empty primal scene with life (excitement and other substitutes for feelings of aliveness) is the experience of 'flirting with danger,' tempting fate by 'flying too close to the flame.'" (p. 1144). Stoller would have us recognize that the art of perversion is in the creation, the flirting, with the carefully crafted and maintained illusion of danger a careful distance from the flame. There persists a delicate balance between the foreclosure of imaginative space through what can be the highly predictable, perseverative patterns of perverse fantasies with the potential to sustain somatic vitality, open imaginative space, challenge sexual shame and anxieties, and "court excess" (Corbett, 2013, p. 27).

Ogden (1989) modified the Kleinian conceptualization of developmental positions to those of modes of experience and relating. He has removed them from the rigid language of pathological fixation, suggesting instead that these modes of experience, while having deep developmental roots, are also life-long, functional modes of relating to the world and those in it. Ogden describes the autistic-contiguous mode as the "experiences of sensation, particularly at the skin surface, that are the principal media for the creation of psychological meaning and the rudiments of the experience of self" (p. 52).

I have gradually come to understand sexual perversions as patterns of somatic/sexual relations (with one's self and/or another) that function to provide cohesion and vitality, a *containing*, *sensate* process, and provide an alternative to a failed or absent containing object/other. Perverse sexualities are compellingly alive in the present, often experienced as beyond conscious choice and control, while often severed from their developmental roots and meanings. Perversions can be a means to squarely face the frailties of the flesh, to bridge the breakdowns of relatedness, and to intensify the edge of existence, a reality that I came to comprehend very slowly over the years of my work with Hank.

Distant, rather than frail, was my first and abiding impression of Hank. Nearing 30, Hank came to see me, complaining of persistent depression and a dread of entering the landmark age of 30, still inhabited by this depression that had haunted him since adolescence. In the initial session I asked Hank (as I ask everyone) if there was anything he needed to know about me. He said no and explained that he could see a great deal of change in the woman at work who had provided him with my name. He saw the changes in her as a direct outcome of her therapy, so that was all he needed to know. It was a kind of foreshadowing of Hank's never asking anything of or about me over the course of our work together.

In the early sessions I felt somehow tested. I couldn't quite grasp the nature of the test but had a deep sense of how tentative was Hank's investment in his therapy. It became clear that I had somehow passed the test when Hank "confessed" that he was gay and that he had really come to see me to resolve his intense conflict about his sexual preference, which he found utterly disgusting. His depression, as he understood it, was directly linked to his inability to maintain sexual interest in women and his refusal to consider a gay lifestyle. Hank was married and had severe bouts of depression after the birth of each of their children. Their marriage was deeply loving and essentially without sex. Hank's wife was aware of his struggle around sexual orientation. At Hanks' suggestion, they separated so that his wife would have "the freedom to find a man who truly enjoyed her body." Significantly, he did not see the separation as an opportunity for him to find a man who would truly enjoy *his* body. Hank and his ex-wife remained active, committed co-parents.

Hank's image of gay men was that of selfish predators "only interested in one thing," which was the one thing in which he could not allow himself interest. He contented himself with occasional gay porn, frequent masturbation, cheap beer, and more expensive marijuana. Outside of his contact with his children and wife, Hank had no real social life or close friends. An engineer in a large IT firm, his solitary lifestyle did not seem that unusual to many of his rather asocial coworkers. My inquiries into his porn and masturbatory fantasies were carefully, politely sidestepped. I did not push. His manner of relating to me was polite but impersonal. I was held at a careful distance, such that there was a subtle but unmistakable deadening of the space between us. My initial impressions were of Hank's fundamental schizoid character style, so I knew that my respect for this distance was necessary. What seemed essential was that Hank had a place and a person with whom he could begin to establish a strong connection to his own vital forces. A focus on our relationship might become central later.

Hank had had very occasional one-night stands with male pickups in gay bars. He found the whole experience sad and disgusting: "I'd rather be alone. It's more self-respecting." He did not believe that men could truly love one another. He'd had one brief relationship with a young man while in college, which he recalled with pleasure and tenderness. Believing at the time that they had confused sex with love, he pressured his young partner to have a celibate relationship with him. When the man insisted on a sexual relationship, Hank ended the relationship altogether. Hank felt deeply that his relentless sexual attraction to men was disgusting and profoundly perverse. In our initial, tentative explorations of what "perverse" meant to him, it seemed that what rendered gay sex perverse for Hank was that he did not believe that sex between men could be loving; it was simply carnal. Such loveless sex, to Hank, was the essence of perversion.

As he came to trust me and the judgment-free space I offered him, he told me that he had twice been in therapy before. The first with a "reparative" (Nicolosi, 1993) therapist recommended by a minister, which successfully reinforced all of his negative self-images while offering behavioral treatment strategies that changed nothing of his sexual fantasies. The second effort was at the local gay and lesbian counseling center where his problem was diagnosed as internalized homophobia, and he was offered a "gay-positive" psychotherapy. Trett (2004) has characterized the goal of gay affirmative models as supporting (even insisting upon) "coming out," in that "full gender/sexual health is equated with the completion of the coming out process and adoption of a congruent gay or lesbian lifestyle" (p. 159). But Trett warns:

> Gay affirmative therapy created a normative position, a fixed inner sexual orientation waiting to "come out" via the mechanism of therapeutic affirmation of its existence. To have same-sex desire and fail either to complete or progress through "the coming out process" meant the subject was in some way not OK. This conceptualization risks providing a therapy oriented toward positions that may not be compatible with the patient's subjectivity and therefore hazardous to the (never complete) human task of self-construction. (p. 161)

This was exactly Hank's experience, and he found no interest in or acceptance of his disgust with his homosexuality from his gay therapist, and he soon quit with no warning or explanation. He made it explicit with me that given his previous therapeutic encounters, he wanted to know nothing about my own sexuality or my views on homosexuality.

Hank was quite close to his parents and siblings—a large family all living in the area. When he told his parents that he had separated from his wife and started therapy again, knowing of Hank's recurrent depressions, his parents expressed concern. This time he told them why he was in treatment, that he feared he was gay. They were quite accepting of his homosexuality and even more so of his refusal to act on it. His mother asked why he didn't just stay married anyway. Hank explained that he didn't think it fair to his wife, whom he thought was entitled to be desired and have sexual intimacy. He had tried it and just couldn't do it. "Well," his mom prompted helpfully, "your father and I haven't had sex for decades. We don't miss it and get along fine." "That was more information than I really wanted, Mom," Hank replied. And with Mom's casual dismissal of sex, Hank and I got a fleeting insight into how it was so easy for him to disregard his own sexual desires.

What impressed me in hearing of this interchange was the existence of a much deeper anxiety about sexuality and intimacy running through the family. Any real discussion or inquiry into Hank's inner world, an intimate conversation, was deflected outward by the suggestion that he just find a nice girl and a return to football games on TV. Perhaps simply enjoying the same television shows should be sufficient to maintain a marriage. Hank took a risk with his parents, but his parents couldn't take it up with him. They were not hostile—they simply couldn't take themselves into his interior world, which is what he so desperately needed. This benign turning away from the interior was mirrored in our work together, as we struggled to hold a space for exploration of Hank's internal world in the sessions.

Hank considered himself "perverse" and wanted nothing more than to be "normal." If Hank's family represented "normality," I found it hard to endorse this as a therapeutic goal. I thought privately to myself that in Hank's case perversity had much more potential than normality.

In one of her earliest writings, McDougall has issued a *Plea for a Measure of Abnormality* (1978/1992), arguing that the unquestioned judgments of deviancy blind therapists to the examination of the pathologies of normalcy. McDougall argued that perversions are an effort to ensure the psychic and bodily survival of the individual. Perversion, seeming to celebrate not only sexuality but transgression, makes many people, psychotherapists included (or perhaps most of all) squeamish, perhaps even a bit envious. Perversion is an easy target for judgment and pathologizing, as McDougall bitingly observed:

> When an analyst, or any other individual, proclaims that this or that theory, practice, or person is "perverse," he may in fact be saying: "Don't look at me, the very model of normality, but cast your eyes over there." The pervert is always someone else! (1991, p. 188)

How often do we sit with our patients (or our colleagues) to systematically and critically examine our notions of "health" and the meanings of normality? An open-minded inquiry into the multi-layered meanings of perversions brings us up against our beliefs about, and investments in, the normal. Schwartz challenges the rooting of normative theories of sexuality in the conventions of developmental models. He argues that such models are "myths of origin for the modern age, the age of science and the idealization of scientific discovery," providing "science-like paradigms of the sources of disturbance, psychopathology, and perversion, the modern era's enlightened equivalents of evil" (1999, p. 556.) Schwartz argues for "reemphasizing the elasticity of the capacity to eroticize" (1995, p. 124).

Bollas delineates a "normotic" personality disorder (1987, pp. 135–156) in which a person "seems unable to experience evolving subjective states within himself." Such a person is extremely "well-adjusted," but is such adjustment "healthy"? Bollas observes:

> the normotic person is nurtured in an environment in which the parent avoids responsiveness to the core of the child's self. . . . Instead of being mirrored by the parent, the child is **deflected**. This is accomplished by diverting the child from the inner and the psychic towards the outer and the material.
>
> Normotic families develop a library of material objects. If a child is working on some inner psychic problem or interest, the family usually has an external concrete object available for the transfer of the psychic into the material. (p. 151, emphasis in the original)

In my work with patients (and my own self-examination) I have found that when children are ignored, deflected, diverted, threatened with a true psychic disaster of emptiness, these children often turn to their own bodies for both solace *and* stimulation. This seemingly paradoxical intertwining of solace and stimulation, calming and exciting, is one of the enduring functions of sexual perversion. Perverse strategies develop from the child's discovery of the autistic, sensate, and ultimately sexual stimulations that declare *I am alive*. The normotic "passes" easily, unobjectionable and unknown; the pervert stands out, objectionable and disquieting.

The interchange (or lack thereof) that followed Hank's "coming out" to his parents shifted my understanding of what Hank needed in his work with me. Like his parents, he could not sustain a long-enough attention to his interior life to begin to grasp what it meant and make decisions from the inside out rather than the outside in. It became clear that within his family, and his own internal object world, there was not so much a condemnation of sex, as an abandonment of it—sex just wasn't to be that important, to be worth the bother. Together, Hank and I would need to come to imbue his sexuality, whatever its ultimate course, with life and meaning.

Unlike his gregarious siblings, Hank was quite introverted and solitary, conveying a distinctly schizoid way of being. Hank had always attributed his introversion to his constant hiding of his homosexuality. As an adolescent, he retreated into the world of reading science fiction, casting himself as a kind of oddball always on the social periphery at school so as to relieve himself of potential social and sexual pressures. Following that interchange with his parents, Hank began to realize that in his introversion, he was typically left alone within his family. In sessions he began to speak of how solitary he was as a child, that no one seemed interested in him or the things that interested him. He spent long periods of time reading science fiction and involved in solitary building projects of one sort or another. He was not so much withdrawn from his family as unknown by them, a pattern that was mirrored in his peer relations at school. But, all things considered, he was a content young man during latency. It was with adolescence and the onset of sexual urges that the trouble began. Still Hank struggled to make the surface look at ease, but there was serious trouble within. He survived high school using studying, endless projects, and religion as suppressants. He had dated girls occasionally to ward off any suspicion, using his religious beliefs as an excuse for "not going any further" with the girls he briefly dated. But his eyes turned toward boys, and his sexual fantasies would not stop, even when he refused to indulge himself in masturbation. His troubles were privately held, as he had no experience within his family to suggest that someone would be interested in his struggles. Hank endured his first rounds of depression in high school unnoticed by those around him.

Once off to college, sex was even harder to avoid, and homosexuality was quite visible and accepted on campus. This did not represent hope to Hank. Approached by a couple of male students, he tried his first gay sex. He thoroughly enjoyed it and was repulsed by his pleasure. He became obsessed with one young man, the one with whom he had felt tenderness, but he cut off the relationship. His depression deepened. Our sessions during this period began to link his continued tendency to deflect the possibilities of friendship or any form of intimacy (no one had ever been invited to his apartment) out of fear that his bachelorhood would be called into question and his sexual preferences suspected.

Hank's solitary nature was inevitably mirrored in our relationship. He would be quite content to spend a session talking about a book he was reading or a movie he had seen (typically alone). I quietly described the subtle but certain distance he kept between us. What was he afraid of with me? I wondered aloud, while never pushing for a reply. He would quietly change the topic whenever I spoke of our relationship. I enjoyed listening to him describe the pleasure he had with his kids and felt great admiration for the care and respect he and his wife offered each other. I lived with my discomfort and his distance, although I could see that my interest in and affection for him was registering in him. Hank was coming to trust that I would not push him into any lifestyle choice and that my primary investment was in understanding the depth and meanings of his conflict.

I struggled with my countertransference. While I had no investment in Hank's being gay or straight, the thought of this hard-working young guy spending the rest of his life alone in varying states of self-loathing was dreadful to me. At the same time, it seemed clear that Hank, from all he said, was indeed gay, and I found myself wanting to offer him books to read to affirm not only accepting perspectives on gay identities but also of gay fathers and family lives. I resisted the urge to direct him. I knew he needed me to provide an antidote to his family by creating a space of interiority. He needed someone who would suffer his struggle with him.

I came up against my Reichian training, which idealized and enshrined sexual relatedness as the crucial sign of true emotional health. I also worried that I was reinforcing Hank's schizoid preference for solitude by keeping myself too quiet and disengaged. I sought consultation as to whether or not to disclose some of my personal reactions and struggles to Hank. My consultant reminded me that both of his previous therapies ended because Hank found them too intrusive and that he had yet to ask me a single question about my thinking or my life. While Hank's aloneness undoubtedly served some defensive functions, it seemed essential that I keep my countertransference to myself, that to take it up with him would be an intrusion of his internal struggle and the space he needed in which to wrestle with himself.

We made no physical contact in our work, no handshake in greeting, no contact at the end of sessions, though there was an unmistakable closeness with each other during some sessions. At the end of one session in which Hank was speaking of his loneliness, as Hank walked to the door, I spontaneously reached out and touched his shoulder. He said nothing, gave no overt response, but I had the sense of his skin and muscles recoiling beneath my fingers.

The next session began as usual. Hank said nothing about my having touched him at the end of the previous session. It was a fleeting touch. I thought perhaps he hadn't noticed. I remembered the reaction of his body and wished he hadn't noticed. I hesitated to bring it up, but fearing I'd made a serious error, I asked him if he'd noticed that I'd touched him as he left the previous week. "Sure did," was his terse reply. "Should we talk about it?" I asked. "Figured you'd say something like that. You first," he replied. I told him what I'd been feeling at the end of the session and that I'd reached to him without forethought. "It was OK," he said, "I know what happens to me matters to you. I took it like that." I described the sense I had of his body recoiling from my hand, my subsequent dismay and discomfort. "Standard procedure on my part, Bill. Nothing personal. You didn't fuck up. I wish I could have liked it, but I hate being touched. I really can't stand it." I expressed my surprise at this accidental discovery and inquired why he'd never told me. "I'm not very proud of this. Makes me feel even more fucked up. Figured we'd get to it eventually or maybe that it would just change without having to talk about it. Even at the office sometimes somebody will be talking and touch my shoulder. I just want to scream, 'Don't touch me!' I hate it, but I guess we've got to talk about it," came Hank's reply. I suggested that we needed to work first, and directly, with his revulsion, with the physicality of his recoiling skin and muscles. We entered the erotic spaces of revulsion. His retreats were filled with shame and dismay. He'd spent years trying to make his body act right, or at least look right. His shame and self-contempt had prevented him from ever allowing this sort of experience and exploration. We explored Hank's revulsion without any further touch.

The recoiling of Hank's body from my touch and his general avoidance of physical contact can, of course, be seen as a defense. Within the Reichian and neo-Reichian traditions, so much part of my foundational training, these bodily defenses were to be confronted and dismantled. I have learned over many years in my work with the body that to prematurely confront and seek to change the defensive patterns within a patient's body process can short-circuit crucial learning. Hank had modified his body throughout his life in response to environmental demands and judgments of one sort or another. I was not about to join that chorus of body judges and body shapers. Our willingness and ability to inhabit Hank's sexual shame and anxiety-drenched spaces together—*not* to change his feelings or alter his behavior—began to give him his body back. This incident, rather ironically, proved to be the beginning of the awakening of his erotic life.

After three years Hank decided to tell me of his porn predilections and masturbatory fantasies. His preference for porn had very little variation (Stoller, 1991a). The movies were sadomasochistic in nature, with the aggressor/top a black male, the submissive/bottom partner white, the sex anal, and Hank identifying with the submissive partner. He often tried other styles of porn, but did not find them arousing. We explored his experience of his own body while watching the action, his experience of his arousal and his orgasm. Typically, his disgust pushed him "to get to the inevitable" (orgasm) as quickly as possible so as to rid himself of his horniness. Having come, the porn was quickly put away and out of mind. He did not wish these fantasies to be a part of himself. He found beer and marijuana to be reasonably effective anti-libidinal drugs. It all felt very depersonalized.

I found myself confused. I had thought of Hank as quite deeply schizoid in his approach to life. Now here were intense, persistent, sadomasochistic fantasies. Was Hank, after all, more masochistic than schizoid? How did his day-to-day solitary life square with these masochistic fantasies? My countertransference, which I could by then see as two-fold, deepened. First there was my identification with his loneliness and isolation, a frequent topic of my own psychotherapies over the years. The second was an extremely negative reaction to a celibate lifestyle, this, I realized through further consultation, being based in my childhood experience of the celibate priests and nuns who were an unfortunate part of my own Catholic upbringing as well as Hank's. I found it difficult not to impose my own experience of the sadistic violence perpetrated by the Catholic valorization of celibacy on Hank's experience. My personal responses were so strong I knew I had to be very careful not to foreclose this fantasy/potential space that we had worked so hard to open. It took both reading (Bennett & Rosario, 1995; Laqueur, 2003) and consultation to keep myself open to Hank's own experience and meaning.

The fears of madness, surrender, "unintegration," or psychosis that Winnicott (1989) suggests often underlie a patient's defenses in psychoanalysis and constantly emerge in deeply erotic moments. For Winnicott, though he never to my knowledge wrote of these experiences in a sexual context, these moments of breaking down were simultaneously terrifying and exhilarating, taking one to an edge of madness that can give birth to creativity and aliveness. Ghent (1990) offers an especially compelling elaboration of Winnicott's ideas in his account of surrender, particularly erotic surrender, as allowing "a quality of liberation and 'letting go' . . . a yearning to be known, recognized, 'penetrated,'" (p. 134). Breaking down and letting in, opening up and being penetrated, the ongoing interplay of pleasure, vulnerability, and motility within adult sexuality, are rarely experienced without the accompaniment of anxiety and/or shame.

Ghent's (1990) essay on masochism, surrender, and submission raises many questions central to this paper; reading Ghent's paper several years ago was in fact the starting point of this chapter. He posits "something like a universal need, wish or longing for what I am calling surrender and that it assumes many forms" (p. 114). He then treads the delicate balances between surrender and submission, penetration and intrusion, discovery and disintegration, excitement and dread, interiority and exteriority. Ghent seeks to capture the sense of one's body coming to life and reality through movement and contact. He underscores the delicacy of the undertaking, that the wish to surrender to another, to feel one's body altered by the impact of another's is nearly always accompanied by the dread of annihilation, disintegration, submission.

Here is the interface of self and other at the juncture of skin and psyche, flesh to flesh. This interface creates first experience of what Anzieu (1989, 1990; Diamond, 2013) conceptualized as the skin ego, the primary membrane for interpersonal interchange. In Anzieu's thinking the skin provides the organic, sensate functions of holding, containing, protection against over-stimulation, individuation, con-sensuality (the integration of differing sensate registers), sexualization, libidinal recharging, and inscription—all of which form the substrate for the developing ego capacities. Ulnik (2007) observes that "the skin can be a [drive] *source*, but it can also be a drive *object*; something which helps to clarify the paradox concerning the skin working as a barrier and at the same time a receptor of stimuli" (p. 25).

Anzieu's theories and clinical approach were fully rooted in the classical Freud-ian traditions of psychoanalysis. From a phenomenological perspective, we see a different take on the skin, that of the skin and "flesh." Frie (2007), in his essay linking Merleau-Ponty's ontology with psychoanalytic theory, observes, "Flesh is the formative medium of object and subject" (p. 62). Heller (2001), a research psychologist at the Laboratory on Affect and Communication in Geneva, uses the notion of "flesh" to capture the experience of the "combination of shared and private bodily sensations" (p. 14). This is the life of the skin, of the lived body, the flesh of the self. There is the potential of a vital, enlivening interchange through skin to skin in a primary, pleasurable eroticism. But the skin, like the flesh, is not always so vitally formed/informed. The skin can be hit, burned, cut, bruised, ignored, left too often untouched, unseen. Skin can grow dead, tough, crusted, inert. Scabbed. Thick skinned. Or thin skinned. The life of one's skin forms and informs *flesh*.

Anita Phillips (1998) suggests that masochism is, in its "eccentric eroticism," an effort to accept and vivify the limits of one's skin/body/*flesh*, providing "the affirmation of the body's frailty as a gateway to intense pleasure" (p. 142). Ghent draws upon Winnicott's writings on the psychosomatic and object relational func-tions of aggression and motility. When things go well enough in the life of an infant, "through motility the world outside the baby is constantly being discov-ered and rediscovered so that contact with the environment is an experience of the individual" (1990, p. 117), fostering what Winnicott termed the indwelling of the psyche in the soma. Things do not, however, always go so well. Ghent suggests, "at least one source of the masochistic syndrome" is "the need for patterned impingement" (p. 118). Patterned impingement, restraint, is what Phillips describes so eloquently:

> Masochism involves a symbolic restriction of the body. At the most basic level, this creates a physical experience of opposition, between sensory deprivation and extending oneself freely in movement. But the meaning of bondage goes further. (1998, p. 139)

In addressing the treatment of masochistic patterns, Ghent cautions:

> We ought also to "tread softly" on patients' masochism and submissiveness. These two are often expressing in a disguised and distorted way a deep yearning to be found and recognized. . . . What is needed in both cases is that the patient get in touch with, and be validated in, the real longing to be recognized, known, perhaps penetrated with enough gentleness that the patient can feel safe enough to discover his or her own motility. . . . (1990, p. 132)

This, too, was the conclusion of Stoller at the end of his studies of masochism.

Hank's typical experience of his use of porn was simply that of action, arousal, and release. His use of porn seemed embedded in realms of literal, concrete *action*. Benjamin (1995) observed:

> To begin with, then, pornographic representations express not the concrete content of desire but rather a relation between sexual excitement and the realm of fantasy. . . . Pornography can therefore be felt as a confrontation with some dangerous and exciting otherness, fictive or real, which has the power to create internal excitement, pleasurable and/or repellent. (pp. 180–181)

Gradually, Hank and I were able to move from the concrete action and release into the exploration of fantasy. Our conversations and my wondering about any fantasies in the shadows of the films, opened a broader experience of himself in his use of porn. He noticed that there was some pleasure, not just arousal, while masturbating, and that there was a disturbing desire "in my skin" to be handled the way the men in the porn handled each other. He wanted to be taken over. While he never said so explicitly, I imagined that many of the pornographic portrayals were of anal sex. When he spoke of the wish to be "taken over," I thought of the complexities of anal sex—so often interwoven with impulses of shame, desire, being desired, power, penetration, being penetrated (Bersani, 1987; Botticelli, 2010; Guss, 2010). I said nothing of my own thoughts and associations; it seemed essential that Hank's narrative unfold in its own time and through his own authorship.

We began to discuss the stories he imagined (which had never been quite conscious until we began to speak of them in session) about the lives of the men in the films. To Hank these men were not ashamed of themselves; they were defiant, flagrant in their desire. He realized that he felt some envy toward them as well as disgust with his own arousal—all very confusing. He was profoundly ashamed of the racism inherent in these scenes but could see that he attributed to the black, lower-class man the force, the freedom, and the will he lacked in himself. He disowned his own aggression and freedom, making them dirty. He could feel his envy for both the black possessor and the white possessed. I asked him to notice the storylines in the porn (not exactly the strong suit of most pornographic films) or to create his own stories for the men in the films. Often in the porn the sexual encounters were one-time-only operations between strangers attracted to each other's bodies, but Hank found himself creating stories in which some of these men continued to see each other.

Our conversations and explorations gradually opened a slight awareness of an emotional experience within him while watching the porn, in addition to the more familiar (and despised) physical arousal. The experience of some emotion made his interest in the porn somewhat more acceptable. He was then able to tell me of his masturbatory fantasy, which was a singular story: He would enter a public men's room; he would be seized from behind by a man (either white or black); he would be bent over the sink, anally raped while the fucker forced him to look in the mirror to see the fucker's face, saying over and over again, "TAKE IT. YOU WANT IT. TAKE IT." The fucker's voice was demanding, humiliating, demeaning. And Hank found it all profoundly arousing. He hated himself for it. But nothing else seemed to work. I asked what he saw in the man's face in the mirror. He'd never noticed, hearing only the taunting voice, but when asked to look and see, he realized that the man's face was full of pleasure and a bit of kindness. He couldn't put the kindness together with the taunting voice or the anal rape. I spoke the same words differently, gently, tenderly, as an invitation, an insistent invitation: *"Take it. You want it. Take it."* Could he hear it that way? He could.

Hank's shame and self-loathing lessened a bit. His fantasies gradually changed in texture from being forced and raped to being *taken*, almost but not quite *wanted*. I continued to keep my countertransference to myself, but in my own fantasies I had Hank going to gay bars, finding some man who wanted Hank enough to overcome Hank's reluctance and disgust. I wanted Hank to finally feel in his body someone else's unbridled desire for him, breaking through and breaking down Hank's disgust.

But this was not to be. Hank was able to go to an occasional bar (though drinking with others still never gave him the same satisfaction as drinking alone) and to some gay social gatherings. He went home with a few guys, never to follow through with anyone. He was able to grant the porn actors in his fantasies the freedom to develop ongoing relationships, but he could not grant this possibility to himself. I hoped that the emergent freedom he could grant the porn characters might gradually become his own. Although his disgust had lessened in his private sexual activities, he still felt disgust in actually being with another man. Hank was now, however, to have a private erotic life that afforded him some pleasure and no small modicum of self-acceptance.

Through all of this, we never spoke directly of our relationship. It seemed to me that to do so risked collapsing the precious potential space that had opened between us and within Hank. At the same time, I had no question but that I had become a significant figure in his internal object world.

After a few months, Hank announced that he had decided to leave therapy. He was no longer depressed, and he had accomplished a great deal of self-understanding and some modicum of self-acceptance. There was more fluidity and emotion in his masturbatory fantasies. But he felt he could go no further. "I know you have more hope for me than I have for myself. I know you want me to have a real lover. But I can't do it. Maybe some day, but not now. I need you to accept this and to let me go with your blessings." Hank had rarely asked anything of me. Now this. So often over the course of our work I had felt as though Hank held me in a kind of blank, depersonalized transference. Suddenly I felt the full force of what I meant to him. My eyes filled with tears as I gave him my heart-felt blessings. We embraced in our goodbye.

I still hope that some time in the future Hank will return to me or some other therapist to be able to allow himself full partnership and sexual intimacy.

Culturally and clinically, masochism and "perversions" have been too often and too easily equated with deviant psychopathologies (Holtzman & Kulish, 2012). Deviance represents a threat to the normative. The normative all too often channels, and ultimately destroys, the capacity for vitality. Deviance is a form of defiance, an effort to sustain life in the face of forces that threaten to collapse it. Something shifts when perversion and erotic "deviance" are viewed not from the perspective of psychopathology but that of marginality, the "spaces from exile" (Phillips, 1998, p. 113). The clinical psychoanalytic literature has been far too often replete with discussions of what the pervert can (must?) learn from the analyst as a "normatist" about the normal. What does the pervert/deviant have to teach the analyst about defiant vitality and living at the margins?

While sexuality was once held to be essential to human nature and wellbeing and at the heart of many psychotherapeutic issues, as reflected in the work of Freud, Reich, Kinsey, and Masters and Johnson, to name those who have had the most profound cultural impact, sex has been moved to the sidelines of most contemporary psychotherapy models. Stripped of its transgressive, disturbing elements, sexuality has been too often domesticated, replaced with idealized visions of attachment, bonding, and attunement. Contemporary models of sexual addiction strip sex of its developmental and unconscious meanings and focus on behavioral control. Psychotherapy without attention to adult sexuality is impoverished.

Our sexualities in all of their diverse manifestations are more of an accomplishment than a defense, an accomplishment in the effort to sustain a somatic and erotic aliveness. I have come to think of our "perverse" sexual fantasies and behaviors as providing the vitalization of sensate saturation as alternatives to psychotic disintegration or neurotic deadening.

Pathological constructions of sexualities and their etiologies narrow vision and heighten anxiety. We are much less likely then to wonder, "What is it like to be in this body?" "What pleasure and meaning does this way of being offer?" "What sorts of conflicts and yearnings are maintained in this body's way of being, through its patterns of sexual expression?" "What is going on in the skin, the muscles, the heart, the flesh, and desires of this person?" When we are able to move beyond our clinical judgments and personal countertransferences—the "eew! factor" (Dimen, 2005)—we can allow crucial unfolding and elaboration of enduring bodily, imagined, and relational motifs, which may or may not be open to change but can always be enriched by engagement and understanding.

Sexuality, in its myriad manifestations, is a refusal to give up on life. For many, like Hank, with "perverse" sexual desires, what life held in store for the young child's body was not so endearing, and pleasure was not so readily found in one's earliest relationships. But the developing body in its own sensate vitality and elaborations in fantasy and action can provide both a means of grounding and containing while seeking to sustain intensity and liveliness. To work successfully with sexual anxieties, conflicts, and fantasies, a therapist must tolerate layers of enigma, the disquiet of patterns of desire that may strike one as profoundly alien and quite possibly frightening or disgusting. It is a primary task of the analyst/therapist to maintain an attitude of bodily curiosity and openness and an intense, mutual searching that will be often aching, sometimes pleasurable, often intimate, and hopefully freeing. In the end this may be all, and the best, we have to offer.

References

Aalberse, M. (2001). Graceful means: Felt gestures and choreographic therapy. In *The flesh of the soul: The body we work with*, ed. M. Heller, pp. 101–132. Bern: Peter Lang.

Akhtar, S. (1992). *Broken structures: Severe personality disorders and their treatment*. Northvale, NJ: Jason Aronson, Inc.

Alvarez, A. (2005). *The writer's voice*. New York: W.W. Norton & Company.

Alvarez, A. (2010). Levels of analytic work and levels of pathology: The work of calibration. *International Journal of Psychoanalysis*. 91: 859–878.

Alvarez, A. (2012). *The thinking heart: Three levels of psychoanalytic therapy with disturbed children*. Hove, UK: Routledge.

Anderson, F.S. (ed.) (2008). *Bodies in treatment: The unspoken dimension*. New York: The Analytic Press.

Anthi, P. (1983). Reconstruction of preverbal experiences. *Journal of the American Psychoanalytic Association*. 31: 33–59.

Anzieu, D. (1989). *The skin ego: A psychoanalytic approach to the self*. New Haven, CT: Yale University Press.

Anzieu, D. (1990). *A skin for thought: Interviews with Gilbert Tarrab on psychology and psychoanalysis* London: Karnac.

Anzieu, D. (2000). *Psychoanalyser*. Paris: Dunod.

Aposhyan, S. (2004). *Body–mind psychotherapy: Principles, techniques, and practical applications*. New York: W.W. Norton & Company.

Aron, L. & Anderson, F.S. (eds.) (1998). *Relational perspectives on the body*. Hillsdale, NJ: The Analytic Press.

Aron, L. & Starr, K. (2013). *A psychotherapy for the people: Toward a progressive psychoanalysis*. New York: Routledge.

Bahrick, L.E. (2004). The development of perception in a multimodal environment. In *Theories of infant development*, eds. G. Bremner & A. Slater, pp. 90–120. Malden, MA: Blackwell Publishing.

Baker, E.F. (1967). *Man in the trap: The causes of blocked sexual energy*. New York: The Macmillan Company.

Beebe, B. & Lachmann, F.M. (2002). *Infant research and adult treatment*. Hillsdale, NJ: The Analytic Press.

Benjamin, J. (1995). *Like subjects, love objects*. New Haven, CT: Yale University Press.

Bennett, P. & Rosario, V.A. (eds.) (1995). *Solitary pleasures: The historical, literary, and artistic discourses of autoeroticism*. New York: Routledge.

Berne, E. (1961). *Transactional analysis in psychotherapy: A systematic individual and social psychiatry*. New York: Grove Press.

Berne, E. (1963). *The structure and dynamics of organizations and groups*. New York: Grove Press.

Berne, E. (1966). *Principles of group treatment*. New York: Oxford University Press.

Berne, E. (1968). Staff–patient–staff conferences. *American Journal of Psychiatry*. 125: 286–293.

Bersani, L. (1987). Is the rectum a grave? In *AIDS: Cultural analysis, cultural activism*, ed. D. Crimp, pp. 197–222. Cambridge, MA: MIT Press.

Bick, E. (1968). The experience of the skin in early object-relations. *International Journal of Psychoanalysis*. 49: 484–486.

Bick, E. (1986). Further considerations on the function of skin in early object relations. *British Journal of Psychotherapy*. 2(4): 292–301.

Billow, R.M. (2000). From countertransference to "passion." *Psychoanalytic Quarterly*. 69: 93–119.

Bloom, K. (2006). *The embodied self: Movement and psychoanalysis*. London: Karnac.

Bollas, C. (1987). *The shadow of the object: Psychoanalysis of unknown thought*. New York: Columbia University Press.

Bollas, C. (1989). *Forces of destiny: Psychoanalysis and human idiom*. Northvale, NJ: Jason Aronson, Inc.

Bollas, C. (1999). *The mystery of things*. London: Routledge.

Bollas, C. (2000). *Hysteria*. London: Routledge.

Bollas, C. (2011). Personal communication. September 20.

Bolognini, S. (1994). Transference: Eroticized, erotic, loving, affectionate. *The International Journal of Psychoanalysis*. 75: 73–86.

Bonasia, E. (2001). The countertransference: Erotic, eroticized and perverse. *The International Journal of Psychoanalysis*. 82: 249–262.

Botticelli, S. (2010). Thinking the unthinkable: Anal sex in theory and practice. *Studies in Gender and Sexuality*. 11: 112–123.

Bowlby, J. (1969). *Attachment and loss, volume I: Attachment*. New York: Basic Books.

Bowlby, J. (1979). *The making and breaking of affectional bonds*. London: Tavistock.

Braatoy, T. (1954). *Fundamentals of psychoanalytic technique*. New York: John Wiley & Sons.

Bronski, M. (2002). Dr. Fell, In *Bringing the plague: Toward a postmodern psychoanalysis*, eds. S. Fairfield, L. Layton, & C. Stack, pp. 279–294.

Brooks, C. (1974). *Sensory awareness: The rediscovery of experience*. New York: Viking Press, Inc.

Bucci, W. (1997a). *Psychoanalysis and cognitive science: A multiple code theory*. New York: Guilford Press.

Bucci, W. (1997b). Symptoms and symbols: A multiple code theory of somatization. *Psychoanalytic Inquiry*. 17: 151–172.

Bucci, W. (2001). Pathways of emotional communication. *Psychoanalytic Inquiry*. 21: 40–70.

Bucci, W. (2002). The referential process, consciousness, and the sense of self. *Psychoanalytic Inquiry*. 22: 766–793.

Bucci, W. (2005). The interplay of subsymbolic and symbolic processes in psychoanalytic treatment: Commentary on paper by Steven H. Knoblauch. *Psychoanalytic Dialogues*. 15: 855–874.

Bucci. W. (2008). The role of bodily experience in emotional organization. In *Bodies in treatment: The unspoken dimension*, ed. F.S. Anderson, pp. 51–76. New York: The Analytic Press.

Bucci, W. (2010). The uncertainty principle in the psychoanalytic process. In *Knowing, not-knowing and sort-of-knowing: Psychoanalysis and the experience of uncertainty*, ed. J. Petrucelli, pp. 203–214. London: Karnac.

Bucci, W. (2011). The role of embodied communication in therapeutic change. In *The implications of embodiment: Cognition and communication*, eds. W. Tschachen & C. Bergoni, pp. 209–229. Charlottesville, VA: Imprint-Academic.

Butterworth, G. (1993). Dynamic approaches to infant perception and action: Old and new theories about the origins of knowledge. In *A Dynamic Systems Approach to Development: Applications*, eds. L.B. Smith & E. Thelan, pp. 171–187. Cambridge, MA: The MIT Press.

Butterworth, G. (1995). An ecological perspective on the origins of self. In *The Body and the Self*, eds. J.L. Bermudez, A. Marcel, & N. Eilan, pp. 87–105. Cambridge, MA: The MIT Press.

Caldwell, C. (1997). *Getting in touch: The guide to new body-centered therapies*. Wheaton, IL: Quest Books.

Caldwell, L. (2005). *Sex and sexuality: Winnicottian perspectives*. London: Karnac.

Casement, P.J. (1982). Some pressures on the analyst for physical contact during the reliving of an early psychic trauma. *International Review of Psycho-Analysis*. 9: 279–286.

Casement, P.J. (2000). The issue of touch: A retrospective overview. *Psychoanalytic Inquiry*. 20(1): 160–184.

Chess, S. & Thomas, A. (1984). *Origins and evaluation of behavior disorder: From infancy to early adult life*. New York: Brunner/Mazel.

Chodorow, N. (2007). Review of *The healer's bent: Solitude and dialogue in the clinical encounter*, by James McLaughlin. *The Psychoanalytic Quarterly*. 76: 617–629.

Clulow, C. (2001). *Adult attachment and couple psychotherapy: The "secure base" in practice and research*. New York: Brunner/Mazel.

Cocks, G. (2001). The devil and the details: Psychoanalysis in the Third Reich. *The Psychoanalytic Review*. 88: 225–244.

Corbett, K. (2013). Shifting sexual cultures, the potential space of online relations, and the promise of psychoanalytic listening. *Journal of the American Psychoanalytic Association*. 61: 25–44.

Cornell, W.F. (1997). Touch and boundaries in transactional analysis: Ethical and transferential considerations. *Transactional Analysis Journal*. 27: 30–37.

Cornell, W.F. (2001). There ain't no cure without sex: The provision of a vital base. *Transactional Analysis Journal*. 31: 233–239.

Cornell, W.F. (2005). Deep in the shed—An analyst's mind at work. Editor's introduction to *The Healer's Bent: Solitude and dialogue in the clinical encounter*, pp. 1–6. Hillsdale, NJ: The Analytic Press.

Cornell, W.F. (2008a). Self in action: The bodily basis of self-organization. In *Bodies in Treatment: The unspoken dimension*, ed. F.S. Anderson, pp. 29–50. New York: The Analytic Press.

Cornell, W.F. (2008b). "My body is unhappy": Somatic foundations of script and script protocol. In *Explorations in transactional analysis: The Meech Lake papers*, pp. 159–170. Pleasanton, CA: TA Press.

Cornell, W.F. (2008c). Solitude, self, and subjectivity: Discussant paper to Lewis Aron's "Relational psychoanalysis: The evolution of a tradition. In *Explorations in transactional analysis: The Meech Lake papers*, pp. 171–175. Pleasanton, CA: TA Press.

Cornell, W.F. (2008d). *Explorations in transactional analysis: The Meech Lake papers*. Pleasanton, CA: TA Press.

Cornell, W.F. (2009a). Stranger to desire: Entering the erotic field. *Studies in gender and sexuality*. 10: 75–92.

Cornell, W.F. (2009b). Response to Shapiro's discussion. *Studies in Gender and Sexuality*. 10: 104–111.

Cornell, W.F. (2010). Searching in the "unsaid seen": McLaughlin's unfinished reflections on the body in psychoanalytic discourse. *American Imago*. 67: 515–540.

Cornell, W.F. (2011). SAMBA, TANGO, PUNK: Commentary on a paper by Steven H. Knoblauch. *Psychoanalytic Dialogues*. 21: 428–436.

Cornell, W.F. & Landaiche, N.M. (2006). Impasse and intimacy: Applying Berne's concept of script protocol. *Transactional Analysis Journal*. 36: 196–213.

Cornell, W.F., Shadbolt, C, & Norton, R. (2007). Live and in limbo: A case study of an in-person transactional analysis consultation. *Transactional Analysis Journal*. 37: 159–171.

Danto, E.A. (2005). *Freud's free clinics—Psychoanalysis and social justice, 1918–1938*. New York: Columbia University Press.

Danto, E.A. (2011). An anxious attachment: Letters from Sigmund Freud to Wilhelm Reich. *Contemporary Psychoanalysis*. 47: 155–166.

Davies, J.M. (1998). Between the disclosure and foreclosure of erotic transference–countertransference: Can psychoanalysis find a place for adult sexuality? *Psychoanalytic Dialogues*. 8: 747–766.

Davis, M & Wallbridge, D. (1981). *Boundary and space: An introduction to the work of D.W. Winnicott*. New York: Brunner/Mazel.

De Masi, F. (2009). *Vulnerability to psychosis*. London: Karnac.

Diamond, D. (2013). *Between skins: The body in psychoanalysis—contemporary developments*. Malden, MA: Wiley-Blackwell.

Diamond, D., Blatt, S.J., & Lichtenberg, J.D. (Eds.) (2007). *Attachment & sexuality*. New York: The Analytic Press.

Diamond, N. (2006). Between touches. In *Touch papers: Dialogues on touch in the psychoanalytic space*, ed. G. Galton, pp. 79–96. London: Karnac.

Dick, K. (1998). *Sick: The life and death of Bob Flanagan, supermasochist*. New York: Avalanche Home Entertainment.

Dimen, M. (1999). Between lust and libido: Sex, psychoanalysis, and the moment before. *Psychoanalytic Dialogues*. 9: 415–440.

Dimen, M. (2001). Perversion is us? Eight notes. *Psychoanalytic Dialogues*. 11: 825–860.

Dimen, M. (2003). *Sexuality intimacy power*. Hillsdale, NJ: The Analytic Press.

Dimen, M. (2005). Sexuality and suffering, or the eew! factor. *Studies in Gender and Sexuality*. 6: 1–18.

Dimen, M. (2010). Lapsus linguae, or a slip of the tongue? A sexual violation in an analytic treatment and its personal and theoretical aftermath. *Contemporary Psychoanalysis*. 47: 35–79.

Dinnerstein, D. (1976). *The mermaid and the minotaur: Sexual arrangements and human malaise*. New York: Harper & Row.

Downing, G. (1996). *Korper und wort in der psychotherapie* [The body and the word in psychotherapy]. Munich: Kosel Verlag.

Eagle, M.N. (2013). *Attachment and psychoanalysis: Theory, research, and clinical implications*. New York: Guilford Press.

Efron, A. (1985). The sexual body: An interdisciplinary perspective. *The Journal of Mind and Behavior*. 6: 1–313.

Eigen, M. (1998). *The psychoanalytic mystic*. Binghamton, NY: ESF Publishers.

Engelman, E. (1976). *Berggasse 19: Sigmund Freud's home and office, Vienna 1938*. New York: Basic Books.

Fast, I. (2006). A body-centered mind. *Contemporary Psychoanalysis*. 42: 273–295.

Federn, E. (1990). *Witnessing psychoanalysis: From Vienna back to Vienna via Buchenwald and the USA*. London: Karnac.

Fenichel, O. (1945). *The psychoanalytic theory of neurosis*. W.W. Norton & Company.

Flanagan, B. (2000). *Bob Flanagan: Supermasochist*. New York: RE/Search Publications.

Fogel, A. (2009). *The psychophysiology of self-awareness: Rediscovering the lost art of body sense*. New York: W.W. Norton & Company.

Fonagy, P. (2001). *Attachment theory and psychoanalysis*. New York: Other Press.

Frank, A. (2013). Unexpected intimacies: Moments of connection, moments of shame. In *Intimacies: A new world of relational life*, eds. A. Frank, C.T. Clough, & S. Seidman, pp. 49–59. London: Routledge.

Frank, G. (1992). Classics revisited: Wilhelm Reich's "On Character Analysis." *International Review of Psycho-analysis*. 19: 51–56.

Freud, L. (2010). *The Studio*. Munich: Hirmer Verlag GmbH.

Frie, R. (2007). The lived body: From Freud to Merleau-Ponty and contemporary psychoanalysis. In *The embodied subject: Minding the body in psychoanalysis*, eds. J.P. Muller & J.G. Tillman, pp. 55–66. Lanham, MD: Jason Aronson.

Gallese, V. & Sinigaglia, C. (2011). How the body in action shapes the self. *Journal of Consciousness Studies*. 18: 117–143.

Galton, G. (Ed.) (2006). *Touch papers: Dialogues on touch in the psychoanalytic space*. London: Karnac.

Gedo. J.E. (1997). The primitive psyche, communication, and the language of the body. *Psychoanalytic Inquiry*. 17: 192–203.

Ghent, E. (1990). Masochism, submission, and surrender: Masochism as a perversion of surrender. *Contemporary Psychoanalysis*. 26: 108–136.

Gilbert, P. & Lennon, K. (1988). *The world, the flesh, and the subject*. Edinburgh: Edinburgh University Press.

Gorkin, M. (1985). Varieties of sexualized countertransference. *Psychoanalytic Review*. 72: 421–440.

Green, A. (1996). Has sexuality anything to do with psychoanalysis? *International Journal of Psychoanalysis*. 76: 871–883.

Green. A. (2000). *Chains of eros: The sexual in psychoanalysis*. London: Rebus Press.

Greenfield, J. (1974). *Wilhelm Reich vs. the U.S.A.* New York: W.W. Norton & Company.

Groddeck, G. (1977). *The meaning of illness: Selected psychoanalytic writings*. New York: International Universities Press.

Guss, J.R. (2010). The danger of desire: Anal sex and the homo/masculine subject. *Studies in Gender and Sexuality*. 10: 124–140.

Hanna, T. (1993). *The body of life: Creating new pathways for sensory awareness and fluid movement*. Rochester, VT: Healing Arts Press.

Hart, S. (2011). *The impact of attachment*. New York: W.W. Norton & Company.

Heller, M. (Ed.) (2001). *The flesh of the soul: The body we work with*. Bern: Peter Lang.

Heller, M. (2012). *Body psychotherapy: History, concepts, and methods.* New York: W.W. Norton & Company.

Hertenstein, M.J. & Weiss, S.J. (2011). *The handbook of touch: Neuroscience, behavioral, and health perspectives.* New York: Springer Publishing Company.

Hinshelwood, R.D. (2004). *Suffering insanity: Psychoanalytic essays on psychosis.* Hove: Brunner-Routledge.

Holmes, J. (1996). *Attachment, intimacy, autonomy: Using attachment theory in adult psychotherapy.* Northvale, NJ: Jason Aronson, Inc.

Holmes, J. (2007). Sense and sensuality: Hedonic intersubjectivity and the erotic imagination. In *Attachment & Sexuality*, eds. D. Diamond, S.J. Blatt, & J.D. Lichtenberg, pp. 137–159. New York: The Analytic Press.

Holtzman, D. & Kulish, N. (2012). *The clinical problem of masochism.* Lanham, MD: Jason Aronson.

Hunter, M. & Struve, J. (1998). *The ethical use of touch in psychotherapy.* Thousand Oaks, CA: SAGE Publications.

Jacobson, L. (2003). On the use of "sexual addiction": The case for "perversion." *Contemporary Psychoanalysis.* 39: 107–133.

Jacoby, R. (1983). *The repression of psychoanalysis: Otto Fenichel and the political Freudians.* Chicago, IL: University of Chicago Press.

Jimenez, J.P. (2004). A psychoanalytical phenomenology of perversion. *Journal of the International Psychoanalytic Association.* 85: 65–82.

Johnson, S.M. (1985). *Characterological transformation: The hard work miracle.* New York: W.W. Norton & Company.

Johnson, S.M. (1994). *Character styles.* New York: W.W. Norton & Company.

Jordan, J.V. (1991). The meaning of mutuality. In *Women's Growth in Connection: Writings from the Stone Center*, eds. J.V. Jordan, A.G. Kaplan, J.B. Miller, I.P. Stiver, & J.L. Surrey, pp. 81–96. New York: Guilford Press.

Josephs, L. (1992). *Character structure and the organization of the self.* New York: Columbia University Press.

Josephs, L. (1995). *Balancing empathy and interpretation: Relational character analysis.* Northvale, NJ: Jason Aronson, Inc.

Karen, R. (1994). *Becoming attached: First relationships and how they shape our capacity to love.* New York: Oxford University Press.

Kelley, C.R. (2004). *Life force: The creative process in man and nature.* Victoria, BC: Trafford.

Kepner, J. (1987). *Body process: A Gestalt approach to working with the body in psychotherapy.* New York: Gestalt Institute of Cleveland Press.

Kernberg, O.F. (1992). *Aggression in personality disorders and perversions.* New Haven, CT: Yale University Press.

Kestenberg-Amighti, J., Loman, S., Lewis, P., & Sossin, K.M. (1999). *The meaning of movement, developmental and clinical perspectives on the Kestenberg movement profile.* Amsterdam: Gordon & Breach.

Khan, M.M.R. (1992). Introduction. In *Through paediatrics to psychoanalysis: Collected papers*, pp. xi–xlviii. London: Karnac.

Klopstech, A. (2000a). Psychoanalysis and body psychotherapies in dialogue. *Bioenergetic Analysis.* 11: 43–54.

Klopstech, A. (2000b). The bioenergetic use of a psychoanalytic conception of cure. *Bioenergetic Analysis.* 11: 55–66.

Knoblauch, S.H. (2005). Body rhythms and the unconscious: Toward an expanding of clinical attention. *Psychoanalytic Dialogues.* 15: 807–827.

Knoblauch, S.H. (2011). Contextualizing attunement within the polyrhythmic weave: The psychoanalytic samba. *Psychoanalytic Dialogues.* 21: 414–427.

Konia, C. (2008). *The emotional plague: The root of human evil.* Princeton, NJ: A.C.O. Press.

Kramer, S. & Akhtar, S. (Eds.) (1992). *When the body speaks: Psychological meanings in kinetic cues.* Northvale, NJ: Aronson.

Krantz, A.M. (2012). Let the body speak: Commentary on paper by Jon Sletvold. *Psychoanalytic Dialogues.* 22: 437–448.

Krystal, H. (1997). Desomatization and the consequences of infantile psychic trauma. *Psychoanalytic Inquiry.* 17: 126–150.

Kuriloff, E.A. (2014). *Contemporary psychoanalysis and the legacy of the Third Reich: History, memory, tradition.* New York: Routledge.

Laban, R. (1960). *The mastery of movement.* London: MacDonald and Evans.

La Barre, F. (2001). *On moving and being moved: Nonverbal behavior in clinical practice.* Hillsdale, NJ: The Analytic Press.

La Barre, F. (2005). The kinetic transference and countertransference. *Contemporary Psychoanalysis.* 41: 249–280.

La Barre, F. (2008). Stuck in vertical: The kinetic temperament in development and interaction. *Psychoanalytic Dialogues.* 18: 411–438.

Laplanche, J. (1995). Seduction, persecution, revelation. *The International Journal of Psychoanalysis,* 76, 663–682.

Laplanche, J. (1997). The theory of seduction and the problem of the other. *The International Journal of Psychoanalysis.* 78: 653–666.

Laplanche, J. (1999). *Essays on otherness.* London: Routledge.

Laqueur, T.W. (2003). *Solitary sex: A cultural history of masturbation.* New York: Zone Books.

Lichtenberg, J.D. (1989). *Psychoanalysis and motivation.* Hillsdale, NJ: The Analytic Press.

Lichtenberg, J.D. & Meares, R. (1996). The role of play in things human. *Psychoanalysis and Psychotherapy.* 13: 5–18.

Lilleskov, R. (1977). Nonverbal aspects of child and adult psychoanalysis. *Journal of the American Psychoanalytic Association.* 27: 207–240.

Liss, J. (1974). *Free to feel.* London: Wildwood House.

Little, M.I. (1990). *Psychotic anxieties and containment: A personal record of an analysis with Winnicott.* Northvale, NJ: Jason Aronson, Inc.

Loewald, H. (1980). *Papers on psychoanalysis.* New Haven, CT: Yale University Press.

Lombardi, R. (2008). The body in the analytic session: Focusing on the body-mind link. *International Journal of Psychoanalysis.* 89: 89–110.

Lombardi, R. (2011). The body, feelings, and the unheard music of the senses. *Contemporary Psychoanalysis.* 47: 3–24.

Lothane, Z. (2001). The deal with the devil to "save" psychoanalysis in Germany. *The Psychoanalytic Review.* 88: 143–154.

Lowen, A. (1975). *Bioenergetics.* New York: Coward, McCann, & Geoghegan, Inc.

Lowen, A. & Lowen, L. (1977). *The vibrant way to health: A manual of bioenergetic exercises.* New York: Harper Colophon Books.

Makari, G. (2009). *Revolution in mind: The creation of psychoanalysis.* New York: Harper Perennial.

Makavejev, D. (1972). *WR: Mysteries of the organism.* New York: Avon Books.

Mancia, M. (2007). *Feeling the words: Neuropsychoanalytic understanding of memory and the unconscious.* London: Routledge.

Mann, D. (1997). *Psychotherapy: An erotic relationship.* London: Routledge.

Maroda, K. (1994). *The power of counter-transference.* Northvale, NJ: Jason Aronson, Inc.

McDougall, J. (1978/1992). *Plea for a measure of abnormality.* New York: Brunner/Mazel.

McDougall, J. (1991). Perversions and deviations in the psychoanalytic attitudes: Their effect on theory and practice. In *Perversions and near-perversions in clinical practice: New psychoanalytic perspectives,* eds. G.I. Fogel & W.A. Myers, pp. 176–204. New Haven, CT: Yale University Press.

McDougall, J. (1995). *The many faces of Eros.* New York: Norton.

McDougall, J. (2000). Sexuality and the neosexual. *Modern Psychoanalysis.* 25(2): 155–166.

McLaughlin, J.T. (1961). The analyst and the Hippocratic oath. *Journal of the American Psychoanalytic Association.* 9: 106–120.

McLaughlin, J.T. (1987). The play of transference: Some reflections on enactment in the psychoanalytic situation. *Journal of the American Psychoanalytic Association.* 35: 557–582.

McLaughlin, J.T. (1989). The relevance of infant observational research for the analytic understanding of adult patients' nonverbal behavior. In *The significance of infant observational research for children, adolescents, and adults,* eds. S. Downing & A. Rothstein, pp. 109–122. Madison, CT: The International Universities Press.

McLaughlin, J.T. (1992/2010). Nonverbal behaviors in the analytic situation: The search for meaning in nonverbal cues. In *When the body speaks: Psychological meanings in kinetic cues,* eds. S. Kramer & S. Akhtar, pp. 131–162. Northvale, NJ: Aronson. [Reprinted, *American Imago.* 67: 487–514.]

McLaughlin, J.T. (1993). Work with patients and the experience of self-analysis. In *Self-analysis,* ed. J. Barron, pp. 63–81. Hillsdale, NJ: The Analytic Press.

McLaughlin, J.T. (1995). Touching limits in the analytic dyad. *Psychoanalytic Quarterly.* 64: 433–465.

McLaughlin, J.T. (2000). The problem and place of physical contact in analytic work: Some reflections on handholding in the analytic situation. *Psychoanalytic Inquiry.* 20: 65–81.

McLaughlin, J.T. (2005). *The healer's bent: Solitude and dialogue in the clinical encounter.* Hillsdale, NJ: The Analytic Press.

Meadow, P.W. (2000). An excursion into sexuality. *Modern Psychoanalysis.* 25: 175–180.

Merleau-Ponty, M. (1969). *The visible and the invisible.* Evanston, IL: Northwestern University Press.

Mitchell. S.A. (1993). *Hope and dread in psychoanalysis.* New York: Basic Books.

Mitchell, S.A. (2002). *Can love last? The fate of romance over time.* New York: W.W. Norton & Company.

Morris, F. (2007). *Louise Bourgeois.* London: Tate Publishing.

Morrison, J. & Goodman, M. (Eds.) (2007). Transactional analysis and the body. *Transactional Analysis Journal.* 37: 246–310.

Nicolosi, J. (1993). *Healing homosexuality: Case stories of reparative therapy.* Northvale, NJ: Jason Aronson, Inc.

Ogden, P., Minton, K., & Pain, C. (2006). *Trauma and the body: A sensorimotor approach to psychotherapy.* New York: W.W. Norton & Company.

Ogden, T.H. (1989). *The primitive edge of experience.* Northvale, NJ: Jason Aronson, Inc.

Ogden, T.H. (1996). The perverse subject of analysis. *The Journal of the American Psychoanalytic Association.* 44: 1121–1146.

Olshan, J. (1994). *Nightswimmer.* New York: Simon and Schuster.

Orbach, S. (2006a). How can we have a body? Desire and corporeality. *Studies in Gender and Sexuality.* 7: 89–111.

Orbach, S. (2006b). Too hot to touch? In *Touch papers: Dialogues on touch in the psychoanalytic space,* ed. G. Galton, pp. xiii–xviii. London: Karnac.

Oxenhandler, N. (2001). *The eros of parenthood: Explorations in light and dark.* New York: St. Martin's Press.

Panksepp, J. (1998). *Affective neuroscience: The foundations of human and animal emotions.* New York: Oxford University Press.

Panksepp, J. (2008a). The affective brain and core-consciousness: How does neural activity generate emotional feelings? In *Handbook of emotions,* eds. M. Lewis, J.M. Haviland, & L.F. Barret, pp. 47–67. New York: Guilford Press.

Panksepp, J. (2008b). Play, ADHD, and the construction of the social brain: Should the first class of the day be recess? *American Journal of Play.* 1: 55–79.

Panksepp, J. (2009). Brain emotional systems and qualities of emotional life: From animal models of affect to implications for psychotherapeutics. In *The healing power of emotion: Affective neuroscience, development, & clinical practice,* eds. D. Fosha, D.J. Siegel, & M.F. Solomon, pp. 1–26. New York: W.W. Norton & Company.

Panksepp, J. & Biven, L. (2012). *The archeology of the mind: Neuroevolutionary origins of human emotions.* New York: W.W. Norton & Company.

Phillips, A. (1988). *Winnicott.* Cambridge, MA: Harvard University Press.

Phillips, A. (1995). The story of the mind. In *The mind object: Precocity and pathology of self-sufficiency,* eds. E.G. Corrigan & P-E. Gordon, pp. 229–240. Northvale, NJ: Jason Aronson, Inc.

Phillips, A. (1998). *A defense of masochism.* London: Faber and Faber.

Pierrakos, J.C. (1987). *Core energetics.* Mendocino, CA: Life Rhythm Publications.

Placzek, B.R. (Ed.) (1981). *Record of a friendship: The correspondence of Wilhelm Reich and A.S. Neil.* New York: Farrar, Straus, and Giroux.

Pulver, S. (1992). Gestures, emblems, and body language: What does it all mean? In *When the body speaks: Psychological meanings in kinetic cues,* eds. S. Kramer & S. Ahktar, pp. 163–177. Northvale, NJ: Jason Aronson, Inc.

Quinodoz, D. (2003). *Words that touch: A psychoanalyst learns to speak.* London: Karnac.

Raphael, C.M. (1970). *Wilhelm Reich misconstrued misesteemed.* Jamaica, NY: The Wilhelm Reich Institute for Orgonomic Studies.

Reich, P. (1973). *A book of dreams.* New York: Harper & Row.

Reich, W. (1920/1975). A case of pubertal breaching of the incest taboo. In *Early writings, volume one,* pp. 65–72. New York: Farrar, Straus, and Giroux.

Reich, W. (1925/1974). *The impulsive character and other writings.* New York: New American Library.

Reich, W. (1926/1980). *Genitality in the theory and therapy of neurosis.* New York: Farrar, Straus, and Giroux.

Reich, W. (1933). *Charakteranalyse.* Berlin: Sexpol Verlag.

Reich, W. (1945). *The sexual revolution: Toward a self-governing character structure.* New York: Orgone Institute Press.

Reich, W. (1948). *Listen, little man!* New York: Orgone Institute Press.

Reich, W. (1949). *Character analysis*, 3rd edition. New York: Orgone Institute Press.

Reich, W. (1953). *The murder of Christ.* New York: The Noonday Press.

Reich, W. (1956). Atoms for peace vs. the Hig: Address to the jury—from the history of Orgonomy. *Orgonomic Medicine.* 2: 22–35.

Reich, W. (1961). *The function of the orgasm.* New York: Farrar, Straus, and Giroux.

Reich, W. (1966). *Sex-Pol essays, 1929–1934* (ed. L. Baxandall). New York: Random House.

Reich. W. (1967). *Reich speaks of Freud: Wilhelm Reich discusses his work and his relationship with Sigmund Freud* (eds. M. Higgins & C.M. Raphael). New York: Farrar, Straus, and Giroux.

Reich. W. (1970). *The mass psychology of fascism.* New York: Farrar, Straus, and Giroux.

Reich, W. (1972/1949). *Character analysis*, 3rd enlarged addition (trans. V.R. Carfagno). New York: The Noonday Press.

Reich, W. (1972). *Sex-Pol essays, 1929–1934.* New York: Random House.

Reich, W. (1973). *The cancer biopathy.* New York: Farrar, Straus, and Giroux.

Reich, W. (1976). *People in trouble: Volume two of the emotional plague of mankind.* New York: Farrar, Straus, and Giroux.

Reich, W. (1983). *Children of the future: On the prevention of sexual pathology.* New York: Farrar, Straus, and Giroux.

Reich, W. (1988). *Passion of youth: An autobiography, 1897–1922.* New York: Farrar, Straus, and Giroux.

Reich, W. (1999). *American Odyssey: Letters and journals, 1940–1947.* New York: Farrar, Straus, and Giroux.

Reich, W. (2012). *Where's the truth? Letters and journals, 1948–1957.* New York: Farrar, Straus, and Giroux.

Reich Rubin, L. (2003). Wilhelm Reich and Anna Freud: His expulsion from psychoanalysis. *International Forum of Psychoanalysis.* 12: 109–117.

Romanyshyn, R.D. (1998). Psychotherapy as grief work. In *The body in psychotherapy: Inquiries in somatic psychology*, eds. D.H. Johnson & I.J. Grand, pp. 43–58. Berkeley, CA: North Atlantic Books.

Rosenfeld, D. (1992). *The psychotic aspects of the personality.* London: Karnac.

Ruderman, E.G., Shane, E, & Shane, M. (Eds.) (2000). On touch in the psychoanalytic literature. *Psychoanalytic Inquiry.* 20: 1–186.

Schafer, R. (1983). *The analytic attitude.* New York: Basic Books.

Schore, A.N. (2003). *Affect regulation and the repair of the self.* New York: W.W. Norton & Company.

Schore, A.N. (2012). *The science of the art of psychotherapy.* New York: W.W. Norton & Company.

Schwartz, D. (1995). Current psychoanalytic discourses on sexuality: Tripping over the body. In *Disorienting sexuality: Psychoanalytic reappraisals of sexual identities*, eds. T. Domenici & R.C. Lesser, pp.115–128. New York: Routledge.

Schwartz, D. (1999). The temptations of normality: Reappraising psychoanalytic theories of sexual development. *Psychoanalytic Psychology.* 16: 554–564.

Searles, H.F. (1960). *The nonhuman environment in normal development and in schizophrenia.* New York: International Universities Press.

Sechehaye, M. (1956). *A new psychotherapy for schizophrenia: Relief of frustrations by symbolic realizations.* New York: Grune & Stratton.

Segal, N. (2009). *Consensuality: Didier Anzieu, gender and the sense of touch.* Amsterdam: Rodopi.

Shabad, P. & Selinger, S.S. (1995). Bracing for disappointment and the counterphobic leap into the future. In *The mind object: Precocity and pathology of self-sufficiency*, eds. E.G. Corrigan & P.-E. Gordon, pp. 209–228. Northvale, NJ: Jason Aronson, Inc.

Shalev, O. & Yerushalmi, H. (2009). Status of sexuality in contemporary psychoanalytic psychotherapy as reported by therapists. *Psychoanalytic Psychology.* 26: 343–361.

Shapiro, D. (1981). *Autonomy and rigid character.* New York: Basic Books.

Shapiro, D. (2000). *Dynamics of character: Self-regulation in psychotherapy.* New York: Basic Books.

Shapiro, S.A. (1996). The embodied analyst in the Victorian consulting room. *Gender and Psychoanalysis: An Interdisciplinary Journal.* 1: 297–322.

Shapiro, S.A. (2009). A rush to action: Embodiment, the analyst's subjectivity, and the interpersonal experience. *Studies in Gender and Sexuality.* 10: 93–103.

Sharaf, M.R. (1983). *Fury on earth: A biography of Wilhelm Reich.* New York: St. Martin's Press/Marek.

Slavin, J. (2012). The innocence of sexuality. In *Relational psychoanalysis: Volume 4, Expansion of theory*, eds. L. Aron & A. Harris, pp. 45–67. New York: Routledge.

Sletvold, J. (2011). "The reading of emotional expression": Wilhelm Reich and the history of embodied analysis. *Psychoanalytic Dialogues.* 21: 453–467.

Sletvold, J. (2012). Training analysts to work with unconscious embodied expressions: Theoretical underpinnings and practical guidelines. *Psychoanalytic Dialogues.* 22: 410–429.

Sletvold, J. (2014). *The embodied analyst: From Freud and Reich to relationality.* London: Routledge.

Smith, E.W.L. (1985). *The body in psychotherapy.* Jefferson, NC: McFarland & Company, Inc.

Smith, E.W.L., Clance, P.R., & Imes, S. (1998). *Touch in psychotherapy: Theory, research, and practice.* New York: Guilford Press.

Sontag, S. (1976). An essay by Susan Sontag. In *Antonin Artaud: Selected writings*, ed. Susan Sontag, pp. xvii–lvii. New York: Farrar, Straus, and Giroux.

Stein, R. (1998a). The poignant, the excessive and the enigmatic in sexuality. *The International Journal of Psychoanalysis.* 79: 253–267.

Stein, R. (1998b). The enigmatic dimension of sexual experience: The "Otherness" of sexuality and primal seduction. *Psychoanalytic Quarterly.* 67: 594–625.

Stein, R. (2005). Why perversion? 'False love' and the perverse pact. *International Journal of Psychoanalysis.* 86: 775–799.

Stein, R. (2007). Moments in Laplanche's theory of sexuality. *Studies in Gender and Sexuality.* 8: 177–200.

Sterba, R.F. (1968). *Introduction to the psychoanalytic theory of libido.* New York: Robert Brunner.

Sterba, R.F. (1982). *Reminiscences of a Viennese psychoanalyst.* Detroit: Wayne State University Press.

Stern, D.B. (1997). *Unformulated experience: From dissociation to imagination in psychoanalysis.* Hillsdale, NJ: The Analytic Press.

Stern, D.N. (1985). *The interpersonal world of the infant: A view from psychoanalysis and developmental psychology.* New York: Basic Books.

Stoller, R.J. (1975). *Perversion: The erotic form of hatred.* London: Maresfield Library.

Stoller, R.J. (1979). *Sexual excitement: Dynamics of erotic life*. London: Maresfield Library.

Stoller, R.J. (1985). *Observing the erotic imagination*. New Haven, CT: Yale University Press.

Stoller, R.J. (1991a). *Porn: Myths for the twentieth century*. New Haven, CT: Yale University Press.

Stoller, R.J. (1991b). *Pain & passion: A psychoanalyst explores the world of S&M*. New York: Plenum Press.

Suslick, A. (1969). Nonverbal communication in the analysis of adults. *Journal of the American Psychoanalytic Association*. 34: 89–97.

Thelan, E. (1995). Motor development: A new synthesis. *American Psychologist*. 50: 79–95.

Thomas, H. (1997). *The shame response to rejection*. Sewickley, PA: Albanel.

Trett, R. (2004). From moral malevolence to autonomous performance. *Transactional Analysis Journal*. 34: 156–169.

Tune, D. (2005). Dilemmas concerning the ethical use of touch in psychotherapy. In *New dimensions in body psychotherapy*, ed. N. Totton, pp. 70–83. Berkshire: Open University Press.

Tustin, F. (1986). *Autistic barriers in neurotic patients*. New Haven, CT: Yale University Press.

Tustin, F. (1990). *The protective shell in children and adults*. London: Karnac.

Ulnik, J. (2007). *Skin in psychoanalysis*. London: Karnac.

Weaver, J.O. (2004). The influence of Elsa Gindler on somatic psychotherapy and Charlotte Selver. *The USA body psychotherapy journal*, 3, 38–47.

White, K. (Ed.) (2004). *Touch attachment and the body*. London: Karnac.

White, K. (Ed.) (2005). *Attachment and sexuality in clinical practice*. London: Karnac.

Widlocher, D. (Ed.) (2002). *Infantile sexuality and attachment*. New York: The Other Press.

Wilson, F.R. (1998). *The hand*. New York: Vintage Books.

Winnicott, D.W. (1949/1992). Mind and its relation to psyche-soma. In *Through paediatrics to psychoanalysis: Collected papers*, pp. 243–254. London: Karnac.

Winnicott, D.W. (1950/1992). Aggression in relation to emotional development. In *Through paediatrics to psychoanalysis: Collected papers*, pp. 204–218. London: Karnac.

Winnicott, D.W. (1960/1965). Ego distortion in terms of True and False self. In *The Maturational processes and the facilitating environment: Studies in a theory of emotional development*, pp. 140–152. Madison, CT: International Universities Press, Inc.

Winnicott, D.W. (1965). *The maturational processes and the facilitating environment: Studies in a theory of emotional development*. Madison, CT: International Universities Press, Inc.

Winnicott. D.W. (1971). *Playing and reality*. London: Tavistock Publications.

Winnicott, D.W. (1986). *Home is where we start from: Essays by a psychoanalyst*. New York: W.W. Norton & Company.

Winnicott, D.W. (1987). *The child, the family, and the outside world*. Reading, MA: Addison-Wesley Publishing Company.

Winnicott, D.W. (1989). *Psychoanalytic explorations*, ed. C. Winnicott, R. Shepherd & M. Davis. Cambridge, MA: Harvard University Press.

Winnicott, D.W. (1992). *Through paediatrics to psychoanalysis: Collected papers*. London: Karnac.

Winnicott, D.W. (2001). *The family and individual development*. London: Routledge.

Whitmont, C. (1972). Body experience and psychological awareness. *Quadrant*. 12: 5–16.

Whitmont, C. (1973). *The Symbolic Quest: Basic concepts of analytical psychology.* New York: Harper & Row.

Zepf, S. & Zepf, J.N. (2010). Wilhelm Reich—A blind seer? *Psychoanalysis, Culture & Society.* 15: 53–69.

Zur, O. (2007). Touch in therapy and the standard of care in psychotherapy and counseling: Bringing clarity to illusive relationships. *The USA Body Psychotherapy Journal.* 6: 61–94.

Index